LITTLE WONDER

LITTLE WONDER

THE EXTRAORDINARY STORY OF LOTTIE DOD THE WORLD'S FIRST FEMALE SPORTS SUPERSTAR

SASHA ABRAMSKY

First published in the United Kingdom in 2021 by

ARENA SPORT
An imprint of Birlinn Limited
West Newington House
10 Newington Road
Edinburgh
EH9 1QS

www.arenasportbooks.co.uk

ISBN: 9781909715912
eBook ISBN: 9781788852920

First published in the United States by Akashic Books in 2020.

British Library Cataloguing-in-Publication Data
A catalogue record for this book is available on request from the British Library.

Designed and typeset by Polaris Publishing, Edinburgh

Printed and bound by CPI Group (UK) Ltd, Croydon CR0 4YY

This book is dedicated to my grandmother Mim,
our Tiny Dancer,
who travelled the world in her eighties
and never grew bored of life's adventures.

And to my children, Sofia and Leo,
who hiked up mountains and climbed on glaciers with me,
while I was writing this book,
with (almost) nary a complaint.

We will stomp to the top
with the wind in our teeth.
George Mallory, mountaineer

"Rambles with a Racket". Lottie Dod album frontispiece at the Wimbledon Lawn Tennis Museum.
©AELTC. Reproduced by kind permission of the Wimbledon Lawn Tennis Museum.

Table of Contents

Introduction 1

Chapter 1: A Family Obsession 24
Chapter 2: Battle of the Sexes 50
Chapter 3: Scaling the Heights in Switzerland 65
Chapter 4: The Grand Tour on Wheels 87
Chapter 5: The Fastest Woman on Earth 95
Chapter 6: Golfing Triumph and Transatlantic Fame 120
Chapter 7: Bull's-Eye at the London Olympics 145
Chapter 8: From Sporting Legend to Wartime Nurse 160
Chapter 9: Singing Her Way into Old Age 182
Chapter 10: The Final Days 213

Acknowledgements 223
Select Bibliography 232
Endnotes 237

Early photograph of tennis champion Lottie Dod, possibly taken at Wimbledon in 1887. The International Tennis Hall of Fame, Inc., is the source and owner of the photograph used in this production.

Introduction

Charlotte Dod, aged eighty-eight, was lying in her bed, in the Birchy Hill Nursing Home[1] in the sleepy southern English village of Sway. It was a peaceful place, quiet, as good as any other spot to spend one's final years. The village had a cluster of houses ranged along a few main streets, a handful of pubs, one church – St Luke's – tennis and archery clubs, and a community choir, all surrounded by the oaks and other trees of the New Forest, England's last major acreage of densely wooded land. Carved out of the forest in places was pastureland, on which grazed herds of cattle, horses and ponies. A few miles to the south were the genteel beach towns, retirement communities and tourist resorts dotting the windswept coast of the English Channel. Towns with names such as Lymington and Milford-on-Sea, Barton-on-Sea and Bournemouth. Their streets were lined with elegant mock-Tudor homes, the fronts cordoned off from prying eyes by tall hedgerows, as well as a fair number of thatched-roof cottages. There were, as well, many guesthouses in these parts, the front porches of which were decorated with hanging baskets of colourful flowers.

Birchy Hill, with its white-painted brick facade and grey-tiled roof, its brick chimneys and elegant curved window bays, had originally been built on a narrow country lane in the mid 1800s as home to three spinster sisters. Its grounds were spacious, the trim, sloping lawns surrounded by trees and thick tangles of blackberry bushes that on one side muffled the street sounds and noises of the village beyond, and on the other served as the outer edge of the New Forest. During the Second World War it had been requisitioned by the army. When the war ended, a male nurse who had served as a military ambulance driver, and his wife, bought the property, refurnished it with second-hand carpets, beds and cupboards picked up on the cheap at estate sales, and opened up a retirement home that specialised in caring for elderly people with chronic physical or mental health conditions.[2] Within ten years, the original house had been expanded into a complex of buildings, and it had upward of thirty-five residents.

Universally known as "Lottie", the elderly woman, who had had to move into Birchy Hill following a decline in her health over the previous years, was listening to a radio broadcast from the second Monday of the Wimbledon tennis tournament. She had been listening all of the previous week too, through days plagued by squalls of rain and endless delays. It was, for Dod, a sacred ritual. Almost certainly she had tuned in to every year of broadcasts since the BBC first began covering the event, by radio in 1927, by television ten years later, in grainy black and white, available for only a few hours each afternoon.

That day, there were four marquee men's matches: on one side of the draw were two round-of-sixteen battles to settle, the first pitting the rising Australian star Roy Emerson against the Mexican Mario Llamas; the other showcasing the Chilean Luis Ayala against the Swede Jan-Erik Lundqvist. Both matches would be played on Court One. On the other side, a round ahead as the championship's schedule had been knocked off-kilter by a higher than usual number of rain showers the previous week, two blockbuster quarter-finals to be played on Centre Court: the number one seed, Neale Fraser, against the American

Earl Buchholz; and then the Italian Nicola Pietrangeli against the United States' up-and-comer Barry MacKay. MacKay was a tall, big-hitting player from Dayton, Ohio, who had risen to number two in the rankings over the past months. There was also one women's round-of-sixteen match still to play, the British star Christine Truman, who had won the French Open the previous year, against the Czech Věra Pužejová. It was scheduled as the third match on Court One, likely to be played in the very last hours of daylight; play at Wimbledon in late June could continue until about nine o'clock at night.

The tennis began promptly at 2.00 p.m.

On Centre Court, Fraser soon found himself in an almighty scrap against Buchholz, losing the first set 4–6, winning the second 6–3, losing the third 4–6, and then having to save five match points in the fourth before pulling back to even the score at 15–15. At that point, cramping so badly that he could hardly stand, and with an old ankle injury from a football game played five years earlier flaring up again, Buchholz had to call it a day.[3] Wimbledon had rarely seen a retirement mid-match at a more dramatic moment. Buoyed by this fierce contest, Fraser would, a few days later, hold the champion's trophy aloft on Centre Court.

Much later, in the gathering dusk, the power player MacKay lost to the Italian in four sets when his serve, which had been unreturnable in the first week of the championships, abandoned him. Seemingly succumbing to stage fright, he hit one double fault after another. His opponent, by contrast, ran down everything, playing, the Associated Press reporter courtside noted approvingly, like a "jungle cat"[4]. When the final shot was hit and Pietrangeli had won, the Italian ran to the net to shake his defeated opponent's hand. As he ran, he threw his racket high into the air in glee. The two men leaned in for the handshake, the heavy wooden racket arced downward through the air, and, in one of the tournament's more bizarre accidents, crashed down on their heads, temporarily dazing both players.[5]

In the other two men's matches, Emerson won in four sets, the last one being 9–7, and Ayala defeated his Swedish opponent in an uneven five-set match that waxed and waned in intensity over the course of several hours.

Meanwhile, in the one women's contest of the day, to the delight of the home crowd, Truman won in straight sets. Maria Bueno, the Brazilian sensation who had won Wimbledon in 1959 and who would go on to win the championships again the following weekend, wasn't playing that Monday afternoon.

Year in, year out, since she had won her first ladies' championship, back in Queen Victoria's jubilee year of 1887, at the ludicrously young age of fifteen years and 285 days, Lottie Dod had made the journey out to the Wimbledon suburbs. First as a player, dubbed by the press "Little Wonder", then as a fan.

She won in 1887 and again in 1888. She took a break from the tournament for the following two years, but when she returned, still a teenager, she was once more unbeatable. The championship was hers in 1891, in 1892 and once more in 1893. In these years, Lottie Dod, who would bicycle over to the courts from the nearby houses in which she stayed during the competition, quite simply made ladies' tennis a one-woman show. "Though young in years, she is ripe in judgement," wrote the commentator W. Methven Brownlee in 1889, in his sweeping overview of the state of tennis. The Little Wonder exhibited, he continued, "the temperament that is best described as 'that sweet calm which is just between'."[6]

Frequently, in the decades after she retired, Dod would bring her young nephews and nieces with her to sit in the front-row seats the All England Lawn Tennis and Croquet Club allotted her, just behind the umpire's chair.[7] When the weather heated up, she would take out her fan – black crenellated paper topping a metal skeleton, decorated with gold floral arrangements and slightly racy portraits of three fleshy women, a bearded man with two devil-like horns watching them from off to their left – and gently fan herself.[8]

The ladies' championships had only begun in 1884, seven years after the first men's competition. A mere three years before that inaugural men's championship, one Major Walter Clopton Wingfield had filed a patent for the portable equipment used to play a game that had some relation in concept to the ancient indoor game of tennis played by Europe's aristocracies since at least the thirteenth century. His patent referenced a design for a "new and improved portable court", in the middle of which a "large oblong net is stretched", with a series of triangular nets, fixed to pegs driven into the ground, arranged alongside the court as side netting to catch wayward balls. The lines of the courts were to be marked out "by paint, coloured cord, or tape". Wingfield was exuberant about the possibilities of his new game. "By this simple apparatus a portable court is obtained," he wrote in his patent application, "by means of which the old game of tennis, which has always been an indoor amusement, and which few can enjoy on account of the great expense of building a brick court, may be made an outdoor one, and played within the reach of all."[9]

The word itself, "tennis", was thought to have originated from the French verb *tenir*, "to hold", a word cried out by the server before he threw the ball up into the air and batted it into play. Over the centuries, it vied with *jeu de paume*, or "game of the palm of the hand", as the name of the game in the Parisian popular imagination. Wingfield called his modified game both lawn tennis and *sphairistike* – the latter being an ancient Greek word meaning something like "skill at playing ball". Others translated it simply as "sphere and stick".[10]

Initially, the military-man-cum-sports-inventor envisioned hourglass-shaped courts, narrowing at the net – which he saw as being about as high as a modern badminton net – and widening out towards the baseline. As for scoring, in a rule book he published in 1874 he advocated that each game be played to fifteen points, making the game a sort of set unto itself, much like it is in the sport of squash today; and averred that only the server could win a point. Lose a point while serving and the ball shifted to the opponent, for him to try his hand at scoring. The following year, however, with the tennis craze spreading like wildfire, the Marylebone Cricket Club (MCC), at the time the leading sports authority in England, took over its rule-making. The MCC adopted the shorter, quicker, 15, 30, 40, game scoring method of the more venerable, ancient royal tennis. It allowed the person not serving to also win points, grouped games into longer first-to-six-game sets and simplified the court structure into the rectangular shape that it has kept ever since. So, too, the wise men of Marylebone lowered the net height down from upward of five feet to its modern level of three and a half feet at the posts, slightly lower towards the middle of the court.

Those basic parameters of the game have survived down the ages. Billie Jean King, John McEnroe, Roger Federer and Rafael Nadal, Venus and Serena Williams . . . all have played, and play, a game structurally almost identical to that codified by the MCC nearly one and a half centuries ago.

Maud Watson, the daughter of a vicar from the London borough of Harrow, won the first two ladies' championships at Wimbledon, in 1884 and 1885. She took home as her prize a silver flower basket valued at twenty guineas.[11] Watson's two-year reign was followed by Blanche Bingley's victory in 1886. Both women were considerably older than Lottie Dod, and both had firmly established themselves as the players to beat on the growing ladies' circuit, the tournaments of which were now dotted around the British Isles: in Dublin, Bath, Cheltenham, London and elsewhere.

A year before Watson's first Wimbledon win, the schoolgirl Dod had started entering doubles tournaments around England. Lottie had learned the game on courts that her parents, Joseph and Margaret, erected on the grounds of Edgeworth House – their sprawling estate, a few miles outside of Liverpool, bought with the profits from Joseph's cotton brokerage business. In those early tournaments, Lottie partnered with her older sister, Ann, nearly nine years her senior.

Ann was good; but her kid sister, only eleven years old when they entered their first competitions, was in another league entirely. Newspapers reported on the child sensation in tones of amazement. "Miss L. Dod, who is only eleven years old, played from the back of the court with both skill and judgement," wrote one reporter after watching Ann and Lottie reach the ladies' doubles final in Manchester in 1883, an achievement that won them two pounds and ten shillings in prize money. Another journalist predicted that "Miss L. Dod should be heard of in the future, as though only eleven years old, she showed really good form, and not only served well but displayed tactics worthy of much older players."[12]

When the younger Dod sister began playing, she was like a tornado, whisking up all her opponents, disorientating them, demoralising them, leaving their tennis in tatters. Her one weakness was that she served underarm, as did most women at the time – though even that fact was partially mitigated by her hitting it fast and low over the net. She would hold two of the "Wimbledon balls", made of rubber and covered with white melton cloth, which the Ayres company sold to the tournaments for 12d per dozen, in her open left palm as she leaned her back forward slightly from the waist and prepared to swing her right arm upward.[13] That relatively weak serve notwithstanding, the rest of her game was fierce, fast. She was a power player decades before power playing became the norm. In an age when tennis was too often played with the delicacy of croquet – "The rallies at that period were very tedious; indeed, it was possible to take a country walk after one began and get back in time to see the end of it," a satirical writer for the *Athenaeum* reminisced in 1909[14] – Dod aimed to end rallies swiftly and brutally. The Little Wonder was one of the pioneers of the idea that backhands and forehands merited different grips; and her ability to shift how she held her cumbersome wooden racket paid huge dividends against her less dexterous opponents. Despite the inelegant, heavy structure of her racket, and the rigidity of the catgut strings, she hit her strokes with sheer ferocity.

The young girl ran down balls that most of her female contemporaries – who played while wearing ornate, skin-concealing outfits that wrapped their torsos tightly and swaddled their bodies from the top of the neck down to just above the feet in layers of underclothes, bodices, dresses, blouses – couldn't, or wouldn't, chase down. Dod, far younger than most of her opponents, could get away with wearing dresses that stopped a few inches above the ankles. As a result, in her first few years on the circuit she had a built-in advantage, her clothing not constricting her mobility quite as much as did the couture of her opponents. But none of that would have mattered a whit had she not also possessed vast wells of talent. The teenage sensation knew how to work the angles, when to hit a drop shot, when to rush the net for a devastating volley, when to pound a ball into the far corner of the court. She played not like a "garden party" player, the society hobbyists for whom she showed considerable contempt in her spoken and written comments on the game, but like an athlete. And she competed to win. "People have frequently asked me if I consider lawn tennis an athletic game," she wrote in 1897, long after she had retired from the sport, in a gold-embossed, hefty tome, *The Encyclopaedia of Sport*, volume 1, edited by the aristocratic sports enthusiast the Earl of Suffolk and Berkshire. "I presume my questioners have never witnessed a hard five-set match between two first-class men, played under a broiling sun. It is doubtful if any game is a severer test of endurance. For ladies, too, it is decidedly a very athletic exercise, always supposing that they go in for it heartily, and do not merely frivol at garden parties."[15]

In her first outing at Wimbledon, in 1887, she faced a sparsely populated field. That year, there were only four other female competitors in the main draw, plus the 1886 champion, Blanche Bingley, waiting to meet the winner of these earlier rounds in the championship match. Crushing her other opponents, the fifteen-year-old Dod easily reached that last round. There, she routed Bingley 6–2, 6–0. Even the fact that Bingley served overarm, her legs and back straight, the low toss-up allowing only a gentle patting of the ball into play,[16] didn't help her against her underarm-serving adversary. The second set lasted a grand total of ten minutes. A reporter on the scene, stunned by the quality of the play he had seen from Dod, her chestnut-brown wavy hair[17] bunched up under her cap as she swung away at the ball, found the new champion so dominating that "in the last set she did almost as she pleased".[18]

Afterwards, the two players, Bingley several inches the taller and wearing a dark dress with ornate crepe laced around the waist, shook hands decorously at the net. Bingley's racket was awkwardly stuffed under her left arm; the champion Dod, with just the hint of a smile on her young face, let hers dangle loosely, casually, pointed down towards the court.[19]

Captivated by her youth and her sheer confidence, the sports journalists of the day, in densely printed, triple-columned publications such as *Pastime,* now took to calling Dod "the Little Wonder".

In addition to publishing lengthy reports on football and tennis, those journals also carried pictorial adverts for rackets with quixotic names like the Smasher, the Never Slack Tennis Bat, the Tête-à-tête, and tennis accoutrements like Jefferies Patent Screw Lawn Tennis Poles and Murston's Patent Star Racket Press. Soon they would be advertising rackets variously called the Dod and the Dod Lawn-Tennis Bat. These bats, raced into production after the Little Wonder's win, were manufactured by Jefferies & Co., a concern based in the East End of London. Their manufacturers claimed that they employed a dense new stringing technique that allowed for the criss-crossed catgut strings to produce as many as 1,200 squares on the face of the racket head.[20]

For the next half decade, Blanche Bingley, who soon after her 1887 loss got married and resumed playing under the name Mrs Hillyard, wasn't able to get a handle on her rival's game. No one else could either. A leading tennis historian, writing decades later, could find only one explanation for Dod's startling success – a most jarring explanation to the modern ear. "Miss Lottie Dod, who was lady champion thirty years ago, and almost as versatile as the present champion," he wrote, "learnt her game, as she learnt other games, in the company of men."[21] Whatever the reason for her success, that she was the best was beyond dispute. In his profile of nine leading players on the circuit, W.

Methven Brownlee included eight men and one woman. The woman was, of course, Miss Lottie Dod.[22]

In the seven years that she would play on the embryonic women's circuit – mainly matches around England and Ireland – she would win forty-one singles tournaments; seven of these garnered Dod championship trophies from the biggest events. She came second in eleven, and third in one. Most of her losses occurred before she turned fifteen.[23] Indeed, from 1887 onwards, she lost only one tournament match to another woman. She also won twenty more tournaments in ladies' and mixed doubles. It was an astonishing record, as near to perfection as any achieved in the long annals of lawn tennis.

Mrs Hillyard eventually won more Wimbledons than did Dod – six to Dod's five. But she only did so during the years Dod wasn't playing: before the Little Wonder came on the scene; again in 1889, the first of two years, in the middle of her tennis-playing career, in which Dod decided not to compete; and several times after Dod's sudden retirement from the game in the mid 1890s, at an age when many up-and-coming players still haven't made their first real mark on the sport. Hillyard didn't stop playing at Wimbledon until she was forty-nine years old, in 1913. Truly, if prizes were awarded for tennis longevity, she would have won them all. Yet when Lottie Dod *was* competing, there might as well have been a chasm separating the ladies' number one player from the number two. Hillyard simply couldn't keep up with the girl from Lower Bebington. In four of the five championship matches Dod played, Blanche Bingley Hillyard was her opponent; all four matches went to Dod, three of them in straight sets.

In those years, the Little Wonder travelled to the three-and-a-half-acre complex of courts on Worple Road. It was a low-key affair, its clubhouse a small, two-storey brick villa, which players would enter through French doors. In the bathroom on the second floor, four washbasins set on marble slabs stood, where tournament participants could rinse the sweat off their faces after a closely fought match.[24]

Around the grass courts at Worple Road, noted A. Wallis Myers, the first great chronicler of the game, at times the spectators were jammed in so tightly that "not even a ferret could squeeze through the centre court crowd". In the early days of the tournament, before the large stadiums were constructed, before women had been admitted to play, people would pay two shillings and sixpence simply to sit or stand wherever they could around the roped-off courts, some perched on chairs they had brought with them, others on piles of heated bricks they rented from hawkers on the grounds.[25] During the rains, they would unfurl huge umbrellas, under which they would shiver while the male players gamely continued. More recently, some semblance of order had been created by the building of the tiered seating, the boxes, the standing areas rising up around the courts. By the thousands, ticket holders, many of them dropped off by London and South Western Railway trains originating from Waterloo, which stopped at the Wimbledon station by the grounds, came to watch the games during the championship week.[26] Each year, it seemed, the sport grew more popular.

In 1922, after years of discussions, the championships finally moved to larger grounds on Church Road, a few miles from the original location, where the All England Lawn Tennis and Croquet Club and its famous tournament have remained ever since.

Dod was always welcomed back to tennis's self-proclaimed cathedral. After all, she had won the prestigious tournament five times before retiring at the age of twenty-one and moving on to other triumphs. To play hockey for the English team. To become the British ladies' golf champion. To train in Switzerland as one of Europe's top iceskaters, reaching a level never before achieved by a woman. To master the most dangerous of toboggan runs, including the Swiss town of St Moritz's notorious Cresta Run. To summit a number of Norway's toughest mountains. And finally to win a silver medal for England in archery at the 1908 London Olympics.

Writing back in 1903, Myers doubted he had "yet seen her equal" in ladies' tennis.[27] She could jerk her opponents around the court like puppets with her forehand. And, observers noted, she volleyed aggressively, with the self-confidence of a man. F.R. Burrow, who presided over Wimbledon as the tournament referee from 1918 to 1936, and who first started watching tennis in the 1880s, wrote in 1937 that so versatile was she, so talented at whatever sport she tried her hand at, that "it is a pity that flying had not then been invented; I feel sure Miss Lottie Dod would have been the first girl to make a solo flight around the world."[28]

Of all the women in sports who followed in Dod's footsteps, the *Guinness Book of World Records* could only find one athlete in the succeeding century-plus to compare her to: Babe Didrikson Zaharias, the great American sportswoman, born forty years after Dod, who in the years surrounding the Second World War competed and won at the highest levels in track and field, golf, basketball and baseball.

Somewhat itinerant in her later decades, Dod had always made a point of going to Wimbledon in June from wherever she happened to be staying at the time, to sit on Centre Court and watch the championships unfold. Until a few years earlier, she had been living with her older brother William in a flat that she owned at 5 Trebovir Road, in London's Earl's Court district. It was an area of grand stone houses, which by mid-century, in the austerity years following the Second World War, had been divided into smaller subunits. Like so much of the great city in those years, it had a faded quality to it, a sense of grandeur misplaced. William Dod, himself an Olympic gold medal-winning archer, and a First World War veteran – in his late forties, he volunteered to fight with the Sportsman's Battalion of the Royal Fusiliers and was sent off to the trenches for a year – had also never married. William and Lottie, the bachelor and spinster siblings, had, since before the Second World War, lived together more or less without a break. Occasionally family members would joke about why neither sibling had married or had children; in private, they may, some members of later Dod generations would subsequently speculate, have wondered whether or not the two Olympians were even interested in pursuing romance.[29]

In 1939, the two siblings moved into a property that William owned in the village of Westward Ho! in Devon. They stayed there throughout the war, and then, some years later, returned to London. But William, four years Lottie's senior, died in October 1954, and a few years after that, Lottie, now well into her eighties, had moved out of the capital to live in genteel retirement on the south coast, to be near her last surviving brother, Anthony, and his wife, Evelyn. Tony had married her shortly before the First World War; Evelyn came from the petite aristocracy, and her father was a vicar of a rectory near Newbury. As the couple aged, they lived quietly in Sway, Tony studying his chess books, Evelyn playing the piano, both regularly attending church. In the evenings, they would read poetry together in their living room. Some days, when their grandchildren were around, they would dust off the large old magic lantern that Tony had bought decades earlier, and put in the slides for the visual images to accompany nursery rhymes and comedic stories.[30]

Lottie had, until recently, remained active and relatively healthy.

In 1960, however, age had finally and fully caught up with her. She had, by that summer, outlived all her siblings. Philip had died in early childhood; Ann, her first tennis partner, had died of cancer back in the 1920s; William had been dead six years now; and, most recently, Tony, with whom she had cycled around Europe in their youth, and climbed some of the Continent's highest peaks, to whom she had moved to Sway to be near, had died at the start of the year. Now, with the summer tennis season underway, Lottie Dod herself was too sick to travel. She was suffering from bronchopneumonia and severe anaemia, and had also recently taken an awful fall in the nursing home, breaking her right femur and pelvis.[31]

To her caregivers at the home, she was likely just another little old lady burdened with ailments and with not too long to live. They probably felt sorry for her, saw how lonely and vulnerable she was, and shuddered inside, hoping that such a fate wouldn't one day befall them. Looking at her, so helpless, so pained, struggling for every breath, they probably couldn't imagine that she had ever been young, had ever been independent. How could they have known that she had once soared like a bird over mountains; that she had once, in riding the Cresta toboggan course in Switzerland, achieved higher speeds than had any other woman on earth at the time? How could they have known that she had once stared into the jaws of massive glacial crevasses, and that she had, for years, graced the tennis courts of Wimbledon like no woman before, and only a rare few after, had done? How could they have known that, in her prime, the old lady could have staked claim to being the greatest sportswoman the world had ever seen?

Lying in her bed in the home in Birchy Hill, far from the Merseyside town of Lower Bebington in which she had been born on 24 September 1871, Dod listened to the plummy voices of the BBC radio commentators. In London that Monday, 27 June, the temperature was hovering at sixty degrees Fahrenheit; it was a blustery, cloudy day, a fairly typical early-summer afternoon in England. It was the sort of weather that Dod as a player had once thrived in. Despite the clouds, the rains held off and the matches continued.

In all likelihood, as she half listened she drifted in and out of consciousness.

By the end of the afternoon, Neale Fraser would have advanced one round further in the journey that would take him to the title the following weekend. (Maria Bueno, not playing that Monday, was practising for her quarter-final match the next day against the Englishwoman Angela Mortimer.)

By the end of that afternoon, too, Dod, the last-but-one surviving champion from tennis's Victorian cradle years, the youngest-ever winner of what would come to be known as the "big four" Grand Slam tennis tournaments, would have died. If she was indeed tuned into the radio commentators reporting from her beloved Wimbledon, she breathed her last listening to the coverage of Fraser's match against Buchholz, before MacKay imploded against the Italian, before Truman wowed the home fans with her win. Lottie's death came in time for the news to reach the later editions of some of the country's evening papers, in time for afternoon editions across the Atlantic to pick the story up off the newswires.

Around the world, a lot had been happening that June: earlier in the month, a group of five young Liverpudlians, boys who had grown up not too far from Dod's childhood home, had performed in concert, using, for the first time, the band name The Beatles. Three of them, John, Paul and George, would stay with the band, recruit Ringo and conquer the world over the coming years; two would drop by the wayside. In Australia and the Soviet Union, major air crashes had claimed dozens of lives. Mid month, Portuguese colonial forces had fired on a crowd of pro-independence protesters in the Mozambican town of Mueda, killing between five and six hundred people. The massacre catalysed resistance to colonial rule, and in the months that followed a number of nationalist groupings crystallised in response. In contrast, a few days afterwards, the Congo, long the blood-soaked crown jewel in the Belgian Empire, was finally granted independence after years of strife. As the space race between the Soviet Union and the United States heated up, recently launched weather satellites began beaming remarkably specific information on weather patterns back to earth. And in New York, an Alfred Hitchcock film titled *Psycho* had premiered in two movie theatres before huge, and terrified, crowds.

Charlotte Dod was long forgotten by that summer of 1960. She was a Victorian relic in the nuclear age. On the rare instances she was talked or written about, by sports commentators and historians, she was always referred to by her childhood nickname of "Lottie", even though she repeatedly made it clear that she loathed the diminutive. Indeed, as far back as 1893, at the ripe old age of twenty-one, she had admonished a reporter for the *Westminster Gazette*, "Pray do not call me Lottie. My name is Charlotte and I hate to be called Lottie in public."[32] In her time, however, under that detested moniker she had been hands down the most famous, most versatile and most accomplished female athlete on earth. She was known throughout the British Isles, and – courtesy of the spreading reach of England's newspapers and periodicals, and the wonders of telegraphy – the wider empire, as Lottie, "the Little Wonder", the youngest person of either sex ever to win a singles trophy at a major tennis tournament. One hundred and fifty years after her birth, that record still stands; it is surely one of the most durable records in all of sports.

But the Little Wonder's last hurrah, her Olympic silver in archery, had been more than half a century earlier. Still photos from that event show her standing ramrod straight, a slightly dour-looking middle-aged lady in a full-length skirt and long-sleeved blouse. She sported a quiver of arrows sticking out from a pouch on her right leg, her left arm was steadying the bow, her right arm pulling back on an arrow, about to let it fly. On her head was what looked to be a double-layered cap, one peak resting on the other. There was almost no cinema footage of her from her two-decade-long sporting career – just a few fleeting, silent seconds of her firing off arrows at bull's-eyes at the 1908 Olympics, the crackly old reel kept in the British Film Institute archives – no extant radio interviews from her heyday. She had peaked just before the era in which sports stars were raised to immortality by visual and audio media. There weren't films about her, she hadn't made her fortune from the sorts of dizzyingly large sports winnings and sponsorship deals that later generations of champions would earn.

During the First World War, Dod worked somewhat anonymously as a nurse on the home front, caring for wounded soldiers evacuated back to London from the Continental killing fields, and in the process winning medals from the Red Cross for her services. After the war, she took up choral singing and piano playing, performing with a well-known London-based group called the Oriana Madrigal Society, and even at one point serenading the king and queen with Bach cantatas in a private chapel at Buckingham Palace.

For decades, she had been a slightly eccentric dowager, unmarried, seemingly – at least according to the late-life memories of her nephew G.E. Worssam – void of romantic feelings.[33] Worssam described her, without elaborating, as a "difficult" lady, and recalled that in their later years the various family members had grown apart. Younger relatives remembered her in old age as a serious, even morose person, someone slow to smile and often sharp-tongued.[34] When a male relative married an older woman, Lottie noted the fact somewhat contemptuously, mentioning that she had once been wooed by a younger man, a guards officer, but had turned him down because of his age.[35] Perhaps, in truth, she had never had the time or inclination for marriage, or for relationships with men, her obsession with sports taking precedence over all things domestic. Perhaps the anecdote that she told a reporter for the *Evening Times-Republican*, a newspaper published in Marshalltown, Iowa, during her tour of the United States in 1904, was in fact autobiographical. "Golf in Scotland is almost a disease. The passions and the perseverance that the Scot brings to golf are quite incredible." She went on to explain, "I heard not long ago of an elderly bachelor in Edinburg [sic] who had played golf from his boyhood up. He was a lawyer, and every minute he could steal from the courts was devoted to the links. This man allowed neither religion nor society nor business to interfere with his daily golf. He had never courted a girl because, he said, golf hadn't allowed him the time."[36]

To an observer in the last years of her life, the elderly spinster Dod might have been a Miss Marple character, easy to underestimate or dismiss; a lioness and precedent breaker disguised as a prim-and-proper, churchgoing mouse.

On the same day that she died in Sway, that 27 June, Harry Pollitt, the long-time general secretary of the Communist Party of Great Britain, passed away of a brain haemorrhage while on a ship that was returning him from a speaking tour in Australia.

The next day, Pollitt's death was widely reported, with long obituaries in many of the newspapers. The communist *Daily Worker* lauded him, somewhat hagiographically, as "a human, loveable man, with a great sense of humour and a seemingly endless store of stories having not only some important political point but also their highly amusing side".[37] Dod's passing, by contrast, was treated as an afterthought. In Scotland, a few hours after her death, the *Aberdeen Evening Express* published three peremptory paragraphs, informing readers, "Miss Lottie Dod, a Wimbledon champion of the 1880s, has died in a south coast nursing home."[38] In England's second city, the *Birmingham Daily Post* published Pollitt's and Dod's obituaries side by side on page four. Pollitt's death merited fifteen paragraphs, spread across two columns, and a photo; Dod's a mere five short paragraphs. So, too, the next morning the London *Guardian*, while mourning the death of "one of the most remarkable sportswomen of the nineteenth century", only gave Dod four paragraphs and a photo. Running down the left two columns of that same page was a huge tribute to Pollitt, detailing the complex twists and turns of a life begun in slum housing in working-class Lancashire, one that included spells in prison and long years as an organiser and party apparatchik. "His life was devoted to what he regarded as a righteous war against the conditions of his childhood," the obituary noted.[39] There was also a front-page news story on his death.

In America the next day, the *New York Times* deemed Dod's death worthy of only three paragraphs, taken off the Reuters newswire, and reported out of the seaside town of

Bournemouth. The tone was decidedly understated: "Lottie Dod, who had been a tennis champion and all-round athlete, died in a nursing home here last night. She was 88 years old." Even the *Minneapolis Star*, which in bold print in its afternoon edition dramatically titled its tribute "Lottie Dod, Old British Athletic Queen, Dies", could only squeeze out five short paragraphs, also taken off the Reuters newswire.[40]

At her death, the one-time sporting superstar's estate was, according to the probate documents, valued at a precariously respectable middle-class £24,013, three shillings, and sixpence.[41]

She was likely buried in a simple ceremony. There were no news reports on her funeral, no indication of top-level representation – no government officials or senior figures within the world of sports came to commemorate the passing of this extraordinary sportswoman.

Over time, the younger generations of relatives would even forget where her body rested. Perhaps hers was one of the several dozen graves in the Sway cemetery on the edge of town that over the years were left untended and eventually became so weathered, so damaged by moss and algae, by rain and wind, that the carved words on the tombstones were no longer legible. Or maybe hers was one of the many graves so overgrown with grass and brambles and moss and weeds in the cemetery surrounding the little brick building that was St Luke's Church, just down the street from the Sway railway station, that it was impossible to see the names of those who lay beneath. Perhaps she had been buried slightly further away, in one of the county-run cemeteries in Lymington or New Milton, each of which had many grave sites that over the decades would become entirely broken down, the stones cracked, the names of their dead long vanished.[42]

Wherever her final resting place, Lottie Dod would be left to navigate eternity alone. Nobody would be there over the years and decades to come to tend her grave or to mourn on the anniversary of her passing.

In her heyday, Dod had been more famous than all but a handful of women in Britain – and most of those who captured more attention from the turn-of-the-century newspapermen were ladies renowned for their titles, their places in high society, rather than for their achievements. Dod, by contrast, was fabled for what she did rather than the title she wore. In her glory years, she had been profiled in and photographed for the leading journals of the age. But even in her lifetime, those writers and photographers had abandoned her as her great accomplishments became but a distant memory from an impossibly long-gone era. She had spent the last decades of her life a silhouette. By the time she died, she had, for nearly half a century already, been shrouded in anonymity.

Lottie Dod's letters and most of her photo albums – a different album for each sport – her hockey stick and alpenstock, one of her archery bows, and other meagre possessions were parceled out to relatives. Her brother Tony's oldest son kept many of these in the cellar of his large farmhouse in the village of Chieveley, in the county of Berkshire. And, as one generation gave way to another and to another after that, over the decades many of these records of her life vanished – disappeared in estate sales, perhaps thrown away as unwanted clutter. What was left of Dod's eighty-eight years were shards, ghostly glimpses, in archives, in collectors' albums, in newspaper morgues, of the larger-than-life achievements of the Little Wonder, that most out-of-the-ordinary Victorian lady.

In 1984, the essayist Kenneth Lash published an imaginary encounter with Woody Allen in which he embarrassed the film director by referencing people whom Allen had never heard of. "'Lottie Dod,' I said, 'Lottie Dod.' I touched him gently on the shoulder and walked away," Lash wrote. "It was doubtful he knew who she was."[43]

ONE

A Family Obsession

Photograph of the young Lottie Dod with friends and family at a local sporting event. Lottie Dod with signature cricket cap standing in the centre of the back row. ©AELTC. Reproduced by kind permission of the Wimbledon Lawn Tennis Museum.

For Joseph Dod, son of William and Mary Ann Heart Dod, the decades after the mid century – a time when the British Empire's expansion seemed limitless, and the ability of England's business class to generate wealth unstoppable – had been good ones.

Joseph was born in Bebington on 25 April 1830, into a large family. Nineteen years separated him from his oldest brother, Henry; and thirteen from his favourite brother, Edward. All told there were ten children, seven of whom survived into adulthood.

Their parents, each of whom could trace their Cheshire lineage back generations, were middle-aged by 1830, having both been born in 1790, just months after the epoch-shaking events of the French Revolution of 1789. William, the son of a butcher, had gone into the wool drapery business in Liverpool shortly after the Napoleonic Wars ended; and by 1827, with a home on Castle Street, in the centre of town, he was wealthy enough to list himself as a gentleman.[1] Over the coming decades, he would acquire much property in the growing city, including a number of cotton warehouses, one of which was a large site on the east side of Cheapside, which he had acquired in 1844.[2]

When the Dods died – William in the summer of 1857, at his son Thomas's house in Lower Bebington, Mary in 1860 – they would be buried in the county they had spent their lifetimes in, in St Hilary's churchyard, in the little town of Wallasey on the mouth of the river Mersey.[3] By the 1860s, their son Joseph, having invested well the considerable inheritance he had come into upon William's death, was firmly established in the cotton business as a broker and a financier.

Before the American Civil War, cotton had poured into the kingdom from the southern slave states – up from a mere handful of bales in 1784, shortly after the end of the American War of Independence, to 128,000 bales on the eve of the 1812 war, to 2.5 million bales in the years leading up to the Civil War.[4] Ships traversed the Atlantic, bringing the millions of pounds in weight of raw cotton that would make the fortune of merchants and factory owners in England. And the port city of Liverpool, which had been central to the transatlantic slave trade in centuries past, became, by the last years of the eighteenth century, the epicentre of this business. A growing number of warehouses were clustered within a few minutes' walk of the large Cotton Exchange Building, opened in 1808, out of which the brokers did their business.[5] By the early 1840s, these merchants were organised into the Liverpool Cotton Brokers' Association and the Liverpool Cotton Association; and they were playing a leading role within the Anti–Corn Law League as free trade exponents in the fierce political debates that roiled England during those early years of Queen Victoria's reign.[6]

As the Industrial Revolution gathered pace in Britain, cotton came to be a crucially important raw product, its conversion into clothing and other textiles providing employment to huge numbers of newly urbanised workers in the counties of Lancashire and Cheshire. Manchester teemed with textile factories; Liverpool with cotton distributers.

"The cotton master", wrote the historian Anthony Howe in 1984, "personified the new force of 'industry'."[7] They were brash young men, chasers of fortune, and unafraid of being seen as the new rich in a class-conscious, aristocratic society. They wore labels – originally thrown their way as pejoratives by members of the older moneyed classes they were displacing – like "cotton lords" and "cottonocracy" as badges of honour, and in the 1850s and 1860s acquired huge fortunes. In Howe's analysis of more than three hundred Lancashire cotton masters, he found that the average value of the estates they left at death was £126,000, the equivalent of many millions of pounds today.

During the American Civil War, Lancashire's cotton barons came increasingly to rely on lower-grade produce from India. That they were able to do so was a testament to their foresight: in the 1850s, as America's domestic situation deteriorated, the Cotton Supply Association had lobbied for increased infrastructure investments and land reforms in the territories of the British Raj, so as to promote, as an alternative source, the growing of cotton there. The strategy worked well enough to keep the British textile industry alive – but not enough to keep it functioning at pre-war levels. For factory workers in Lancashire, 1861 to 1865 were known as the "Cotton Famine" years, times of underemployment and hunger. Yet for the few hundred men, Dod among them, who controlled the cotton supply chains through the Liverpool market, the famine was more an inconvenience than a catastrophe. They had, for years now, been spreading their investments, moving into banking in Liverpool and nearby Manchester, setting up department stores, taking positions in the newly important rubber industry.

After the war ended, American cotton again flowed copiously into England, factory technologies increased productivity by leaps and bounds, and the elite merchants of Liverpool found that they had more money than they knew what to do with.

Joseph Dod navigated these market shifts well. He imported cotton and sold it to the mills that were fuelling the growth of Lancashire's cities, and he used some of his profits to go into banking in Liverpool, which netted him still more money. During the American Civil War, as he diversified his business he also began importing large quantities of Canadian seed oat, which he advertised for sale in local newspapers.[8]

By the time he married Margaret Aspinall, ten years his junior, on Thursday, 11 September 1862, in a ceremony presided over by the elderly Reverend A. Knox[9] at St Mary's Church in Birkenhead, Joseph, still only in his early thirties, was an extremely wealthy man.[10] Like so many of his cotton-broker peers, in addition to investing well he began spending some of that money on luxurious living conditions. The cotton lords, Anthony Howe wrote, largely abandoned the political field in those years, foregoing the agitation of the Anti–Corn Law decade early in Victoria's reign, when they had made their mark as impassioned free traders, and instead "succumbed to the discovery of Europe, the hunt, yachting, London society, fishing and shooting in Scotland, and mock country-house life". Howe wrote of "elaborate dinners, capacious wine cellars, plentiful servants, extensive travel abroad", of a preoccupation with cricket, billiards and other fashionable sports.[11]

Joseph and Margaret Dod seemed determined to live up to this image. They moved into a sprawling Cheshire county estate, which they named Edgeworth House, a few miles outside of Liverpool and near the home of Joseph's brother Thomas. The name Edgeworth, according to family legend, was chosen as an homage to one of Joseph's ancestors, Sir Anthony Dod of Edge, an English archer who performed heroically during the fabled battle of Agincourt against the French in 1415 and was knighted on the field of victory by Henry V that very evening.[12]

Edgeworth's buildings were Gothic brick with stone entranceways, the rooms heated by ornate stone fireplaces that vented through high, thin chimneys, the grounds spacious enough for large outdoor social gatherings and an array of sports facilities. The floors were wooden, the noise muffled by thick, patterned rugs. In one corner of the dining room – a space cluttered with heavy upholstered chairs, high-backed wooden seats and china vases, with ornately carved tables draped with thick tablecloths, and Romanesque statues – was a small organ. On the wall to the right of the organ, the young couple hung two small oil paintings: one of little sailboats in an ocean, the other delineating the fierce waves of the sea crashing against a wooded shore.[13] Over the years, as the family grew, the mantelpiece above the fireplace would come to host several framed photographic portraits of individual family members, as well as one featuring two of the children standing next to each other, a small clock and several additional vases.

In 1863, Joseph and Margaret's first child, a girl whom they named Ann, was born. Four more children followed over the next nine years: William, Anthony, Charlotte – likely named after the dead wife of Joseph's older brother Edward, a woman who had died in 1860 at the age of only thirty-seven – and Philip. The latter, born a year after Charlotte, would die in infancy in the late spring of 1873; the rest would grow up in Edgeworth House, taught from a young age to engage heartily with the world of sports that Joseph and Margaret held in such regard.

Well-to-do Victorians had, in recent decades, become increasingly obsessed with physical exercise. Some had installed portable gymnasiums in their homes, in which they did a series of exercises intended to limber up leg muscles, expand chests and strengthen aching backs.[14] Others, modifying exercise regimens encountered by colonial soldiers in India, began swinging bottle-shaped wooden "Indian clubs" in a set of calisthenic exercises that looked something like a combination of weightlifting and the swinging of batons by latter-day cheerleaders.[15] From the 1860s on, a number of exercise machines patented by doctors in Sweden, the German states and elsewhere began being imported into Britain. Weightlifting became popularised, for women as well as men. And over the coming decades, gymnastics, acrobatics, rope climbing and the use of rowing machines to strengthen one's abs would all become widely accepted parts of the fitness craze for health-conscious Victorians.[16] By the century's end, wealthy young people were competing in a rash of new sports, both individual and team-based.

The four young Dods learned to shoot rifles and arrows, to run, to swim, to play an array of ball games – from cricket and billiards to the new fad of lawn tennis.

William would notch up considerable success as both an archer and a big game hunter – in which capacity, on a transatlantic ship taking him on one of his overseas trips, he met the great poet and novelist Rudyard Kipling, who reportedly asked him about the odd spelling of his last name, and then muttered grumpily that he guessed "if it was good enough for God, it's good enough for Dod".[17] Ann would thrive as a tennis and billiards player. Anthony, who as a young man spent months roaming around Europe with Lottie by bicycle and climbing mountains with her in Switzerland and Norway, would eventually carve out a niche as a highly skilled chess player, able to hold his own with the world's best. In 1889, he was the Liverpool Chess Club champion, a position he ceded to William three years later; to commemorate their wins, both brothers were presented with a huge silver trophy plate resting in a bed of red velvet, depicting an ancient Greek scene of a half-naked woman lounging in a temple, surrounded by three female courtiers. So good did Anthony become at the game that he would eventually be able to blindfold himself and play multiple games simultaneously, his photographic memory enabling him to keep perfect track of what was happening on each board.[18] Lottie . . . well, Lottie would be quite simply the greatest sportswoman of her, maybe of any, era.

Shortly after Major Wingfield patented his lawn tennis gear and published his pamphlet laying down the key rules of the new game, Joseph ordered some of the kits from Wingfield's agent and had them installed on Edgeworth's grassy grounds just to the east of the house.[19] He would, in all likelihood, have hired gardeners to closely crop the lawn, using the efficient mowing machines developed by the Gloucestershire tinkerer Edwin Budding in the 1830s. He would have presided over the laying of the canvas lines delineating the courts, the hammering of poles into the ground on which to attach the nets. He would have ordered boxes of the new sport's felt balls with a vulcanised rubber core. By now, Dod was fashioning himself as a man of leisure. When, in 1877, he was summoned to sit on a local grand jury, several of his fellow jurors labelled themselves brokers – of cotton, of metal, of timber; Joseph, by contrast, along with half a dozen of the other more well-to-do jury members, insisted that "gentleman" be listed next to his name.[20] He was, in his mid forties, a man defined by his wealth and the accoutrements that accompanied financial good fortune.

Perhaps, like so many other country estates of the time, those newly repurposed gardens in the Dods' Edgeworth home had previously boasted croquet lawns; perhaps, too, when the croquet fad dissipated in the early 1870s, the lawns remained vacant, waiting for the next craze to come along and claim them.

There were at the time many candidates to fit that bill. For hundreds of years, royals had played a game of "tennis" that involved bats, hard balls, and indoor courts with high nets and various eaves for the ball to rebound off. In the walls of the courts were holes, situated at various strategic points, for the ball to be batted into. It was in some ways a precursor to more modern racket games and also to such sports as basketball and lacrosse. More recently, a series of outdoor variants on the game had been tried out – some played one-against-one, others involving teams of up to twelve people, with the object of getting the ball down long outdoor fields. A sports genealogist could trace a family tree for tennis that encompasses everything from the modern sports of badminton, squash and lawn tennis, through to a series of evolutionary dead ends that fizzled out somewhere in the nineteenth century.

Wingfield, however, had luck and considerable self-promotional skills on his side. When he rolled out his new idea for a sport in 1874, he gave it two names. The first was "lawn tennis", the second "*sphairistike*". Classically educated, he couldn't resist the ancient Greek reference. The awkward name didn't stick; but the game itself did. Aided by an extraordinarily effective public relations campaign – Wingfield used his army contacts to secure enthusiastic articles about his invention in various military journals, daily papers, society magazines and sports periodicals – the fad took off like wildfire. Within months of Wingfield having been granted his patent, it was a sensation, something that a great many society people wanted in on.

The Dod children, boys and girls alike, homeschooled by a series of governesses and tutors, were given free rein to play on the newly installed courts whenever they liked. They were also expected to help out in cutting, rolling and marking those courts, fenced off from the surrounding trees and scrubs, in putting up and taking down the nets each day, and in cleaning the tennis balls, at the end of a day's use, on the doormats to the house.[21] Ann and young Lottie, perhaps four or five years old when tennis arrived at Edgeworth, took to the game especially well. It would hardly be a stretch to say that the younger girl in particular grew up on those courts, that from both of their early childhoods Lottie Dod and tennis were inextricably linked together. When she wasn't playing on the courts she would go off to one of the corners of the estate and hit a ball against a wall again and again and again, harder and harder and harder, honing her reflexes as the ball bounced back at her fast and low.[22]

But then tragedy struck the Dod family. On 30 November 1879, when Lottie was only eight years old, Joseph died. A brief death notice was published in the *Liverpool Mercury* two days later, with details of the funeral arrangements and the hint that "friends will accept this intimation".[23] He was interred, at eleven o'clock on the morning of 3 December, in a family vault in Bebington Cemetery, in the same place his infant son Philip was buried, and where Margaret's father, John Aspinall, and Margaret herself would ultimately be laid to rest.[24]

After her husband's death, Margaret seems to have viewed Edgeworth as a world unto itself. Within its boundaries she felt in control, able to be the elegant hostess, the graceful, well-provided-for widow. In his will, handwritten in black ink, his neat script leaning slightly to the right, Joseph had left the house and its furnishings, its paintings and most of his book collection to his wife. The exception was some of his father's books, which he bequeathed to his brother Thomas.

Despite the fact that in the 1860s and 1870s the Dods had splurged on fine living and elaborate sports grounds, Joseph had also been careful to nurture his finances. He was, perhaps, cognisant of the Dod family crest and motto: a serpent wrapped around a wheatsheaf, underneath which was the Latin phrase *In Copia Cautus*, which translates to "In Plenty Be Cautious". In other words, don't tempt fate by overspending.[25] Now, Joseph's widow and children were to reap the benefits of his financial good sense. In addition to the house and its contents, his will had established an annuity of £200 to be given to Margaret, so long as she didn't remarry, for the rest of her life. He had also authorised two additional payments each year of £200 from the proceeds of the auctioning off of parts of his estate. He had provided for all four of his children equally, their money to be invested, until they reached the age of maturity, in government bonds, property and what were seen as safe industries such as railways and canal construction, both in England and abroad. While they were minors, the estate would cover their education and other expenses. Once they reached adulthood, what was left of the money would be released to them – and Joseph specified that in the case of his daughters, the wealth would transfer directly to them rather than to any husbands they might acquire along the way. Beyond these specific details, as well as a few minor bequests to local hospitals and to a handful of other relatives, the additional elements of Joseph's estate, presented to the local court a few months after his death by his executors, totalled up to just under £8,000. That was the equivalent of nearly £1 million in today's currency.[26]

With no incentive to remarry, the wealthy widow lived with her four children, a young housemaid named Harriet Jane Picton, originally from Liverpool, and a live-in cook named Jane Jones. They played their role of leisured country gentry well. On the grounds of their large estate, the Dods kept brown shorthorn cows, some of which they would periodically offer up for sale, the ads posted in local newspapers.[27]

Relatives would stop by to talk and to play; on Joseph's side of the family alone, Lottie and her siblings had twenty-six first and second cousins, many of whom lived within a few miles of Edgeworth. Friends, including the teenage Joshua Pim, who would go on to become a medical doctor, and also a two-time Wimbledon champion shortly after Lottie retired from the game, would come to spend weekends at the house. They arrived early in the afternoon on bicycles or in pony traps,[28] riding up the gravelled, tree-lined drive to the stone steps leading to the entrance to the house; they came to play tennis and billiards and all the other sports that had come to define the estate. For a couple of hours the hosts and their visitors would exercise, and then all the young people would sit down in the dining room to eat scones lathered with thick Cornish cream, delivered by the milkman the previous evening, and a variety of country jams. Margaret would pour dark-brown tea for the guests, and, according to the writer Gwen Robyns, who spoke to Lottie late in her life about those long-gone days, the crowd "talked of nothing but tennis and the forthcoming county championship. They were not pat-ball parties. Tennis was a serious matter. And at the end of the day, fortified by home-made lemonade for the girls and beer for the boys, everyone went home."[29]

Outside, however, the world increasingly appeared to Margaret to be a frightening, unpredictable place, one that she had an obligation to protect her four surviving children from experiencing.

Increasingly controlling as she aged, the widow Margaret insisted her children be homeschooled, rather than going off to school and university.

For Ann and Lottie, Margaret and Joseph's choosing to educate them via privately hired governesses, and Margaret's carrying on with this practice after her husband's death, would have been a fairly ordinary decision. After all, into the second half of the nineteenth century, up to forty per cent of women in England remained illiterate and unschooled – not until the 1880 Elementary Education Act was it made mandatory for children of both sexes aged from five to ten to attend schools; and for the upper classes, while a few girls' boarding schools, such as the Cheltenham Ladies' College, had opened in the middle decades of the nineteenth century, no widespread system of quality schooling for girls yet existed. Thus, for those who wanted their daughters to be schooled in the classics, to learn music and art, and to engage intellectually with the broader world, tutors remained the easiest option.[30] But for the boys, there were myriad choices outside of the home. Most towns had private education establishments, either secular or church-based, and around the country there was a network of elite boarding schools catering to families with the sorts of resources that the Dods now had. That William and Anthony were tutored at Edgeworth spoke more to the preferences of their parents, to the extraordinarily close-knit nature of the family, than to any innate need for homeschooling.

As the 1880s got underway, the Dod children, with their mother hovering in the background, were something of a world unto themselves. They were a sporting equivalent of the Mitfords a generation later, that obsessive, self-enclosed family, each sibling of which would go on to make their mark in the world of politics or literature; or perhaps of the Durrells, homeschooled on islands around the Mediterranean, one of the siblings going on to become a top novelist, another a brilliant naturalist. In sports, the Dod children were free to go their own way; in matters of love and life, however, Margaret's presence was inescapable. She wanted, her grandchildren surmised decades later in conversations with the writer Jeffrey Pearson, to always be in control.

Later, when Ann, William, Tony and Lottie had finished their education, Margaret made it emotionally difficult for them, as young adults, to leave the family home, to fledge from the Edgeworth nest. In the late 1880s, family legend had it, she wouldn't give her blessing for twenty-six-year-old Ann's wedding to Ernest Worssam, an already well-established brewer and manager with the Whitbread beer company. The couple eloped instead; afterwards, for months on end, Ann wrote near-daily letters to her mother asking forgiveness. The envelopes were all returned unopened, discovered by her family after her death from cancer nearly forty years later, when they went through her possessions. Surviving portrait photographs of Margaret show a stern-looking woman, her posture ramrod straight, her floral-patterned dark dress buttoned up all the way to her chin. The Dod matron's hair is pulled up into a severe bun under her ornate, lacy hat; her mouth is turned down slightly at the edges. In the one family photograph that Lottie Dod pasted into her album, a photo with Margaret, the four children and a family friend named R.O. Rawlins, the matriarch is looking down, deliberately avoiding eye contact with the cameraman. In none of the surviving sepia images does Margaret look like a woman who wore life lightly; in none of them is there even the hint of a smile.

The Dod materfamilias made it clear that it would be socially unacceptable for her children to work for a living – which family lore had it was why, as the century wound down, neither William nor Tony were willing to make money from their manifest skills as photographers and wood-carvers. It simply wasn't the gentlemanly thing to do to profit from such gifts. Thus, as their cousins went off into the world to become civil engineers, architects and dentists – to go into business as manufacturers of chemicals, timber merchants, accountants, and estate agents – the four Dod siblings, each one sitting on a comfortable inheritance from Joseph, were left to find ways to fill their time in rural Cheshire.[31]

Given the constraints placed on how they could live their lives, the obsession with sports that all four embraced may well have been the only way the children could escape their mother's control. Margaret expected her grown children to stay with her in Edgeworth House, only begrudgingly letting them explore beyond Cheshire's somewhat claustrophobic confines.

Ann seems to have done what she could to make her environs lighter. She turned her room into an art studio; filled its bookshelves with dozens of heavy tomes piled somewhat haphazardly; brought in a display case in which she housed small vases, statuettes and flowers; and hung a huge Japanese paper fan above it. She covered her floor with intricately woven rugs and crowded the room with a cream-coloured armchair, with tables stacked with hand-painted plates and with numerous family photos. Around the top of the walls, she painted a line of birds – geese, ducks and several other species. And underneath these she hung her own paintings, including a seashore scene and a close-up of an old man pouring water from a jug into a glass.[32] But, when she wasn't in her art studio, she still had to make her way through daily life under Margaret's close watch.

When Ann began taking her younger sister out on the road to play tennis tournaments from the early 1880s on, it may well have been a reaction to the cloistered environment that Margaret was imposing at Edgeworth, largely an excuse for the children to get some fresh air. If that was the case, for the sporting world it was a fortuitous decision. By the summer of 1883, the young girl, beating much older competitors in tournaments in Dublin, in northern England and elsewhere, had already been noticed by a number of sports journalists. After all, none of them had ever seen an eleven-year-old, the age Lottie was that spring when she first won matches at the Northern championships, so comprehensively beating her grown opponents in a sporting contest.

For the Dod brothers, William and Anthony, as well, tennis was an escape hatch. Both began entering tournaments in northern England, sometimes in singles, other times playing doubles together; and both began racking up respectable, if not spectacular, records. At times, it seemed, the entire family was tennis obsessed. Tony, a thin, somewhat sickly-looking adolescent, in a well-tailored bespoke wool suit, posed for formal photographs with his racket resting nattily just off to his side. When Margaret's father, John Aspinall, an elderly man with a long white beard, his shoulders slightly stooped, his hands clasped behind his back as he walked, travelled with his grandchildren to the nearby castle at Normanston – a mid Victorian folly designed to look like a medieval fortress – they made a point to take a photograph of him on the tennis courts with William.

In the summer of 1885, still only thirteen years of age, Lottie won a tournament at Waterloo. Then, heading north, she competed again in the prestigious Northern championships in Manchester, an event that attracted all the top women in the game. She got to the final, where she gave the reigning Wimbledon champion, Maud Watson, a considerable scare before eventually losing 8–6, 7–5. The following year, however, in the ancient Roman city of Bath, Dod got her revenge, with a straight-sets 7–5, 6–4 victory over Watson in the finals. It was the first time since 1881 that any player had beaten her in a singles match.[33] "Miss Dod is wonderful with her returns and promises exceedingly well for the future, only now being thirteen years old," a writer on the scene opined, getting her age wrong by a year.[34] Another wrote that the fourteen-year-old returned all of Watson's shots "with such force and judgement that her opponent was fairly run off her legs". The crowd left restraint to one side. They cheered the young girl wildly, giddy with the promise and poise she brought to the game.

That same summer, all four Dod siblings showed up for the Northern championships. In the ladies' singles, Lottie got to the championship match before succumbing to Maud Watson, 7–5, 6–3. In the ladies' doubles, Ann and Lottie demolished their opponents to take a well-earned victory. In the mixed doubles, Lottie partnered with Harry Grove, and made it all the way to the championship match before losing to the indefatigable William Renshaw – already a multiple Wimbledon champion – and his partner, Miss M. Bracewell. Finally, in the men's doubles,

William and Tony paired up; they didn't win, but they did make it to the final of the consolation tournament, a parallel event for teams knocked out in the early rounds of the main draw.[35] It is doubtful that any set of four siblings was ever before, or since, so successful in a single major tennis tournament.

With Wimbledon and all the other prestige tournaments now open to women, the sports commentators of the day felt that it was only a matter of time before the teenage sensation Lottie Dod made her mark in them too. "As to the destination of the Ladies' Challenge Cup, there is, on present appearances, little scope for conjecture," a *Pastime* writer opined in mid 1887. "Everything points to the success of Miss Lottie Dod, whose recent career victory has been quite unchecked, and to whom the coming years promise an increase of strength and speed, as well as of skill and experience."[36]

By now, Lottie knew her own worth, knew that she was destined for sporting greatness. She bought a dull-red scrapbook with thick, cream-coloured pages. In it, she began carefully gluing every article sent her way on her and her siblings' sporting accomplishments. She also took a heavy black leather photo album, given to her by the family friend R.O. Rawlins, a dapper-looking man with a moustache waxed to two fine points,[37] and dedicated it to tennis. On the inside of the front cover, she titled it *Rambles with a Racket from Edgeworth*. The two words beginning with *R* were lined up one above the other, with a single large *R* sufficing for both words. The stem of the capitalised letter was carefully penned by the young girl to look like a wooden net post, with the interior of the letter, as well as the surrounding space on the page, a series of grid-like lines meant to resemble the edge of a tennis net. Over the coming years, she would glue into that album dozens of photos, ranging from intimate family scenes with her siblings and friends on the fenced courts at Edgeworth, to images immortalising her greatest public triumphs. She would also, as her successes mounted, jealously hoard her trophies and championship cups, filling her room in Edgeworth with so many of them that a visitor once noted it had become a "perfect storehouse" for her prizes.[38]

The year 1887 was a crowded one. For literature buffs, it would come to be defined by the writer Arthur Conan Doyle publishing, in the November release of the magazine *Beeton's Christmas Annual,* the novel *A Study in Scarlet,* which introduced his inspired creation, one Sherlock Holmes, and his sidekick, Dr Watson, to the reading public.

But while Sherlock Holmes's debut would prove to be a sensation, by far the biggest event of that year was the queen's jubilee celebration. As the months of 1887 rolled towards 20 June, the fiftieth anniversary of Victoria's ascension to the throne, so the British Isles were decked out in an extraordinary display of gilded pageantry. After all, in the long history of the kingdom, only three prior monarchs had ruled for fifty years or more – and in each of those previous instances the celebrations had been somewhat muted: Henry III marked fifty years as king during a time of civil strife and hunger, after years of unsuccessful wars in France, and decades of simmering rebellion and discontent at home; Edward III's reign had been scarred by devastating plague epidemics; and George III, by 1810, had lost the American colonies, lost his mind, and ruled over a kingdom that had spent much of the previous twenty years, and huge amounts of economic capital, fighting the Napoleonic Wars.

In 1887, by contrast, Britain was at the height of its powers, its imperial reach spanning the globe, its wealth massively amplified by the Industrial Revolution. Victoria, crowned empress of India by order of Parliament eleven years earlier, was far and away the most recognised public figure on earth.

That spring and summer, in the months surrounding the actual anniversary of Victoria's becoming queen, the shops of London were filled with jubilee paraphernalia – commemorative pottery pieces, medals, books rushed into print to honour every aspect of the empress-queen's life. Periodicals and magazines published special issues. Poets from across the empire wrote celebratory odes, often sycophantic in tone. Hymns specially composed for the occasion were sung in churches throughout the land. And from the awnings of pubs and shops hung flags and bunting, as well as images of the long-reigning queen.

As the anniversary date neared, a sort of fever-pitch hysteria, an unreflective glorifying in empire, descended on London. While there were scattered political protests, notably by those calling for Irish independence, by and large the atmosphere was pure boosterism. Flags and anthems. Pomp and circumstance. Every day brought new celebrations, each one outdoing the next. There were soirees at Buckingham Palace with dozens of European monarchs, princes and princesses sitting in attendance. There were gatherings in Hyde Park, in which tens of thousands of schoolchildren were given meat pies, sweet buns, and oranges in honour of the queen. There were military parades. New hospitals were opened. In May, Victoria even attended a special performance of Buffalo Bill's Wild West Show.[39] She was, reportedly, enchanted.

From the town of St John, in Canada's New Brunswick province, the poet William Peters Dole sent the words of his "Carmen Acadium: Ode for the Jubilee Year of the Reign of Queen Victoria." "Now let glad song arise and pious prayer, / Let merry feast and grave solemnity / Shew to the world a mighty nation's jubilee." Dole extolled the virtues of the globe-encompassing empire, uncritically positing Britannia's role in the world as being to bring enlightenment to troubled, backward lands – lands that now stretched from the "Orient" to the "sacred Ganges" and the "Abode of Snow", all the way to "Africa's dark coasts, / Where slavery and horrid heathen rites / From age to age have trod man to the ground."[40]

On 21 June, with royalty and political luminaries gathered from around the world to pay tribute to Victoria, the ageing sovereign was conveyed to Westminster Abbey in an open landau, the four-wheel carriage – the wheels painted a vivid red, the body of the vehicle black – drawn through central London by six large horses from the royal stables. She was guarded on her journey by an escort of turbaned Indian cavalry and British guardsmen, some sporting red uniforms and plumed hats, others dark-blue uniforms. Some reports from the day mention seventeen princes, from Russia, Britain, Prussia and elsewhere among the mounted bodyguard.

Slowly they proceeded from the palace, through Trafalgar Square and on to Westminster Abbey. Red, white and blue bunting, the colours of the Union Jack, hung from all the public buildings and surrounded Trafalgar Square's famous lions. Under shop awnings, dotted around the square, and atop the roofs of the grand stone buildings, the museums and churches and offices that had been erected around the periphery of Nelson's Column, countless thousands of Londoners stood and cheered.[41] Victoria sat on the rear bench of the landau, looking forward, her two younger consorts facing her from the opposite bench. As the procession moved at a snail's pace through the throngs, the portly figure stared ahead, calmly, regally, taking in the hullabaloo.

Inside Westminster Abbey, 10,000 invited guests awaited Queen Victoria's arrival. The high priests of the Anglican Church stood to one side of the altar, all wearing their ceremonial robes, some deep reds, others a lush hue of gold. Opposite them, the women in flowing gowns, the men in full military regalia, stood invited royalty, including the Hawaiian queen, Kapiʻolani, and her sister-in-law Liliiʻuokalani, the Belgian queen, Marie Henrietta, and Grand Duchess Augusta of Mecklenburg-Strelitz. Beyond them, arrayed down the more than 30,000 square feet of the abbey's interior, thousands upon thousands of guests stood in rapt attention as Victoria entered the echoing, cavernous church, its stone columns soaring more than 200 feet into the air above. On the second and third floors, from the galleries ranged around the nave and over the aisles that snaked between the ancient columns, thousands more leaned forward to see the spectacle below.[42]

That evening, after the religious services held in Westminster Abbey and around the country had concluded, great bonfires blazed in celebration from hilltops around the British Isles. Photos from the time show large oxen, their torsos wrapped in Union Jack cloths, being led to huge pits, there to be slaughtered, roasted over the spit and eaten in village-wide festivities. Elsewhere, huge "royal barons of beef", weighing close to 200 pounds and carried in on litters by upward of ten liveried servers, were dished up in town halls and manor houses to gathered local elites, the platters ornamented with Union Jacks. Plum pudding and great crates of cider were distributed to the less affluent townsfolk outside.[43]

In the days following the jubilee, London's celebrations continued unabated. The Guildhall held a ball, at which were served up aspics of lobster and eels, pies, roast meats, pastries, meringues and copious amounts of alcohol.[44] In the capital city's great public parks, patriotically themed Punch and Judy shows, marionettes and other spectacles entertained the huge crowds.[45]

Eleven days after Victoria's jubilee, that summer's Wimbledon championships commenced. Dod was coming off a hat-trick, having won the Irish championships, Bath and the Northern championships earlier in the season. She was by now the undisputed number one in women's tennis. Flush with victory, she headed to the grounds at Worple Road.

In addition to the eponymous strawberries and cream of Wimbledon, vendors at the event were also likely selling cherries jubilee, a newly popular dessert of pitted Bing cherries cooked in syrup and then, tableside, flambéed in brandy, offered up atop a vanilla ice. The concoction had been crafted by a leading French chef of the era to honour the queen and her well-known love for cherry dishes, and that summer it was all the rage in London.

When Dod took to the court, wearing a pleated skirt, layered on the outside with a polo-necked "overdress", a sprig of white heather pinned to her bodice for good luck, she exuded both a steely purpose and a devastating pose. Her eyes were blue-grey; she was tall and muscular; and she gave off a "coolness and presence of mind" that made it "almost impossible" for her opponents to "disconcert or unnerve her".[46]

It was a hot Monday afternoon, perhaps slightly humid. The clouds that would later in the evening roll in to take the edge off the heat were still far off.[47] Dod stood just inside of the baseline, waiting to receive serve, her eyes supremely focused on her opponent. Behind her hovered a small ball boy in a suit and bowler hat,[48] and the umpire sat high in a chair adjacent to the net. The court, to a modern eye, would have looked narrow, for there weren't doubles lines back then. By default, each court was singles only, and when doubles matches were to be played, extra lines were added in – the benefits of Wingfield's patented portable system, the canvas lines easy to fold up and put away after each match, fully on display.

Ranged around the teenager were hundreds of spectators, many of the women standing close to the court under white parasols, the men in top hats, some of the younger boys in bowlers.[49] They were kept back from trespassing too close by knee-level ropes that separated spectators from players. Above and behind these front-row observers rose the newly constructed stands, holding perhaps upward of 1,000 more cheering fans. As occurred at so many of the tournaments Dod had entered over the past few years, locals in nearby houses were leaning out of upper storey windows, hoping to get a glimpse of the unfolding drama.

In the first few years of the championships, there had been twelve courts in a three-by-four grid. A handful of the spectators were lucky enough to get tiered bench seats under the one awning, emblazoned with a large decal for the tennis kit manufacturer F.H. Ayres.[50] Most, however, simply sat or stood around the perimeter of the grounds, at court level, trying to get nearest to whichever match held their fancy. In 1881, two of those courts had been combined to create a larger central locale on which the most high-profile matches were played. It became known, informally, as Centre Court, and the name stuck. Over the next several years, three stands were constructed around that court; at first temporary, ramshackle affairs, little more than canopies and a few tiers of seats; then more permanent structures. In 1886, the year before Dod made her debut, the three stands, with their canopy roofs held up by metal posts, had been joined together at the corners. It was a squat affair – the surrounding trees towered over the stands – giving little indication of the temple-like quality that the Centre Court stadium would come to embody over the coming decades. But it did at least provide some measure of shade and comfort for the tennis enthusiasts who were, in increasing numbers, flocking to

Wimbledon each year.[51]

From that very first match, it was clear that Wimbledon had a new star at hand. Using a wooden racket, the head of which flattened out at the top – a racket that weighed a little under a pound,[52] its handle wrapped in a strip of tightly bound brown leather – she played a raw, powerful game. Seemingly, she took pleasure in blasting her opponents out of contention. The tennis correspondent for *Pastime*, surprised by the teenager's ferocity, informed readers that Dod had "fully convinced us that none of the ladies now playing can hope to dispossess her of her position without completely altering their style of play". The crowd loved it. Much as large sports audiences today chant the names of their heroes and heroines, so back in the 1880s they did the same for the new star of Wimbledon. "Lot-tie! Lot-tie!" they shouted out, slowly, rhythmically, as she skewered her hapless opponents.[53]

A year later, Dod cemented her reputation by successfully defending her Wimbledon title. Once again, she routed her nearest rival, Blanche Bingley Hillyard. Once more, the newspapers waxed rhapsodic about her abilities. "Nothing but praise can be written. She appears to improve at every successive meeting at which she competes," *Pastime* purred. "Her play on Saturday was far superior to any previously shown by a lady. Her forehand stroke across the court is, for pace and length, almost unapproachable, even among the men players."[54]

Dod's meteoric rise, and the coverage the newspapers and magazines of the late 1880s accorded it, was tapping into a powerful new force in late Victorian society. Sports culture had taken off with a vengeance in that decade in both Britain and the United States. The new individual and team sports of the age, from tennis to football, from cycling to baseball, were all capable of furnishing new mass-culture heroes for the rapidly changing and urbanising era. For women, sports, along with the adventurous pastime of travel writing, afforded an escape from at least some of the strictures of Victorian life. Take, for example, the *New York World* reporter Nellie Bly, the globe-trotting young American who had so famously beaten Phileas Fogg's fictive eighty days for circumnavigating the globe. Or Freya Stark, the young Englishwoman who began travelling to some of the most far-flung places on earth and chronicling her adventures in a series of well-received books. Or consider the accolades accorded the American sharpshooter Annie Oakley.

In the Victorian world, women were hemmed in (literally) in terms of what they could do . . . except in those odd instances when they weren't. Someone like Lottie Dod, improbable as her achievements were, captured the late Victorian imagination as surely as did the exploits of Nellie Bly. Such women were allowed to be transgressive, to do what were thought of as men's jobs, to accomplish what were thought of as inherently male achievements. And, in so doing, in resonating so deeply with the public's imagination, they helped shatter the stereotypes of what women were and what they could and couldn't do.

Dod was by now the object of something approaching fan adoration. After her second Wimbledon victory, the *New York World* had a special correspondent in London write up a glowing portrait of the champion and her fans. Titled "The Girls Go See Champion Lottie Dod and Get Points on Style", it reported that "it is quite a fad with society girls to go in parties to see Lottie Dod play tennis. A London girl asked her the other day the secret of her success. 'Well,' said the pretty championess, 'I never lose my head in a game, and experience has taught me never to lose my temper. I think tennis a capital game to teach a girl self-control.'" Rich American girls in London on their grand European tours would corner Dod at garden parties and beg her to visit them across the sea.[55]

That same year, an anonymous scribe, writing under the pseudonym of Thomas Moore, wrote a satirical poem on the inability of Scottish lasses to defeat Dod on the tennis court:

Weep Weep Hibernia,
Let thy tears
Bedew the verdant sod.
For vanished are thy
hopes and fears
Before Miss Lottie Dod!
Miss Martin – had you
Played as well
As we have seen you play,
Another tale we had to tell,
Than must be told today.
But who can face that skating sling
That sends the ball like bird-on-wing
And drives it to the very spot
Where, at the moment, ye are not.[56]

TWO

Battle of the Sexes

The young Wimbledon champion posing with her racket. The International Tennis Hall of Fame, Inc., is the source and owner of the photograph used in this production.

The summer of her second Wimbledon win, in 1888, Lottie Dod, now aged sixteen, invited three of the best male tennis players of her age to a series of sporting duels. This was a full eighty-five years before sports' most famous battle of the sexes, when, in 1973, an ageing Bobby Riggs challenged Billie Jean King to a tennis match and had his head very publicly handed to him on a plate in a bling-filled, $100,000, winner-take-all, globally televised match in the Houston Astrodome. The sporting world of the 1880s, the fans, the reporters, none had ever seen anything quite like what Dod was proposing. In the Victorian imagination, such a matchup was almost inconceivable, a pairing that was fundamentally against the natural order – but the Little Wonder, flush with her string of victories, supremely confident as to her abilities, believed that she could triumph.

Harry Grove, a Londoner nine years Dod's senior, had won the Scottish championships in 1887 and reached the finals again the next year. As for the Renshaw brothers, the twins William and Ernest, they had utterly dominated Wimbledon since the start of the decade. William had won the tournament six times in a row, from 1881, six months after the twins celebrated their twentieth birthdays, to 1886, and would win one more championship in 1889. In his first win, William had demolished the reigning champion, Reverend J.T. Hartley, 6–0, 6–1, 6–1, in a match that lasted only thirty-seven minutes. It would establish a speed record for a Wimbledon men's final that has never since been beaten.[1] Ernest had lost to his brother in several of the Wimbledon finals, though would partially redeem himself by winning the tournament in 1888. And the pair had combined into a formidable team that had won five Wimbledon men's doubles titles. Their matches routinely drew huge crowds and ecstatic commentary from sports reporters.

"The match was of a most obstinate character, both brothers playing the hard volleys known as the Renshaw smashes to perfection," reported a *Morning Post* writer of the 1883 Wimbledon final, watched by an estimated 2,000 people, which William eventually won in five sets. "Considerable excitement prevailed, as both were in excellent condition and playing in fine form, hard volleying and rapid service being the order of the day." Three years later, the *Derby Mercury* waxed rhapsodic about the "immense concourse of spectators" who came to watch William Renshaw play.[2]

All three men knew that their female opponent, Dod, was a skilled player; indeed, Ernest Renshaw had partnered with her over the previous year to win several major mixed doubles events. They had a good, friendly rapport. And Grove had also, at times, played mixed doubles with the teenager. In Exmouth that summer, after Ernest and Lottie won a tournament together, a friend's camera had caught them sitting on a bench, casually talking. Ernest was wearing white trousers, spats, a white shirt, a checkered jacket and a matching cravat. His face was dominated by a delicate moustache and intense, soulful eyes. Lottie was smiling; a rarity in her photos from the period, she looked relaxed, happy.[3]

The men Dod challenged probably figured that the unorthodox contests could only bolster their already high profiles in the rapidly growing sports culture of the era. And so they eagerly accepted her throw down.

Despite Miss Dod's already remarkable résumé, the three gentlemen were confident that they could dispatch her with a minimum of fuss. After all, Lottie had two strikes against her: she was, quite obviously, a girl; and, following on from that, she would have to wear long skirts and all the other clothing that made it so difficult for women athletes to move fast. Ernest Renshaw knew, from first-hand experience, that this was a hindrance, since he had once, on a dare, dressed up in women's clothing to play a friendly few games against Blanche Bingley.[4] In fact, so bullish were they that, in an age in which many matches were played with handicaps, much like golf is today, they offered the girl what they assumed would be a sporting chance, something to keep the attendees a bit on edge before they put the girl in the awkward cricket cap back in her rightful, subservient place.

Each game would, Grove and the Renshaws stated in accepting the dare, begin with Dod ahead 30–0. (William had boasted that against any other woman he would even offer 40–0 head starts, essentially meaning he'd have to win at least the first three points of every game in order to thread a path to victory.[5]) They also offered her "bisques", a sort of second chance then in vogue in handicapped tennis matches, in which the weaker player could request two or three point replays each set, allowing them to scrub a few poorly played points at vital interludes in a game.

Since in tennis the scoring was 15, 30, 40, game, the Wimbledon ladies' champion would need only two points to win each game; her opponent, by contrast, would need four. Dod accepted the conditions. Dressed in an ankle-length white dress, the sleeves down to her wrists, the body of the dress up to the middle of her neck, with a corset underneath, her legs covered in thick black stockings, her feet clad in the sort of clunky black leather shoes worn by washerwomen, her head protected from the sun by a delicate white cricket cap, she set to work. The Little Wonder employed her powerful forehand to the full, chasing down balls in the far corners of the court, charging the net whenever possible to end the rally with one of her signature devastating volleys. For tennis cognoscenti, her game was something to marvel at. The tennis chronicler A. Wallis Myer called her simply "the incomparable Miss Dod".[6]

In the first match, played in northern England on the Monday following the end of a draining weeklong tournament, the girl took on Ernest Renshaw. Local papers had heavily publicised the event, which was billed as a charity exhibition with ticket proceeds going to the regional dispensary, and with additional mixed doubles matches featuring the two stars thrown in as a bonus. Dod won the first set at a dash, crushing her mixed doubles partner 6–2. But then, according to the reports from the grounds, she flagged. Perhaps the week of tennis had caught up with her; perhaps Renshaw, realising he had a real match on his hands, simply raised his game one vital notch. He perceived, a commentator acerbically reported, "that he had no ordinary lady opponent, and from that moment every stroke was keenly contested, both players doing their utmost to gain the victory".[7] Whatever the reason, he won, but only just. The final score was 2–6, 7–5, 7–5. Newspapers noted the "brilliancy" of Dod's play, the astounding hand-eye coordination she showed at the net. She ran her opponent around the court so hard that it almost seemed, they wrote, as if Renshaw's opponent were a man.

Later that summer, in between regular matches at a tournament in Scarborough, the exhibitions resumed.

First, the teenager wiped the floor with Grove, beating him 1–6, 6–0, 6–3. Then she took on the six-time Wimbledon champion – a man who for years had been the fiercest player on the lawn tennis circuit, a hero who travelled throughout the British Isles from one tournament to the next, routinely humbling his opponents. By the end of that match, Dod had proven her point. In demolishing William Renshaw 6–2, 6–4, she had shown that women, those delicate, fragile flowers of the Victorian imagination, were more than capable of holding their own in the most physical of domains.[8] The newspapers gushed about her "remarkable feats" in taking down the best male players of her era.

* * *

As the dreary rains of a sodden English July and August continued, the news focus shifted. The English public became engrossed in reading about the onset of a series of grizzly East End murders that would soon come to be known as the Jack the Ripper killings. Temporarily, sports, the Irish question, the growing movement for women's suffrage, and pretty much everything else took a backseat. Purple prose poured forth on the slashing horrors that were unfolding on the darkened, narrow streets of the old districts coming off the River Thames in the eastern precincts of London.

Time seemed to slow to a crawl. Each day from 31 August, when the first of a series of victims' bodies was discovered, new and ghastly revelations surfaced. The women, most of them prostitutes, had had their throats slashed, their abdomens and genitals cut. Some of them had had their internal organs removed. As the police started to put the pieces of the puzzle together, they found murders dating all the way back to April that appeared to fit the pattern of a serial killer.

The papers provided the unknown murderer daily coverage, guessing as to his motives, his identity, his status in society. The *Illustrated Police News* carried lurid stories with headlines such as "Ready for the Whitechapel Fiend, Women Secretly Armed."[9] And a guessing game began: who was the crazed killer stalking the women of the East End, what were his motivations, where would he strike next? In September, news organisations started receiving letters from the perpetrator, signed "Jack the Ripper". It was a moniker that would come to be a byword, down the centuries, for depravity. In mid October, one of his missives, titled "From Hell", arrived along with half a kidney, thought to be from one of his victims.[10]

Once the killer had named himself, the country, and much of the rest of the world, became utterly obsessed. In Scotland, the *Courier and Argus* reported that one of the canine entrants in a rabbit-coursing match had been named after the killer, and that, when he lost, the crowd "cheered lustily", with one of the spectators announcing, "He cannot rip rabbits anyhow."[11] In Yorkshire, the *York Herald* reported "further murders threatened by 'Jack the Ripper'", and in the next column over detailed how an East End woman who lived in the vicinity of the killings had been so "excited and effected" by them that she had hung herself in her own home.[12] Throughout the East End, the police flooded neighbourhoods, hoping to flush out the murderer in his lair. They rounded up scores of known criminals, looking for a break in the case. They chased one lead after another, provided to them by informants. When the Ripper's victims were buried, huge crowds lined the streets, following the hearses to the cemeteries and uttering what a *Bristol Mercury and Daily Post* reporter termed "loud and frequent" threats against the unknown killer. Across the Atlantic, the *Cincinnati Enquirer*, reporting on the murderer's penchant for removing body parts from his victims, came up with what may well have been the most lurid subhead of all: "Theory That the Murderer Is Gloating over a Bubbling Cauldron of Hell-Broth Made of Gory Ingredients".[13]

Soon, newspapers were reporting copycat assaults as far afield as Paris.[14] In Bradford, a woman named Maria Coroner was fined £20 for "breach of the peace" after she sent out a series of threatening letters that she signed "Jack the Ripper".[15]

Amid the horrors and the fear, sport must have been a most welcome diversion. In addition to increasingly breathless reports of dastardly crimes and bloody killings – most of them having nothing to do with the Ripper – the newspapers managed to keep up a steady flow of sports coverage. Next to the story about Maria Coroner, for example, was a long report on a shooting competition. There were still plentiful column inches in the major newspapers devoted to football, cricket, billiards, bowling – even if the front pages were otherwise occupied with murder and mayhem.

Lottie Dod kept her focus; she continued to win. The tournament season in England and Ireland ran until mid October. And in one event after the next, Dod now pulverised her opponents. She beat them in regular matches, and she beat them, again and again and again, in handicapped events, in which her opponents started off with a two-point advantage. She beat them in singles, in ladies' doubles, in mixed doubles. On the rare instances when an opponent kept close to her, eventually Dod would always pull off a break. When a set went the duration, her opponents would, almost without fail, blink first. That summer, she won several sets 11–9, 10–8 and 9–7. The only opponent to win one of these extended sets against her was Blanche Hillyard, who managed to squeeze out a 10–8 first set against Dod in Bath that May before collapsing 6–3, 6–0 over the following two sets.[16] Adding insult to injury, Lottie then partnered with her sister, Ann, to win the ladies' doubles, easily beating Hillyard and her partner in the first round of that tournament. Afterwards, the two sisters and their friend Mrs Bagnall-Wild posed for photographs on the wooden chairs courtside, the sisters sitting straight, wearing feathered hats and holding parasols by their sides. They looked regal, unapproachable.

The past couple of years, the writer W. Methven Brownlee wrote as the season wound down, had been "simply a triumphal procession" for the teenager. She and Maud Watson had together built ladies' tennis into a mass spectator sport. "To these two players, the ladies of the lawn tennis world owe everything,"

Brownlee gushed. But in reality, by late 1888 it really was only a one-woman show. "It was not now a question of getting a set against her," the commentator wrote of Dod. "It was the satisfaction of getting a game."[17]

The next year, however, there was a shocking absence.

The Little Wonder didn't play Wimbledon in 1889, nor did she play in 1890 either. The public reason given was that, in the first instance, she was yachting, and in the second, she simply didn't feel like playing. In private, however, the story may well have been less happy: the spring of 1889, Lottie's older sister, Ann, had fallen in love with an older man, a senior employee of the Whitbread brewing company, while on a trip through the Scottish isles, and had asked her widowed mother for her blessing to get married. Instead, Margaret, who had minutely controlled her children's lives from the time Joseph died in 1879, refused to even contemplate such a union. Fearing she would be forever trapped at Edgeworth, gradually growing into an old maid, on 2 September 1889, Ann eloped to Chertsey, where she and Ernest Worssam married.[18]

Nearly a century later, her children and Tony's children told Jeffrey Pearson, a Cheshire-based author working on a short book about Dod at the time, that they believed in the wake of this scandal – first the spring and summer romance, then the elopement – Margaret had simply refused to allow Lottie to travel down to London to compete.[19]

Possibly adding salt to the wound was the patronising way in which male reporters of the day greeted the proud young lady's every success. Repeatedly, they wrote of Lottie as a tomboy, as somebody who wasn't quite as womanly as she should be – or, if they acknowledged that she was womanly, they said it almost as a forced afterthought. They felt that they had a right to comment on everything from her weight to her muscle tone to the complexion of her skin. "Miss Lottie Dod, the well-known lady tennis player, and joint champion of England with Mr. J.C. Kay in the mixed doubles, lives near Liverpool," one anonymous commentator wrote in a tennis guide published in 1891. "She is twenty years of age and weighs one hundred and sixty pounds; is healthy, ruddy, and as strong as a man." To smooth out the backhanded compliments, the author then felt compelled to add, "But with all her training [she] has not lost a particle of her womanliness."[20]

It couldn't have felt good to know that, no matter how extraordinary her athletic achievements, the journalists who dogged her every sporting move would always find some way to explain her successes in terms of the men she was surrounded by. Thirteen years after she had been labelled "ruddy, and as strong as a man", an article in the *Montgomery Advertiser*, published in the US state of Alabama after she wrapped up an American golf tour, would couch her myriad triumphs this way: "The champion woman golf player of Great Britain is Miss Charlotte Dod, a slender and very athletic young lady who has been practicing outdoor games and sports of all kinds since her childhood. She had two or three athletic brothers to coach her in her games, which was a great advantage."[21] Not to be outdone, the *Dispatch* in Moline, Illinois, informed its readers, "The young lady had advantage over most girls in that she had big brothers devoted to outdoor games. These gentlemen kindly coached their sister in her athletic training. It is a wonderful help when the athletic girl has such brothers."[22]

None of the articles mentioned Ann, the sibling who had actually been most responsible for her emergence as a sporting superstar. Ann, who had taken her on train trips around England to compete in tennis tournaments, who had been her doubles partner during her first years on the circuit. And Lottie herself, who surely knew all too well the debt she owed the older woman, felt at times compelled in public to pander to this demeaning narrative. In 1899, she went so far as to argue that her brother Tony had been her primary playmate as a child, and that "perhaps it is because I have mostly played with men that I have learned to play such a strong game . . . the average man's stroke is undoubtedly much more powerful and swift than that of even the most expert women players".[23] After all, in an era in which women couldn't vote and had almost no independent property rights, few of the reading public would have been willing to accept that women could, or should, compete on an equal basis with men in any arena of public life. Many would, quite probably, have agreed with the *Pastime* essayist who, three years before Dod had won her first Wimbledon title, penned a piece essentially arguing that while most women couldn't play a good game of tennis, they could – and should – flirt with male commentators and officials well enough to convince them to overlook their sporting flaws. They should be judged as adornments rather than on their sporting merits. "Lawn tennis, unlike most popular sports, places the critic in an exceedingly delicate position, inasmuch as he has to deal not only with the successes and failings of men, but also with the merits and mistakes of those of the fair sex who adorn the game by participating in it," he wrote. "He must, indeed, be a hard-hearted scribe who could resist the soft supplication 'not to mention that miss' or to record 'all those faults,' and we cannot be surprised that our reporters – faithfully as they usually portray events – occasionally plead 'extenuating circumstances' when the stern editor wishes to know why so few remarks have been made on the play." The author, carried away by his own fantasy, went on to write of how male umpires might get distracted by the "natty little shoes" of female servers, forgiving their foot faults when faced with the "pretty pouts" of female competitors. "Truly, man shows his weakness when he is in possession of the umpire's chair in a ladies' match!"[24]

In her heart of hearts, however, while she occasionally pandered to public prejudice, Dod never seemed truly able to accept the inferiority of women in tennis or in anything else. She might not have defended her Wimbledon title in 1889, but she was still entering and winning other tournaments, mostly in northern England, within a relatively easy train ride of Edgeworth. In Liverpool, she trounced Hillyard in the championship match, and also won the ladies' doubles. In Northumberland, she won in singles and in mixed doubles. Then, as a follow-up, she challenged yet another leading male player, H.G. Pease, to yet another battle of the sexes, this time a one-set exhibition match.

Dod's handicap against Pease was only a one-point head start in each game. It didn't matter; she ran away with the set 6–2. Most likely, she would have won even had they played on equal terms. Time and again, she ripped unreturnable crosscourt forehands. "When this movement came off, as it did nine cases out of ten, Pease could do little more than smile, though whether sarcastically at his own inability to return, or at the skill of his fair opponent, one cannot say," wrote one of the journalists present courtside. "What was most striking, however, was the ease with which Miss Dod played. Without making much show of activity, she seemed always to be just where the ball was returned to."[25]

Two years after her second Wimbledon win, and coming off an extended absence from the game, Dod was asked by the editors of *The Badminton Library*, a series of books devoted to covering the era's most popular sports, to compile her thoughts about women in tennis. She eagerly accepted the assignment.

The resulting essay, seven pages in length, was a window into Dod's true thinking on the topic, brilliantly attacking the idea that women couldn't excel in sports. Not yet nineteen, she wrote with style and emotional force. "For some years after its introduction the game was evidently thought beyond them [ladies] both as regards body and mind. There were piteous moans about the weight of the balls, and pathetic appeals not to spoil it as croquet had been spoiled, by making it too scientific. It was represented, not it may be hoped by ladies, but on their behalf, that no lady could understand tennis scoring."[26]

The teenage sensation, who had now played four matches against top male players and won three of them, was scathing about these critics. Of the editor of the *Field*, a journal with an outsize influence over how the sport was viewed, she wrote that "he was invested with the prerogative of an irresponsible despot"; and that, moreover, his narrow ideas about women in tennis had been "conclusively disproved" by the quality of the matches then being played by lady competitors.

"To thee a woman's services are due," she announced, as a stand-alone line at the start of her essay, quoting act four of Shakespeare's play *King Lear*. She had made her point: Dod wanted to be judged on her own terms. Not as a freak show adjunct to the male contestants at Wimbledon and the other events on the tennis circuit, but as an athlete who would rise or fall based on her own skills and her own ability to compete.

In 1891, after more than two years of on-again, off-again presence at the major tournaments, the young Bebingtonian returned full-time to the circuit. She promptly took up where she had left off in late 1888, swatting away all her challengers.

That year, she won every match she played. She did the same in 1892. The same again in 1893.

She was, by now, far and away the most famous female athlete in England, probably in the world. The well-known London society photographers W. & D. Downey invited her to their studios on Ebury Street, in one of the most fashionable neighbourhoods of central London, to pose for a series of portraits. She showed up in a simple, crenellated white dress, the material from her shoulders up to the top of her neck a doily pattern, held tight with a metal clasp high up on her throat. She wore her signature cricket cap, under which was bunched her wavy brown hair, now somewhat longer than it had been when she first won Wimbledon as a slightly awkward fifteen-year-old. As the photographer took one image after the next, she looked off to the left, her lips, dimpled at the corners, showing just the trace of a quizzical smile.[27]

In early July 1893, Dod played her fifth Wimbledon title match. Yet again, she faced her archrival, Mrs Hillyard. This time around, on a rainy, windy Sunday afternoon, Hillyard managed to pull out all the stops. She drove balls deep into the court, ran her opponent from side to side. For the first time in a final, Dod seemed to have lost her way. Battling the wind, she struggled to get the ball into court. The defending champion lost the first set 6–8.

Digging deeper than she had ever had to do before, however, Dod put in a bravura performance in the second, pummelling Hillyard and racing to a 6–1 victory. Perhaps the winds had died down, leaving just a steady drizzle; those were the conditions, commentators observed, in which Dod particularly thrived. "The English climate generally enabled her to take a speedy and complete revenge," Wallis Myers wrote, referring to those rare occasions in which an opponent opened up an early lead against Dod. And once in her element, Myers noted, she quickly picked up steam and became "the beau ideal of what a lady-champion should be", an unstoppable force of nature "absolutely without a weak point".[28] Hillyard, however, refused to give up, and in the final set, the two women duelled fiercely, each staying on serve for the first six games. At one point, Dod fell heavily, and it wasn't clear if she would be able to go on. She stopped, took a few minutes, regrouped, and then put in some of the most punishing tennis the sports journalists and audience members gathered around the court had ever seen. The quality of the play at Worple Road, reporters noted with astonishment, seemed to get better and better as each game passed. Hillyard kept probing, firing off shots deep into Dod's backhand corner. Dod, wrote the *Pastime* writer on the spot, responded with "marvelous backhand returns". In his opinion, "No other lady player is strong enough on the backhand side to return such well-placed drives with such unfailing accuracy." Dod won the final set 6–4.

It was to be her last competitive tennis match. Ten years after she had debuted as a little girl in a small tournament in northern England, the now twenty-one-year-old slipped away, disappearing Garbo-like from the world she had so completely dominated. Not that she didn't like the trappings of victory – her stash of prizes showcased in her Edgeworth bedroom was proof of the fierce pride she felt in her accomplishments; but she had never wanted to be what she derisively termed a "pot hunter", someone who only stayed with a sport that she had conquered in order to collect even more trophies. Simply coasting, staying atop a game in which she had no true competitors, held little appeal for the Little Wonder. In fact, she said somewhat haughtily, she found the idea of sticking with one game her whole life "appalling".[29]

THREE

Scaling the Heights in Switzerland

An Elizabeth Main photograph of Dod and two companions during the first-ever winter ascent of the Swiss Drei Blumen, 23 February 1896. Courtesy of the Martin and Osa Johnson Safari Museum.

Lottie Dod's absence from the public eye didn't last long. While she never aggressively courted the media in the same way as did Babe Didrikson – the great American track and field star, golfer, basketball and baseball player, and quintessential self-promoter – more than a quarter of a century later, she did know how to hold her own in the spotlight.

Hers was a world increasingly fascinated by the sporting hero, by the unlikely accomplishment against the odds. Figures

like Thomas Stevens, who in 1887 circumnavigated the globe
on a penny farthing bicycle, captured the attention of writers
at the growing number of mass-circulation newspapers and
magazines, and through them the imagination of the populace.
Or Nellie Bly, the globetrotting *New York World* journalist.
Or impresarios such as Buffalo Bill, whose Wild West Show
opened in London two months before Dod won her first
Wimbledon title, thrilling crowds with the performers' derring-
do. Or the cricketer William Gilbert Grace, who played for an
extraordinary forty-four consecutive seasons in the nineteenth
and early twentieth centuries.

Dod, with her effortless transition from one sport to the
next, with her breaking of one record after another, with her
ability to compete against the best of male athletes, was tailor-
made for stardom.

Throughout the 1890s and into the early twentieth century,
reporters sought out the Little Wonder to ask her opinion on
everything from the quality of tennis played to the sorts of
clothing female athletes should wear. She wasn't shy in giving
her responses. "How can they ever hope to play a sound
game when their dresses impede the free movement of every
limb?" she asked, perhaps recalling how, when she first won
Wimbledon, she was helped by the fact that as a young teenager
she "only" had to wear a dress that fell to the top of her ankles,
rather than one that cascaded all the way down to her shoes. "In
many cases, their very breathing is rendered difficult. A suitable
dress is sorely needed, and hearty indeed would be the thanks of
puzzled lady-players to the individual who invented an easy and
pretty costume." Sports doctors at the time believed that female
athletes should wear woollen dresses and corsets, specifically
intended to make the athletes perspire as much as possible. In
advertisements placed in sports publications, one Dr Jaeger

went so far as to argue that the more the overdressed athlete perspired, "the better will be her digestion, her complexion, and her health in general".[1] Dod, by contrast, wanted loose, flowing clothes, garments that hung lightly off the shoulders rather than pinching a player tightly around the waist.[2] Elsewhere, she wrote, a touch coquettishly, that such a dress "must be becoming, or very few of us would care to wear it".[3]

So, too, editors of sports anthologies requested her writings on technique and training. Dod, still in her twenties but already a doyenne of the sports world, was only too happy to oblige. In setting up shots, she wrote, there should be "no stiffness of arm or elbow, no aiming after grace and effect; for all strokes, if made correctly, allowing the free, easy movement of the body, are naturally graceful". She described the importance of timing, of keeping one's eye on the ball, of not hitting it too early while the bounce was still on the rise. She suggested that young ladies should have the confidence to hit strong backhands, rather than trying to run around the ball to take it on the forehand side. Finally, the great champion warned young players not to overpractise and thus grow "stale", while at the same time urging them not to take their skills for granted and getting "consequently careless".[4]

Over the fifteen years following Dod's last Wimbledon triumph, despite suffering intense bouts of sciatica, some so severe that they would take her out of commission for months at a time, she would perform, at an international level, in a dizzying array of sports. She seemed almost fanatically driven in her athletic ambitions.

In 1893, the twenty-one-year-old Dod, who had dabbled with golf for seven years already, was a spectator at the inaugural championships held by the Ladies' Golf Union (LGU) at the

Lytham & St Annes golf course. There, she befriended the LGU's honorary secretary, Miss Issette Pearson, as well as the glamorous golfing enthusiast Lady Margaret Scott, daughter of the third Earl of Eldon, who was two and a half years Lottie's junior and would win the British ladies' amateur championship three times running; in that first tournament, the young aristocrat defeated Pearson to take the trophy.[5] The year following, in 1894, Lottie was a founding member of the Moreton Golf Club – where she would rapidly establish a course record of seventy-four, six under par. (A few years later, she would take her best round down two more, to seventy-two.)[6] In 1895, her confidence on the golf links now blossoming, Dod participated in the third LGU national competition, rather than simply watching from the sidelines again; this time around, it was she who, by a narrow margin, fell victim to Lady Margaret Scott's imperious game.[7] Huge crowds followed the players around the links as they fought for dominance. And those same huge crowds cheered raucously for Dod and for Scott as they went toe to toe from one hole to the next, the duelling players tied till very late in the day.

Over the next decade, the Little Wonder would compete in and win top-level golf tournaments in Britain and overseas, traversing the country from Gullane, in the north of Scotland, on the links of which sportsmen had played golf from the midseventeenth century on, to Devon in the south.

By the century's end, the erstwhile tennis champion had racked up two bronze medals in the national golf championships,[8] and won numerous smaller tournaments. At one such event, hundreds of shipyard workers, hardened working-class men, took the day off from their jobs so that they could see her in action.

Went one anonymous ditty that did the rounds in 1894:

Now Lottie Dod
So Neatly Shod
Steps forth upon the tee –
On tennis green
She is the queen
At golf what will she be?[9]

The answer to that question was *pretty damn good*. In one tournament after the next, she stole the show. The authors of *Our Lady of the Green*, the first manual intended for female golfers, called her "a brilliant player and a magnificent driver", and marvelled at how she could play herself out of difficult situations that "would dismay most golfers".[10] Even when she lost, as she sometimes did, her critics in the media tended to frame the defeat as an aberration, reassuring readers that it was only a matter of time before she fully found her form. "She is more erratic than her many friends wished to see her. It is difficult to say where she failed, except in steadiness," wrote one reporter following a disappointing performance from Dod in May 1899. "But there is little doubt that she can play a far finer game."[11]

Yet, while golf was a staple during those years, to the chagrin of the *Golfer's Magazine* it was by no means her only sporting outlet. "She has been a champion in lawn tennis," a writer noted in the magazine's September 1899 issue. "She plays tennis yet, but she ought to discard these frivolities and take up golf seriously," the author opined.[12] Dod discarded the advice. Instead of focusing on one sport to the exclusion of all else, the Little Wonder now spun off in a dozen different directions at once.

The young lady kept illustrious company. Where once she had gone yachting for diversion, after she stopped playing tennis she and her brother Tony began spending more and more time in the Swiss Alps. Perhaps in Switzerland, high up in the clean mountain air, the snowy peaks soaring skyward, she felt she could truly escape her ageing mother's domineering presence, not to mention the expectations of her legion of fans in Britain.

Twenty-five years earlier, Queen Victoria, coming off seven years of seclusion and all-consuming mourning for the death of her beloved husband, Prince Albert, had arranged a semi-secret trip to the Swiss mountains. She had, during those years, largely withdrawn from public life, her nerves frayed to the breaking point. Indeed, so incapable was the sovereign of maintaining her duties that republican rumblings had grown in the kingdom from whispers into roars. Victoria's closest political advisers, her doctors, her courtiers, all realised that she needed to find some dramatic way to regroup emotionally, in order to steel herself for fights over the coming years that would determine the future of the monarchy. They recommended a getaway to the mountains of Switzerland, a landscape that Albert himself, as a young man, had adored.

Victoria took their advice. In the early summer of 1868, travelling not in her official capacity of queen, but under one of her other titles, "the Countess of Kent", she decamped with a small retinue for several weeks of hiking, boating and other outdoor activities in the Alps.

There, walking in the mountains, fishing in the crystalline lakes and taking in glacial vistas the likes of which she had never before seen, Britain's queen found a reason to live once more. In her diary entries and letters, she waxed lyrical about the landscape. "We were in the greatest admiration of the splendid panorama before us," she noted in her diary entry for 23 August. "All the mountains so softly lit up, white with snow and with the loveliest blue tints . . . The air is most beautiful and light, and enabled me to accomplish what was quite a long walk for me."[13]

Subsequently, as news of Victoria's travels spread, Switzerland had become one of the most fashionable stopping points on the grand tour. In the years following, tourist resorts, spas and hotels rushed to take advantage of the English elite's willingness to part with large sums of money in their Alpine environs.

By the 1890s, there were flourishing English ex-pat communities in many of the most desirable Swiss towns. Among them was a particularly colourful character, Elizabeth Main, later known more widely as Lizzie Le Blond, the top female mountaineer of her day, a skilled photographer and one of the first women anywhere on earth to take up the new art form of cinematography.

Main, originally from an upper-class Irish family, had been twice widowed already by the time the Dods met her. Her first husband, Colonel Frederick Gustavus Burnaby, had been one of the era's most celebrated soldiers and adventurers. Burnaby had become something of a celebrity in the 1860s as a hot-air balloonist, had subsequently joined the Royal Horse Guards as a member of the detail protecting Queen Victoria, and went on to make a literary name for himself writing about his extensive travels in Europe, in Asia Minor and throughout the British Empire. By the 1870s, when he was still only a captain, he was sufficiently famous that the society artist James Tissot decided to paint his portrait. In Tissot's canvas, Burnaby sits on a sofa covered in a white fabric, a pile of books by his side. He is wearing his black horse guard's uniform, a thick red stripe up each leg, gold brocade on the jacket, a white sash crossing his chest from the left shoulder towards the right side of his waist. The soldier has a long cigarette dangling loosely from the fingers of his left hand; and the ends of his moustache are perfectly oiled into two fine, wire-thin points. On the wall behind him is visible the bottom half of a map of the world. By his feet rests his shining copper body armour.[14]

In 1885, Burnaby was one of the most famous casualties of the hard fighting in the Sudan, dying in mid January at the battle of Abu Klea. His widow, who had had a bout with lung disease and had, from 1881 on, relocated to Switzerland for at least part of each year to give herself the better health prospects thought to come with the clean mountain air, subsequently remarried – this time to a young doctor named John Frederic Main. But in 1892, the good doctor, too, had died. Main, now in her early thirties and twice bereaved, enjoying her life in Switzerland and the freedom she felt climbing in the Alps, saw no reason to return to Britain. Instead, she threw herself into a life of mountaineering and into the rarefied social scene first of Chamonix and then of the St Moritz resort, in the mountains of south-eastern Switzerland.[15]

The glamorous young widow hobnobbed with the social and artistic elites at the resort: Arthur Conan Doyle, whom she photographed in Viking horns; two of the American artist James Whistler's muses; Ralph Pulitzer, son of the famous New York newspaperman Joseph; and Bertie Dwyer, a dashing toboggan specialist, his hair carefully parted on the left side of his head, who had recently won the prestigious Symonds Shield in Davos – all were part of her crowd. So, too, could be found the famous Italian pastoral artist Giovanni Segantini, who, with his long wavy hair, massive beard, and wool jacket, looked more than a little like a Russian anarchist revolutionary. Segantini, whose paintings highlighted grazing cattle against mountain backdrops, women bathing in Alpine lakes and vast, snowy landscapes, was wont to pose heroically, his barrel chest puffed out, standing with one foot forward in the middle of the wilderness. It made for marvellous imagery. Almost as marvellous, in fact, as his famous painting *The Punishment of Lust*, showing two partially clad sirens locked in a permanent floating knot, hovering painfully above the barren snowscape. Segantini loved the mountains around St Moritz – loved them so passionately that a few years later he decamped to a hut high up in the mountains to paint in solitude for several weeks. It would prove to be an unfortunate decision; some say he caught pneumonia in his hideaway and, unable to hike back down to the valley below, died a miserable, lonely death in his eyrie.[16] The Cuban American socialite and fabled beauty Doña Maria Consuelo Yznaga y Clement, who had married a British aristocrat and was now known as the Duchess of Manchester, would also show up during the season with her equally glamorous twin daughters, Lady Alice Montagu and Lady Jacqueline Mary Alva Montagu. After the latter died suddenly in 1895, the duchess and Lady Alice continued to visit the Swiss spa.[17] There were wealthy Canadian businessmen and their wives, French *vicomtes*, barons, Italian princes, English ladies with their waiting maids in tow, members of the British peerage and retired military officers. There were society figures from New York, Odessa, Rome, Vienna, Hamburg, London, Edinburgh, even Buenos Aires.[18]

In the middle of the decade, Lottie Dod, five-time Wimbledon champion, fell pell-mell into this crowd.[19]

For months on end in the years following her withdrawal from the tennis world, Lottie, along with Tony and sometimes William, could be found skating in St Moritz. She played tennis with a wide circle of friends, both male and female, when the weather was calm enough, and ice hockey or even ice cricket – a skating adaptation of cricket, played on the frozen lake – when it wasn't. She might well have taken part in the annual friendly games between denizens of St Moritz and hockey and ice cricket players from the nearby rival resort of Davos.[20] Sepia photos taken by Main, now mottled with age, show her on the ice in an ankle-length black skirt, a white blouse and what looks to be a straw hat, the snow-covered peaks as backdrop.[21] Of all the people on earth, quite likely no one understood Dod's obsession with the conquest of new sports in new locales better than did Main. "Who cares to triumph over a foe that shows no fight?" Main would write in one of her many books, *Moutaineering in the Land of the Midnight Sun*. "The exhilaration of the struggle – that is what makes life worth living; and nowhere as in the mountains is a man so quickly and completely brought into the thick of a battle where mind and body alike must put forth their best energies in order to win against nature's opposition."[22]

St Moritz had made a name for itself in recent years because of its sanatorium, a retreat to which well-heeled consumptives would flock to try to repair their ravaged lungs. In the wake of the aristocratic tuberculosis sufferers, other tourists, lured by their praise of the mountain air, followed. They took a train to the valley town of Chur, and from there a series of yellow carriages pulled by four-horse teams, and, for the steeper passes, small yellow-and-black two-person sledges, attached to a single horse. "The driver cracks his whip, and the vehicle moves off, and soon begins laboriously to mount the long incline to Churwalden," Main wrote in her 1886 book, *High Life and Towers of Silence*. Some of the smaller sledges were controlled by a driver standing on a board attached to the back of the vehicle. Others had no drivers; an official would simply crack his whip once the sledge was loaded, scream "*Vorwärts!*" and the trained horses would set off in the direction of the next village along the route, the sledge veering uncomfortably as the horse attempted to navigate the deep snow.[23] Their baggage would follow on other sledges. Atop the Julier Pass – far above the tree line, the surrounding rocky peaks soaring upward, each one seemingly more wild than what had come before – near the standing ruins of a Roman column,[24] the rattled passengers would stop at what Main described as a "dingy little inn", where they would gulp down "most uninviting coffee". And then the sledges would continue down the final slopes to St Moritz; as they did so, the little blots that were tobogganists on the icy streets of the town far below would gradually become larger. When they finally arrived at the post – the stopping point for sledges in the centre of the little community – they would decamp from the vehicles, and slowly trudge the last few yards to the hotel that would be their home for the winter season.

Soon, the grand Kulm Hotel – an imposing cluster of five-storey yellow stone buildings next to the breathtaking Lake St. Moritz, behind which soared snow-covered mountains, its wood-panelled dining rooms and clubs exuding taste and exclusivity and opulence – had become a must-see stop on the winter tour. Affluent sportsmen and sportswomen from around the world would spend months living in its elegant rooms and perfecting their athletic skills on its well-tended grounds. The hotel's colonnaded lobby boasted a stained-glass window ceiling, and its bar area housed a large grand piano on which local musicians would play tunes to entertain the guests. Arrayed in the hallways and other public areas were intricately carved wooden benches and chests, some hundreds of years old, the fruits of owner Johannes Badrutt's obsession with collecting antique furniture. In 1879, its Grand Restaurant was the first place in Switzerland to install electric lighting, when Badrutt – who worked in a dark office on the hotel's ground floor, and whose whole family lived above, in a room reached by a small stone spiral staircase hidden behind a narrow door in the office – rigged up a hydroelectric system to generate power for his sprawling properties. As guests sat at long wooden tables, twenty-four diners at each, in a cavernous room that could seat hundreds, the bulbs of Badrutt's chandeliers, hanging from the high wood-panelled ceiling, were lit up by the newly harnessed electricity. It must have produced an incredible sensation, a feeling that at St Moritz anything was possible: night could even, at the flick of a switch, be turned to day. Ten years later, the year Badrutt died, the hotel scored another first when it became the first building in Switzerland to install a public telephone. By the time Dod arrived, the hotel had notched up two additional records: it now boasted a nine-hole golf course, the highest fairway in the Alps, a few hundred yards up the hill from the main hotel; and, in the basement, it had opened the Alps' first sports bar, the Sunny Bar, with a long, elaborately carved wooden counter and four arched windows looking directly out over the dark green-blue waters of the lake. When the tobogganists, skaters, mountaineers and ice hockey players who were drawn to the town wanted to celebrate, it was down the stairs of the Kulm they trooped, there to drink from the hotel's quite extraordinary wine cellar, one of the most valuable in all of Europe.[25]

Near the grounds of the hotel had been hosted the first European-wide skating championships in 1882 and bobsled competition in 1890.

Now, with Tony immersed in his winter photography, Lottie was looking for new athletic conquests. For more than two hours a day over a two-month period she trained each morning, in order to pass the ladies' skating test. She learned how to perform "inside backs", skating backward into a rotation, the torso still, the rotation coming from the legs and outstretched arms. She perfected her "back outside edges", again skating backward, this time the ridge on the outer edge of her boots gripping the ice. And she learned how to please the judges with effortlessly executed "serpentine lines", long, graceful S-shaped curves, from one side of the ice to the other.[26]

For much of the rest of Dod's waking hours, when she wasn't practising for the challenging skating test, she could be found exploring the nearby Alps and attending local activities, such as the New Year's Day ice-skating festivities and "Fete Day" on 1 March – in which locals rode around in sleighs designed to look like giant ice skates, sitting in the boot of the skate[27] – with her friend Elizabeth Main.

Main had been living in the Kulm for several years now, in a luxurious suite paid for out of the inheritance left her by her father years earlier. She didn't travel light. Elizabeth Main brought with her her life's clutter: her living room at the hotel was filled to overflowing with photos, some framed atop a glass display case packed with crystals, porcelain and small Chinese statues; others cascading off a heavy, overstuffed bureau. It was a room filled with mementos stacked higgledy-piggledy, and with surprising curios.[28] She also had long, coiled mountaineering ropes, ice axes and all the other paraphernalia for her summiting adventures. Main would, when the mood struck, often wake up at two in the morning and, in the bitterly cold, moonlit night, set off, either by herself or with her long-time guide and friend from the town of St Nicholas, Joseph Imboden, to climb a nearby peak. Imboden, whose father had tried to discourage him from climbing by apprenticing him to a boot maker, had been drawn to the mountains his whole life; at the age of sixteen he had run away from his boot-making job, and he had been a guide ever since.[29]

In the evenings, Main would attend photography clubs,

public lectures, musical soirees – decidedly amateur "theatricals" heavy on fancy dress, powdered wigs and pantomime-like escapades. In its high-ceilinged ballroom, the hotel would host charity galas and fetes.

Now, the Dod siblings took their own suites too, heavily panelled rooms with high, ornate wooden ceilings, built-in floor-to-ceiling bookshelves and cupboards, deep bathtubs in which they could soak themselves after a long day on the mountains and windows overlooking the lake.

Skating was all the rage that year among the fashionable ex-pat community living in St Moritz and in the nearby resorts of Davos and Chamonix. Every Sunday morning, Lizzie Main, Lottie and Tony Dod, and the others would traipse to the local Protestant churches, the one in St Moritz a little stone building with a simple, tall spire, nestled in the valley against the edge of the lake. These houses of worship had been built by subscriptions raised among the English residents over the past several years. There, the skating-obsessed worshippers could be seen in the pews, surreptitiously practising, their feet pushing off from the ground at a ten to three o'clock motion as the service droned on.[30]

On 15 January 1896, four male judges – all staples in the local English community – Doctor Holland, Reverend C. Watson, Harold Topham and General Grove, got dressed up in their woollen trousers tucked into long socks, donned their sports jackets and their formal hats and skated out on to the ice to grade Lottie's performance.[31] Off to the side, Tony stood with his camera covered in a black drape, attached to a tall tripod. His left hand was stationed under the draping, ready to press down on the camera shutter as his younger sister, wearing a long, crenellated dark skirt, a white blouse and a straw hat, performed her drills. Perched next to his right foot on the ice was a leather satchel, in which he kept all his miscellaneous photography gear.

The Little Wonder passed with flying colours.

Now, not content with having aced the female skating test, Dod decided that she would become as good as the best men in the sport. True to form, the next year, coached by her erstwhile cycling companion, mountaineer and champion toboggan racer Harold Topham – who had been one of the judges for her ladies' test – she passed the far more rigorous men's exam. Main, who was there with her dogs taking photographs of her friend that day, 16 January 1897, had been the first lady ever to pass this test, back in 1889. Now Dod was taking it to the next level.[32] She elegantly skated "z's to a centre" with one Mr R. Readhead, winner of the Davos Skating Challenge Bowl for two successive years; did a series of figure eights, described at the time as "eights to a centre"; and executed to perfection tight "D turns". By day's end, Lottie Dod had been recognised as a skater who could hold her own with the best men of the era.

When the storied Lottie Dod came to St Moritz, Elizabeth Main must have known she had found a kindred spirit. As the winter snows gave way to milder spring weather, Main adored taking photos of her new friend on one of the hotel's three tennis courts – an umpire sitting, legs crossed, in a raised chair next to the court, the hotel a few hundred yards off to the south-west, craggy Alps seemingly immediately behind the baseline, the lake a few hundred feet below. Sometimes she even managed to pull off the complicated technical feat of capturing the ball in motion, fresh off Dod's strings. In many of these photos, the Wimbledon champion bestrides the net in her mixed doubles matches, her left leg pulled far back under the hem of her long black dress, her left foot raised up on to its toes, as she springs into a volley. The weight of her body is pushing forward on her planted right foot. Arms outstretched to balance her and add force to the upcoming shot, Dod is throwing all of herself into the point. There's nothing dainty or "ladylike" about the image. One sees an athlete, pure and simple.

Dod, always looking to improve her technique, would have adapted her swing to neutralise the fact that, at well over a mile above sea level, the tennis balls in St Moritz flew off the racket strings far faster and further than they usually did. She would have shortened the backswing, perhaps hit the ball flatter, maybe tried out some slice or backspin to keep the ball from soaring out behind the baseline. Perhaps the first few times she played, the high altitude would have left her breathless and perspiring; soon, however, her lungs would have become used to the thinner air – she was, after all, a supremely well-conditioned athlete; and then she would have felt like she could fly: the pure Alpine air would have filled her lungs; and she would have been able to run around the court, the short, cropped grass of which was covered with a thin layer of sand, with vast reserves of energy.[33]

In some of Main's photos, Dod is even serving overarm, a radical departure for the champion who had won Wimbledon five times using the older-fashioned underarm serve. Again the motion is forceful, modern. One can almost hear the thwack of the ball meeting the racket as it begins to fall from the apex of the toss. Despite the full-length dress she is wearing, one can practically see her leg muscles as she bends into the toss, her abdominal muscles as she stretches up towards the ball, her upper arm muscles as she makes contact with the felt-covered rubber projectile. Even from nearly 130 years removed, one can see the concentration on her face as she looks to place her serve where her opponent won't reach it. In another particularly beautiful image, Lottie Dod, in an ankle-length black dress and broad-rimmed black hat, is smiling broadly, practically dancing towards Main as she returns to the baseline, presumably having just won a point at the net.[34]

One of the handwritten notes that Main penned to accompany her photos, carefully glued into hefty albums, mentions that Dod had sprained her wrist; and in the photo that goes with the note, there is Dod, walking through a snowy pine forest, hiding her injured arm under a huge, hooded cape, almost as if she's embarrassed to show vulnerability. She had, apparently, been violently thrown from a toboggan.

In 1895, along with William and Tony, Dod began mountain climbing with Elizabeth. That year and the next, the companions took long walks in the snowy passes, accompanied by a large Bernese dog named Pluto.[35] They clambered over the Morteratsch glacier, carefully navigating its complex, potentially deadly series of crevasses. They roamed deep into ice caves.

In the Val Roseg, they crossed frozen rivers, the surfaces of which were covered in deep, soft snow. Near the village of Samedan, they found a wonderland of ice speckled with a light covering of freshly fallen snow, all framed by dramatic, windswept bushes, the branches covered in ice crystals.

In the early spring, as the snows began to melt, they encountered grazing cattle and the first blooms of yellow, purple and white flower–speckled broad meadows, the long grasses blowing in the fierce winds that came down off the glacier-covered peaks surrounding Lake Sils. Far into the valley, in a landscape dominated by tall conifers – the thick roots of which protruded on the rutted paths and made walking the mountain routes above the lake particularly treacherous – along the banks of fast-flowing rivers, they would have come across ancient villages. The houses were squat affairs, some of stone, others of logs; their roofs were made out of thick slate slabs layered atop each other. Farming families lived there, cutting grass for hay in the summers, keeping herds of cattle for milk and for meat. Outside each house were huge piles of chopped wood, fuel for the long, cold, dark winter months.[36]

Sometimes they dressed like Victorian gentlemen and ladies out for a stroll, their clothes desperately formal, their only concession to their environment stout walking sticks. On other days, particularly when they were away from view, the ladies replaced their impractical dresses with clothes tailored more appropriately for climbing. Main wrote that she would choose skirts "of the lightest possible material", so that they "could be rolled up and carried in a knapsack".[37] Come lunchtime, they would sit down on fallen branches, or directly on to the snow or ice, take out their wicker baskets and leather bags filled with food and bottles or tin gourds of wine, and picnic, eating directly from the oil paper wrappings, Pluto nuzzling up to them, hoping to get a bite.[38] When the weather was particularly cold, they found, through trial and error, that the best way to keep their wine from freezing was to wrap the tin gourds in flannel bags stuffed with cotton wool insulation. Their biscuits and cognac didn't need such elaborate protections; they seemed, wrote Main happily, "quite proof against congelation".[39]

Main taught Dod how to use an alpenstock, essentially a rock-cutting axe that allowed the user to carve out little ridges, on which to grab on to while scaling a rock face. They started using ropes, rappelling up and down steep, icy, rocky crags. In some of Main's photos, her companions are dangling off these ropes, seemingly hanging above the void. "Miss Lottie Dod tries mountaineering," Main observed coquettishly in one of her album notations.

Dod, restless, always eager for something new, was a quick

learner. Over the next two years, before they had a bitter falling-out, the pair summited some of Europe's most difficult peaks, in Switzerland, Norway and elsewhere.[40] They walked together in snowbanks, just about at the tree line, Lottie sandwiched between a guide with a walking stick in front of her and the dog, Pluto, behind her. Other than these three beings, and Main off to the side with her camera, there was just snow as far as the eye could see and, on the adjacent slope, a smattering of trees.

They snaked their way along narrow rock ledges; used ropes to pull themselves up vertical cliffs. Main painstakingly documented the expeditions. In one image, Imboden can be seen atop a rocky ledge, looking out over the void, the sky starting to cloud over. Behind him, attached by ropes, Dod, in a long skirt and blouse, is pulling herself up the edge of the rock face, her back bowed, her eyes looking down as her feet seek a grip. "Never mind your womenkind!" Main scribbled cheekily underneath the photo. In another of her mementos, they can be seen with no ropes, using handholds to pull themselves up a rock face the gradient of which is more than forty-five degrees. Far below the climbers can be seen the vague outline of a tree-studded valley.[41]

Not content with climbing these peaks in the spring and summer months, when the weather was mild and the rocks largely ice-free, they also began a daring series of ascents during the harshest season of the year. On 13 February 1896, with local guides Martin Schocher and Christian Schnitzler, they summited the Zwei Schwestern or "Two Sisters" peak, also known to the local Romansh-speaking population simply as Las Sours. It was a brutal climb: hours up the sides of the slopes rising from the nearby village of Pontresina; and then, as an extraordinary vista unfolded before their eyes – on one side lakes strung like beads on a necklace along a narrow valley in between mountains, and, off to the left, soaring glacier-covered peaks – they ascended up an ever-steeper terrain of scree and loose boulders. The path wound its way around the mountain, one hairpin bend after another after another, the slope at times so steep they would have had to walk almost doubled over simply to propel themselves forward.

Eventually, exhausted, most likely panting for breath in the increasingly thin air, they reached a hut. From there, they could see an immense glacial range off to their right, and the steep, barren slopes of the Two Sisters to their left. They rested at the hut, drank hot drinks to try to warm their freezing bodies, and finally set off again. At a fast pace, it was a couple of hours walking still, ploughing through snowfields; trudging up the steep face of the first of the Two Sisters; finally, as they neared the almost vertical final ascent, tying themselves together with ropes, and one at a time scrabbling up the rocks, looking for handholds from one moment to the next. At the top, they sat on a ledge barely large enough to hold all of them at once and looked over the valley, and its speck-like villages, far below.[42]

Six days later, with Tony along for the climb as well, they made the first-ever winter ascent of Piz Zupò,[43] a craggy 13,000-foot peak, reached via the Morteratsch glacier, that soared over both the surrounding mountains and the cloud cover below. On the glacier itself, there were enormous "glacier tables", random arrangements of chunks of ice that Main felt looked like tables resting on their legs. She posed one of the hikers by the ice furniture to give her audience a sense of scale. Each table was at least the height of an adult human. It was a violent, unpredictable glacier, the huge ice floes rutted and cracked, with immense crevasses capable of forever disappearing a hiker in an instant, and towering, cathedral-like turrets of ice.[44]

The top of Zupò, exposed entirely to the elements and far above the tree line, was dominated by a series of brutally steep ridges, the snowbanks sweeping downward like waves breaking from their crest. Even though 1896 was a peculiarly mild winter, the shallow snows allowing for first winter summits of many Swiss peaks, nevertheless temperatures at the top could plunge to twenty degrees below freezing, sometimes even colder.[45]

Main and the Dods reached that peak wearing their regular woollen hiking clothes, their boots with nails in the soles to help them grip, their ropes and ice axes. Had they succumbed to the frigid air or fallen into the deep snowdrifts, had they slid off an icy ridge or dropped into a crevasse, no one would have known where they were; and even if they did, they wouldn't have been able to rescue them.

They were living as close to the edge as one could choose to live. They were, in modern parlance, feeding off the adrenaline rush that comes with tempting fate. And each time they succeeded in conquering another peak, so the urge to go still further, to risk still more, intensified.

Resting a few days after this extreme climb, on the morning of 23 February the women began another ascent. That evening, Lottie, Elizabeth, Tony and their guide Martin Schocher were the first climbers to ever summit the Swiss Drei Blumen or "Three Flowers" peak in winter, Main boasted in her album notes. It wasn't all smooth sailing; near the top, climbing up a cracked rock edifice that looked like a gigantic jigsaw puzzle with each of the pieces fitting together but slightly loose, one of the climbers, attempting to scale a near-vertical rock face, lost their grip on the tiny hand and footholds. The embarrassed member of the troupe had to be hauled up the rock face by the rope they were hanging from by a clearly exhausted Schocher.[46] Again, however, they were rewarded by views the likes of which few people had ever seen: a huge, snowy panorama extended below them. Everything was silent, apart from the roaring of the wind in their ears.

FOUR

The Grand Tour on Wheels

An Elizabeth Main photograph of Dod taken during the European bike tour, spring 1896. Courtesy of the Martin and Osa Johnson Safari Museum.

The experience of summiting these peaks had drawn Main and the Dods ever closer; for a while it seemed their every action was coordinated. Where Main went, the Dods did too. When the Dods took up new sports and hobbies, including endurance bicycling, Main swiftly joined in the fun.

Come spring, with the St Moritz season winding down, the friends looked for other adventures.

In early March 1896, Lottie and her brother Tony set off by train for Rome, to join Main on a bicycling tour that would, over the next three months, take them through Italy, back to Switzerland, Italy again, San Marino, France and finally England. For some weeks they were joined, too, by Harold Topham, their tobogganist friend and general sporting enthusiast, and someone whom Main may have been romantically involved with before the expedition began. Somewhere in France, on the road from Évien to Territet, Main handed over her camera to another friend, possibly either the photographer Robert Bly or one L. Oppenheim, whom Main had nicknamed both "the strongman" and "Mr Red". With that fifth person aiming the camera straight at them, the four of them rode abreast down the street, each with one hand on the neighbouring bike's handlebars, forming a human chain on wheels.

They had, in careful detail, mapped out their own personal grand tour, one that would take them on bikes and trains through some of Europe's most stunning and dramatic mountain, lake and coastal landscapes. It would encompass great cities from Rome to Florence to Milan, Geneva to Paris to London, and would allow Main to photograph many of the most famous Roman and Greek ruins in Italy – from the destroyed city of Pompeii to the Greek temple of Neptune at Paestum.

Tony was something of a show-off on his bike. On occasion, like a vaudevillian emoting for the crowd, he would stand atop the seat, arms leaning forward to grasp the handlebars, or coast side-saddle, both his legs swivelled rigidly out to the left. Perhaps, in these tricks, the youngest Dod son was recalling weekend parties to which the four siblings had been invited in Cheshire some years earlier, in which guests had ridden bicycles down the capacious halls of stately homes, sometimes using the two-wheelers as proxies for horses in impromptu indoor games of polo.[1] As well as being the resident trickster, Tony was also the designated Sherpa of the group. "In addition to his own luggage," Main wrote, "Tony usually carried the camera, the string bag containing lunch, our books and maps, and any other trifles he could possess himself of."[2] He wore, on these journeys, light-coloured flannel trousers tucked into his woollen socks, simple leather shoes, a cream-coloured jacket, a white shirt, a cravat and a beige cap. His moustache was trim. Approaching thirty, he looked the quintessential late Victorian gentleman-adventurer. The women wore their long dresses, their formal hats, their gloves.

The cycling was hard. Some days, they would force themselves over high mountain passes, or walk their bikes slowly along muddy, rutted mule paths. More than once, the only way up steep mountains was by pushing their bikes, laden with their bags, up rough-hewn stone steps carved into the sides of the slopes. One afternoon, in fierce headwinds, they were forced to walk their bikes twenty miles uphill.[3] Other days, they would set out early, cycling tens of miles along country lanes from one city to the next. Come lunchtime, they would stop by the side of the road and picnic amid the flowers. On occasion, they would pluck bouquets of narcissi from the fields.

When they arrived in each town, they would book into a local hotel and stay for a few days, their hours filled with sightseeing, either in the city itself or on exhausting day trips to neighbouring villages and natural wonders. Over the Gorges du Trient, they crossed a ramshackle wooden bridge, high above the waters at the bottom of the gorge, which looked like it could crumble at any moment, casting them into the abyss.

In Rome, which they sojourned in for long periods at the start of their trip and again in early April, they toured the Colosseum, the Via Appia, the Vatican – walking the cobbles of St Peter's Square to find different angles to photograph the great basilica. They visited the Baths of Caracalla, and marvelled at the surviving floor mosaics there and also the huge scale of the arches that once held up the great edifice of the bathhouse. Tony stood at the base of one of the arches, a mere human speck against the stone, to provide a sense of scale. They wandered through the ruins of the Forum, stopped at the Arch of Titus. They went to see the little boats docked along the banks of the Tiber, and strolled through the city's parks, through the Jewish ghetto, up to the Trevi Fountain.

There was something almost frantic in their itinerary, as if they were determined to see absolutely everything of note listed in the popular guidebooks of the time, published by newly flourishing travel companies such as Thomas Cook, Murray's and Baedeker. "On the fifth [of April], we go to Frascati and Tusculum," Main noted. And then, as if it was self-evident why, she tersely added, "The amphitheatre."

In Milan they went to see a tomb within which were interred the remains of one of the infamous Renaissance-era Borgias.

When they arrived in Florence early in the fourth week of March, the quartet splurged on rooms at the Hotel Grande Bretagne, from the windows of which they could look out over the famous Ponte Vecchio, and the covered way leading to the magnificent Uffizi Palace. The hotel was a luxurious, five-storey affair, ranged against the built-up riverbank, an Italian flag fluttering from the roof, the sort of place those with means went to honeymoon. At street level, little stores and restaurants perched under green canopies.[4] Each day, they lunched at a small restaurant opposite the simple rectangular edifice of the Orsanmichele church, converted in the late 1300s from a grain market into a house of worship, its roof red tiled, its windows arched Gothic-style. They ascended the steps of the campanile to take in the views of the city below. They marvelled at Giovanni da Bologna's *Rape of the Sabines*, one of the greatest sculptures of the sixteenth century. It was thirteen feet tall, carved out of a single piece of marble, and depicted a Roman soldier grabbing a young Sabine woman away from her helpless husband. The three figures were entwined together, their fates inexorably linked, their emotions etched eternally, agonisingly, into the marble.

On the road between Florence and Perugia, on 25 March, as the friends struggled through a late-season snowstorm, they suddenly came upon the vast ruins of the Aqua Claudia, the arches of the aqueduct mere silhouettes in the swirling snow. Two weeks later, as they made their way north through Italy towards the tiny republic of San Marino and its dramatic cliff-edge buildings, they "had a hard day over a high pass to Spoleto"; then on to Terni, where tall waterfalls appeared equally suddenly and dramatically out of what looked like a sea of rising, early-springtime mist; and finally to Assisi, to visit the monastery where St Francis had once resided. They refreshed themselves in a hotel, and then continued on again, this time to Ravenna, the western centre of governance in the late, declining Roman Empire after Rome had been sacked by the barbarians.

Their pace was hectic, exhausting. Why stay still when there was an entire world to see?

* * *

Over the next two months, the crew took trains, bicycles and rowboats as they continued on their journey. They went into Switzerland to explore, by foot, the brutal, still-snow-covered Pennine peaks, some of them needle-sharp at the summit, surrounding the town of Zermatt. They sojourned for a week by the Italian lakes, visiting Como, Lake Maggiore and other significant sights. They rowed along the reed-lined Rhône river and the canal near Villeneuve; sometimes they exchanged their oars for punts, and, like Oxford students on a leisurely afternoon out, took it in turns to stand up and use their long poles to push their way along the shallow waters. On occasion, when the waters were too shallow for either rowing or punting, one of them would hop out on to the towpath to the side of the canal and pull the boat along until they reached deeper waters. Often, they would let the vessel drift while they sat under a white awning, unpacked their picnic bags and ate a leisurely lunch.

Slowing down somewhat, the quartet then spent three weeks in the Lake Geneva area,[5] including a few leisurely days in a cosy lakefront hotel in the town of Geneva itself, watching the waters lap gently against the pebbled shore, enchanted by the little boats that locals sailed a mere stone's throw away from the water's edge. Some days, they themselves took a little boat with two sloped sails far out into the middle of the lake.

In the village of Territet, they rode the funicular railway, constructed thirteen years earlier, up the mountain to Glion. It was known to be a harrowing ride, the anxiety it provoked only just redeemed by the stunning views from the top. Once the brakes on the car were released when leaving the station, the funicular worked by gravity alone; two cars, both attached to a single cable above, rode the narrow, steep rail, one going up, the other down. Under each was a water tank, filled at the top of the ride. As the first car descended from Glion, its extra weight from the water pulled up the other car – which had, once it reached the bottom, dumped its water into Lake Geneva. At the midpoint, the single rail on which both cars rode temporarily split in two, allowing the cars to pass each other without crashing. Think about it too much, and one probably wouldn't risk the ride. Put one's fear to the back of one's mind, however, and the payoff was magnificent: a thrill seeker's ride up the side of a mountain, the thick, dark-green vegetation encroaching right up to the side of the tracks, and, from the top, a view of the entire lake, the sun glinting off the deep water, surrounded by snowcapped mountains.

Finally, in late May, two days before they were booked on to a ship that would take them across the English Channel, the bicyclists stopped briefly in Paris to wrap up their Continental wanderings. The streets were extraordinarily crowded, filled with other cyclists, with horse-drawn carriages, with men and women and children promenading along the tree-lined boulevards. Surprisingly, however, the city didn't seem to leave too much of an impression; Main took few photos but, unlike in Rome, they didn't go on a whirlwind sightseeing tour. Instead, they quickly headed to the Channel, crossed over to England, and by the morning of the twenty-ninth were bicycling through the thronged centre of London and into Hyde Park, the pathways of the famous leisure playground packed both with pedestrians enjoying a day in the springtime sun and also what appeared to be hundreds upon hundreds of bicycles and horse-drawn carriages. It was, if possible, even more crowded than had been Paris.

Their trip was almost over. Through the course of the next week, they made their way slowly around southern England. Finally, on 9 June, three months after they had first settled into their hotel in Rome to plan out their route, they called it quits. "The party breaks up," Main noted somewhat forlornly in her album, in the margins next to one final photograph of Tony Dod doing stunts on his bike in the gardens of what looks to be a country house.

FIVE

The Fastest Woman on Earth

An Elizabeth Main photograph of Lottie Dod training for her ice-skating test in St Moritz. Courtesy of the Martin and Osa Johnson Safari Museum.

It would, of course, take more than the ending of an individual trip to break up the kind of party, the rolling celebration of life and adventure, such as the one the Dods and Main now lived for. And so, the next winter, the snows of St Moritz would draw them back.

Three years earlier, on 24 February 1894, a bluebell morning, the sky cloudless, the sun glinting off the ice and snow, Lottie and Tony's friend Harold Topham had hurtled down the Cresta Run, across the snowfields from the Kulm Hotel, on a steel-skeleton toboggan. He did so three times in quick succession. It was the annual Grand National race, and competitors were in town from England, the United States, Canada and elsewhere.

Each year since the run's inauguration in January 1885 – nine weeks after workers hired by Peter Badrutt, son of Johannes, the original owner of the Kulm Hotel, started carving the runs out of the Alpine snow – daredevils had gathered in St Moritz to try their hand at this new sport. As soon as the season began, just before Christmas, they would flock its way, each trying to outdo their rivals in terms of sheer speed. The competitors would lug their toboggans a short walk down the hill from the tennis courts, heading away from St Moritz and the lake, and would then hurtle downhill, towards Celerina, the next village along the valley. They would weave in and out of the shadows cast by tall pine trees, the fragrant purple, white, yellow and pink wildflowers of summer now long buried beneath the snowbanks, and then out into the broad expanses, the sudden visibility of the sheer lines of the mountainsides, sloping left to right in front of them at the end of the valley, signifying that they were approaching the finish line.

The Grand National race, held at the height of the season, was the event in which the best of the best of them competed.

Topham set off from the top in an unorthodox style, running across the steep start line, the nails embedded in his shoes gripping the ice, his toboggan tucked under his arm. As the slope steepened, he leaned down, placed the sledge on the ice, and without slowing leaped on to its cushion and began the descent. It proved to be a winning method. He navigated the three-quarter-mile course, its sometimes-deadly turns, its steep descents, its icy straights, to perfection. By the end of the second run it was clear that, barring a disaster, no one would catch him on the final go-around. And sure enough, they didn't. Topham was in a league of his own, flying down parts of the course at an astonishing seventy miles per hour.[1] That year, the only real drama in the third run was who would take the bronze and silver positions.

In a photo taken at the bottom of the course, as one of the riders crosses the finish line, four women can be seen, all in long black dresses, capes and hats, the one in the foreground with a parasol leaning forward. They were enthusiastically trying to capture in their minds' eyes that exact moment in which the tape was crossed and the timer waved his flag, signalling to the stopwatch keeper at the start line hundreds of feet above to stop his clock.[2] Its entirely possible one of those four women was Lottie Dod. Certainly she would have been at the Cresta that day, watching her friends compete.

Now, three years later, Dod asked Topham whether he would be willing to coach her in this new and terrifying sport too.

Over the past ten years, tobogganing had developed in leaps and bounds. Riders had moved from short, wooden sledges, on which they sat as they steered down the mountain, to longer, lower and far faster steel-skeleton constructions, where they lay down on their bellies and rode the run head first. The steel-skeleton vehicles were only five inches off the ice, their grooved runners a mere eighteen millimetres wide. As the riders sped head first on a flat cushion laid atop the centre board, down the infamous, twisting Cresta Run, they picked up incredible speeds. In some of the straighter parts of the course, such as the steep Cresta Leap, they could gobble up forty yards in a little over one second. Sir Theodore Andrea Cook, a race participant and author, wrote that these were speeds "which can scarcely be credited by any one but an eye-witness of the actual performances".[3]

Good tobogganers like Topham would reach seventy miles

per hour, the ice mere inches from their noses. It was, like so many other sports in the late Victorian period, thought to be the exclusive preserve of well-heeled gentlemen-adventurers. Indeed, towards the end of his book on the Cresta, Cook had specifically warned women off trying it, arguing that while the fair sex was capable of sitting upright on a wooden sledge and navigating gentler parts of the course, they were constitutionally incapable of lying head first on a fast steel skeleton and completing the whole thing. Cook warned that the "tempestuous petticoat" that custom dictated women wear would get tangled up in the equipment, and that no woman should attempt the "One Tree Leap" and other particularly challenging parts near the top of the run. Perhaps, when writing this, he was thinking of an insult then in vogue in society circles. The three daughters of the aged Queen Victoria who had remained in England as adults – Lenchen, Louise, and Beatrice – were, in those years, disparagingly referred to as "the Petticoats".[4] Ladies, he cautioned, "should be sedulously encouraged, both at the beginning of the season and after the 'Grand National' is over, to ride steadily and confidently from the 'Junction' [halfway down the course] . . . to the finish". And even then, he noted solicitously, the ride was "not without its risks".[5] All through the mid 1890s, women such as Lottie's childhood friend Mrs Pennington Legh had tackled portions of the run. None, however, had gone all the way.

Lottie Dod, who had recently returned to the tennis courts to play an exhibition match in which she had soundly beaten another leading male tennis player, the Scotsman S. Hillier, in yet another battle of the sexes, was having none of it.[6] Petticoats be damned, she decided she would be the first woman ever to make it down the run.

For weeks on end, Topham explained to Dod how to steer

the sledge with subtle shifts in her body weight, how to brake by letting the iron toe screwed into each boot descend on to the ice to force the pace to slow through friction. Oversteer, and the rider would crash into the sides. Get it right, and you could propel yourself down the three-quarters-of-a-mile run at least as fast as the fastest locomotive train on earth, the ice an exhilarating blur as you sped along the run. "It descends 500 feet," wrote Topham in a sports encyclopedia entry a few years later. "There are no two corners alike, no two consecutive gradients which are similar, and no section which is actually straight."

Cars had been invented and popularised in the early 1890s; but by Thanksgiving 1895, at the first American automobile race, held in Chicago and sponsored by a local newspaper, the winner managed to eke out an average of only 7.3 miles per hour.[7] Motorcycles weren't yet much faster. A horse at full gallop might reach thirty miles per hour over a sustained distance, maybe even as high as fifty for a very short duration. And a few trains – notably the one that took Nellie Bly east across the American continent in early 1890 on the final leg of her mad dash to circumnavigate the globe faster than anyone had ever done before – had reached sustained speeds of sixty miles per hour. But those were the exception; mostly locomotives chugged along at a far slower rate. And so, if you were a true speed demon in the 1890s, there was no place on earth you could go at greater speed than at the new toboggan run in Switzerland. Dod wanted her part of this.

Harold Topham, as experienced in ice sports as any man on earth, was in awe at the new run, as devilish in its journey as the most ornate of roller coasters would be in theme parks a century later. It was a wild beast, on the verge of being untamable, its entire length kept as sheet ice by crews throwing bucket after bucket of water on to the packed snow. "Of the corners, several are almost right angles, and one, at least, is hardly more than a prolonged curve. Where the corner is most abrupt, there we find the steeper and higher bank." If a rider lost control on the Shuttlecock, an infamous corkscrew turn halfway down, they would plunge out on to a crash bank of soft snow and straw, instantly earning membership in the forlorn "Shuttlecock Club".[8] At the bottom of the course, as the gradient bottomed out, riders frequently would catch air, flying scores of feet above the snow before landing in the soft snowbanks at the far end of the run. Tony Dod took particular pleasure in using his high-speed camera to capture the exact moment riders became airborne. When they shakily got to their feet and turned to look back up the slope, they saw a huge, humpbacked massif looming up above them; the buildings of St Moritz, from down in the valley, couldn't be seen; they were hidden behind the soaring pine trees that the riders had just navigated their course through.

All of this respect for the course Topham imparted to his student. He taught Lottie to master every detail, not to leave anything to chance.

The winter of 1896/7, that season in which Dod conquered the Cresta, the fastest man completed the run in what was then a stunning 69.2 seconds.[9] Dod was slower – and, while she likely went head first down parts of the course during her training, when she did it top to bottom in one go, she did so sitting upright.[10] But her time was largely beside the point; in completing a course thought to be impossible for members of her fair and fragile sex, she had more than proven herself once again.

It was a remarkable achievement. Until her top-to-bottom run, no woman had successfully navigated the sometimes-deadly course, and only a handful, in 1895, had reached the bottom from their midcourse starting position. Thirty-two years after her triumph, with only a few additional women having conquered the Cresta in the intervening decades, the St Moritz Tobogganing Club formally banned women from racing; the ostensible reason was that lying face down on a speeding sledge for prolonged periods could trigger breast cancer. The ban stood from 1929 through to the end of 2018.

Even today, more than 120 years after Dod's success, with women once again allowed, they are in practice heavily discouraged by the club from trying the run, and are kept strictly separate from their male counterparts. "Ladies may ride the Cresta Run at times set out in the Notice pertaining to Rule 8b," the rules state somewhat snootily, making sure that women cannot go down the run at times set aside for men.

After navigating the Cresta successfully several times, sometime later that winter Dod was violently thrown from her toboggan on one of the trickier turns of the run. She hurt her wrist and was lucky not to have done more damage. It would be the last time she ventured down its brutal slopes.[11]

Now, she turned elsewhere to sate her taste for danger. In her mid twenties, Dod's appetite for new challenges was seemingly unquenchable. She took part in curling contests on the ice; in often-brutal ice hockey games; even in the local speciality of ice cricket. She accompanied Harold Topham on "ice sailing" expeditions, in which ice skaters would hold a huge sail and pick up tremendous speeds skating across the lake. And, along with Main and three men, she rode five-person bobsledges down steep mountainsides. But what really excited her was climbing.

Despite being relatively new to the world of mountaineering, she determined that she would ascend some of Europe's toughest peaks, both in Switzerland and in Norway. Main found the Little

Wonder's tenacity exhilarating. She fondly nicknamed her "the Novice", and then quickly explained how inappropriate such a name actually was, given Dod's enthusiasm. "The Novice," she wrote, "[is] a young lady who has taken to climbing with an avidity that makes her title as unsuitable as is that of King of the Gypsies to the sturdy Spanish beggar who hangs around the door of the Alhambra."[12]

Along with Tony – now enduring the nickname "Bones" – Elizabeth Main, and their long-time mountaineering guide in Switzerland, Joseph Imboden, Lottie Dod returned to England and prepared to head north.

Imboden's oldest son, Roman, who had been guiding mountaineers from the time he was thirteen years old, had recently died in a grisly accident atop the Lyskamm peak in the Swiss Alps – the younger Imboden, aged twenty-seven, along with two other climbers, had been standing on a snowy cornice jutting out from the rocks when it broke off, plunging them hundreds of feet to their deaths. Shortly afterwards, his battered body was buried in a little cemetery in Zermatt, filled with the marble tombstones and simple stone crosses marking the graves of mountaineers who had died while climbing. Nearby was a tiny chapel where special prayers were routinely offered up to protect climbers from the dangers of avalanches.[13] "By his English friends," the wording on his tombstone said, "as a mark of their appreciation for his sterling qualities as a man and a guide."[14] In his death, Roman had joined a growing group of legendary climbers who had, over the past few decades, as mountaineering grew in popularity, died while trying to summit ever-harder peaks. There was Jean-Antoine Carrel, who met his end falling from the Matterhorn; there was Mummery, who died in the Himalayas; there were Donkin, Fox and their Swiss guides, who were killed while climbing in the Caucasus; and many others too – climbers buried by vast avalanches of rock and snow; adventurers trying out the new sport of skiing who had fallen into crevasses; ill-equipped tourists who hadn't taken seriously enough the dangers of ice movements on the glacial fields, or sudden shifts in the weather high up on the slopes.

In the wake of the tragedy, Joseph himself, while he remained as avid a climber as ever, had recoiled temporarily from doing more ascents in Switzerland – as had Elizabeth Main, who had been extremely close friends with Roman. When she had first heard the awful news, while sitting and writing at a dinner table in the salon at the Hotel Zermatt, she had been inconsolable.

Now, months later, still consumed by grief, both Joseph Imboden and Elizabeth Main had decided to heal themselves by climbing in parts unknown. For Main, climbing was more a meditation than a sport. It was how she centered herself. "It takes [the mountaineer] amongst the grandest scenery in the world," she wrote a few years later, explaining the allure. "It shows him the forces of nature let loose in the blinding snowstorm, or the roaring of an avalanche. It lifts him above all the petty fiction of daily life, and takes him where the atmosphere is always pure, and the outlook calm and wide."[15]

And so, with Baedeker travel guidebooks in hand, the quartet decided upon the destination of southern and central Norway.[16]

Imboden, a wiry, moustachioed, guru-like character, his cheeks and the skin surrounding his eyes creased with wrinkles from long hours exposed to the elements, knew Main's formidable skills on the mountains. He had, after all, been her friend and guide for years. She, in turn, considered him to be their most "devoted philosopher and friend in every circumstance which may arise". As for Lottie, while the old mountaineer could see that she clearly hadn't much experience climbing, her enthusiasm, as demonstrated by her recent exploits with Main in the Alps, was self-evident. Suggesting that she do the mountaineering equivalent of throwing herself into a pool at the deep end in order to learn to swim, the Swiss guide recommended she attempt Skagastølstind, a brutally difficult climb in the Hurrungane range, and the third-highest peak in all of Norway. It had first been summited only twenty-one years earlier, and the first woman to reach its top, the Norwegian climber Therese Bertheau, had only done so in 1894.[17] Main, looking on at the scene as her guide gently ribbed the one-time Wimbledon champion, reported mischievously, "The Novice opened her eyes at this programme, but was, as ever, obedient."[18]

Main, Imboden, Lottie and Tony took a train to Hull, a port city in Yorkshire, its estuary leading out over twenty-five miles into the rough waters of the open North Sea. In their Zermatt knapsacks, mountaineering bags with numerous separate compartments to make it easy to retrieve necessary equipment, were packed a variety of potted meats, jams, tinned soups and, for the picnics they anticipated taking in the valleys abutting the fjords, several bottles of wine. Tony brought with him, in addition to his camera equipment, a pair of powerful binoculars.[19] In Hull, on a fine summer evening in July 1897, they boarded the *Eldorado* steamer that would take them to the Norwegian port of Bergen. It was a long journey, but a fairly popular one; there were at least three commercial steamers, as well as several mail boats, making regular runs between the two cities that year.[20]

The boat headed slowly north, the seas surprisingly calm, continuing all through the night, then through the next day, and finally arriving in Bergen the following evening. The waters abutting the small but lively town were filled with steamships and masted vessels, and on the cobbled wharf was a large fish market, the wares laid out on tables lined along the street, customers crowded in to buy the freshly caught produce.[21] There were shrimp, crabs, huge slabs of salmon. Some days, the fishermen – each in yellow canvas hats, oiled to waterproof them – would row up to the piers in their skiffs, and ladies, baskets in hand, would descend the stone steps to the water's edge to choose whole fish directly from the piles in the bottoms of the boats.[22] There likely would have also been sausage sellers lining the docks, with the sausages filled with exotic meats such as whale, reindeer and moose. Overhead, gulls circled and squawked noisily, swooping down on to the streets to take leftover pickings from the fish sellers.

Bergen, on Norway's south-western coast, had once played a prominent role in the trading systems of the Hanseatic League, which had dominated the economy of northern Europe 500 years earlier. Colourful brick and stone houses with arched windows and steep, slate-tiled roofs topped with solid stone chimneys – trophy homes lived in during those bygone centuries by wealthy league traders – lined the old wharf. They ranged in height from four to six storeys. Coming off the docks as well were a series of three-storey, rough-hewn wooden warehouses, dating to the early eighteenth century, their lofts with gabled windows built out over the narrow, dark alleyways that they inhabited. The entrances to each warehouse were heavy, painted iron doors, each swinging on huge hinges.

In the centre of the pretty little town were museums and churches; elegant, manicured gardens and lakes; and numerous copper statues, now green with age, celebrating leading citizens, burghers, from times past.

Rising up off the central city, a dense warren of smaller abodes were nestled against the mountains that rose steeply off the fjord. Seven mountains were ranged around the city – and from the top of one of them, in the little community of Fløyen, visitors could sit and drink coffee and look down on Bergen's impressive old streets far below. On sunny days, one could trek up steep rocky mountain paths – narrowing at points to just a few feet wide – from Fløyen to Ulriken, and then down the side of the mountains again to the outskirts of Bergen. It was a hard half day's hike, six hours at a fast trot. But, as locals were careful to warn tourists, the weather could change in an instant; fierce winds and drenching, freezing rains could suddenly come in off the sea, turning the route into a treacherous, slippery, muddy morass; and dense, rapidly developing fogs could make it all but impossible to keep sight of the trails. When the fogs were particularly bad, one's hiking companions would disappear away entirely into the mist at a distance of no more than twenty or thirty feet.

By the 1890s, Bergen's glory days were behind it, though for music aficionados such as Lottie Dod, who had studied singing and piano to a high level as a child, it boasted a famous resident: the composer Edvard Grieg had been born there in 1843, and fifty-four years later he was still living in a small wooden country house, a couple miles from the old Hanseatic League centre, that he and his wife, Nina, had named Troldhaugen. It was a simple home, the walls, floors and ceilings of which were unpainted pine boards; its exterior was painted a pale yellow, the windowsills and gables a dark green; and despite the large steel stove in the living room, it was largely uninsulated from the cold. During the brutal Norwegian winters, the Griegs would decamp south on concert tours of Germany, Holland, Denmark, Great Britain and elsewhere in Europe. Come summertime, they would return home.

Troldhaugen was, when the Dods, Main and Imboden arrived in Bergen, as much a part of the tourism circuit as the grand buildings lining the old town's seafront. The Griegs had, that summer, recently returned from a particularly frenetic tour, one that had taken them to Berlin, Amsterdam, Copenhagen, Edinburgh and London, among a slew of other major European cities. Now they were playing host again. One after another, music lovers would traipse out to the house, its cluttered living room – the walls of which were filled with photographs and paintings – dominated by a Steinway grand, bought for Nina and Edvard by friends to celebrate their twenty-fifth wedding anniversary a few years earlier. There, they would be served tea by Nina and would, if they were lucky, talk music with the great man himself.

To escape the endless parade of visitors, Grieg, a short, tubercular man, his head covered in a shock of thick wavy hair, would sit and compose his music in a red-painted hut overlooking the waters of the fjord, down the fern-covered hillside from the main building. He had always been inspired by his country's landscape, and despite his ill health and his collapsed left lung, had, for years now, spent time exploring the wild Jotunheim region, with its preternaturally beautiful glaciers and jagged mountains. In his music, his great piano pieces, his vocal works, his concerti, he sought to capture all of that natural majesty. It was a legacy, a twinning of sometimes dramatic, sometimes simply whimsical piano and choral music with fierce, wild, natural imagery, that Lottie Dod in particular would have utterly loved. Perhaps, as she and her companions whiled away the days in Bergen, the young lady might have made her excuses for a few hours and made the pilgrimage out to Troldhaugen.[23]

The four mountaineers stayed a few days in a little hotel, poring over their Baedekers, talking over ascent routes with local guides, likely dining in the elegant restaurants that speckled the old wharf area. They wanted to get north, towards the intimidating string of granite mountains and seemingly endless forests topped by tundra plateaus in the sparsely populated centre of the country. It was, they knew, a spectacular locale, with some of Europe's largest glaciers and steepest peaks within a few days' journey of the town they were now in.

One morning later that week, having determined the summits they wanted to conquer, and with a nasty, cold rain falling on the little town, the foursome headed back to the docks and boarded another steamer. Their boat would head up the coast, the slew of islands running north of Bergen off to the ship's right; then it would turn east into the deep blue waters of the 120-mile-long Sognefjord. All told, it would be a thirty-one-hour journey to Skjolden, at the north-eastern head of the fjord and its secondary tributaries of Aurlands and Lustra. As they sailed north-east, the hills became mountains and the slopes morphed into cliffs. In the V-shaped spaces between the craggy, corded peaks, low-lying clouds swirled.

The Sognefjord boat ride took them along a stunning, narrow body of water, the banks covered by a verdant turf, the mountains coming off each side fiercely, shockingly steep. At the lower reaches of the granite inclines were clusters of birch trees, pines, red alders and short, squat rowans. Little hamlets of houses and red churches with grey slate roofs nestled at these lower levels, the structures insignificant against the vastness. A few small orchards were being tended on the grounds surrounding some of the homes. Above them, above the tree line, the jagged cliffs were largely bare, the rocks dark and foreboding. Cascading waterfalls tumbled down thousands of feet towards the fjord below. Off to the sides, rivers rushed through mountain gorges, their waters swollen into rapids with the snowmelt.

At the village of Balestrand, Sognefjord spread out into a

large bay, off which were a series of smaller, narrower secondary fjords. The boat continued east along the Aurlandsfjord, then cut north on the Lustrafjord, past Sogndal, Solvorn, Gaupne, on to Luster, and finally, at the very end of the fjord, Skjolden. The waters became shallower in the last few miles, the colour of the surface a lighter, almost tropical shade of blue. By contrast, the closer they got to the water's end, so the mountains got fiercer, higher.

Unfortunately, however, for much of the journey that spectacular scenery was an irrelevance to Dod and her companions: throughout the boat trip, the weather was foul, the rain so cold that it repeatedly drove them belowdecks to seek succour in the saloon. On the higher peaks, hidden in the swirling clouds, snows were likely falling – as they do fairly often in the mountainous inland reaches of Norway in early July.

As if by magic, however, with the steamer making the final approach to Skjolden, the clouds lifted and a brilliant sun swathed the fjord. In the bright light, the mountains, the bases of which were a mossy deep green in the summer months, formed perfect reflections in the fjord's waters. Behind the little town, with its cluster of small inns and cafés ranged along the shoreline, loomed a huge, narrow ridge, looking like the profiled forehead of a gigantic pachyderm. Off to either side, other mountains cascaded into the distance. Just east of Skjolden, a series of high waterfalls could be seen hurtling down the cliffs.[24]

After all the rain and cold, it put the four of them in a glorious mood. They grabbed their bags – Bones carrying the most, a load that Main described fulsomely, in a subsequent essay titled "Mountaineering in the Land of the Vikings", as containing "cameras, wraps, bottles of wine, and sticks of chocolate, all muddied together in glorious confusion" – hurried down the pier, past the little wooden building that served as the shipping company offices, and briskly walked up the steep hill to Solheim's hotel. It was, they found, a "cosy" place, the grounds of which contained seemingly endless amounts of raspberry and redcurrant bushes. The delicious berries were ripened to perfection in the early-summer warmth, and there for the picking of hotel guests. In nearby waters, the guests also had permission to fish.

In the hot afternoon sun the next day, they lay under shade trees in the garden, Joseph sitting up periodically to puff on his pipe,[25] and watched the waters of the fjord glittering in the light, the shadows of the mountains dancing atop the liquid surface. It was as dramatic a vista as one could wish to see.

Dod and her compadres left at dawn, striding in the cool air through the valley and up rough mountain paths towards the tiny village of Turtagrø, an isolated hamlet just above the tree line, roughly ten miles into the mountains. There were no roads there; the terrifyingly steep paved route up to Turtagrø, one hairpin bend after the next after the next, for nearly ten miles, wouldn't be carved out of the rocks until 1938. And so, to reach it, they hiked up to the tree line, beyond which the birches wouldn't grow, impossibly sharp peaks and glaciers towering above them. The route was convoluted; they had to stick to barely discernible pathways between the steep, crevassed cliffs; had to avoid stumbling into fast-flowing rivers. Nothing about this landscape was easy.

Two decades earlier, the mountaineering legend William Cecil Slingsby – a broad-shouldered, grey-blue-eyed, bearded Yorkshireman, known as "Mister Cee-cil" to his friends, who would one day introduce the sport of skiing to the resort towns of the Swiss Alps[26] – had traversed this same route in his quest to become the first person to summit Skagastølstind. He reported starting up a "steep, zigzagging cattle path . . . into the Maradal, a short valley headed by the Maradalsbrae . . . the finest glacier in the range of the Horungtinder". At 1,300 feet, the tall trees petered out, replaced by dwarf willows. Far below, Slingsby's group could see the "foaming river Utla . . . here a tempestuous rapid, there a deep pool". There were large bear tracks pockmarking the snow.[27]

Reaching Turtagrø, a small crop of wooden buildings in a desolate, rocky mountain bowl, which Tony believed to be "the best climbing station in the Horingen region",[28] Dod's group found they had a choice of two hotels. The larger one was somewhat grandiosely named the White House; since Slingsby had popularised extreme climbs in the region, it had been an epicentre for the mountaineering set. On some days, scores of people, a mix of local villagers, guides and a handful of climbers, could be seen congregated on the mossy grounds out front of the hotel.[29] It looked too flashy for their taste, as if it was trying a little too hard to impress the smattering of tourists who would, in recent years, arrive each summer climbing season to try their luck on the local peaks; they chose, instead, the other inn, a nameless little place behind the White House, two storey high on piled slate foundations, in which they spent a quiet evening. From their windows, facing southward, they could see down the steep valley and gorge at the end of which, hidden from view, was Skjolden. When they stepped out on to the veranda of the building, they could look towards the large White House, and behind it and off to the left a series of sharp peaks, their tops appearing and disappearing again as the mists shifted.[30]

It stayed light until well after midnight, and after just a brief darkness, the sun began rising once more over the epic landscape when it was not yet three in the morning.

The next day, they began to climb again through a long, gently ascending valley, with a series of flat-topped massifs off to their left and jagged, snow-and-ice-covered peaks to their right, from which long waterfalls cascaded. The paths were waterlogged from the recent rains, the deep mud mixed unpleasantly with a slurry of waste from the cows and sheep pasturing in the flatlands. Within minutes, their boots would have been saturated.

At the end of the valley, after more than an hour of traipsing through the marshy mud, the gradual slope suddenly gave way to a steep gradient up towards the snow line and, beyond that, the glaciers.[31] They clambered up, scrambling along the sides of waterfalls, looking for safe routes from one boulder to the next, careful not to fall on the sometimes-slick rocks. A few hours from Turtagrø they passed a glistening lake, above which rose huge cliffs of black rock, "on which", Main observed, "cling wildly distorted glaciers with the bluest tones in their seracs [ridges of ice] and crevasses which I have ever seen." Slingsby, twenty years earlier, had been similarly awed by these cliffs, writing that they "form a colossal and nearly perpendicular wall between 2,000 and 3,000 feet in height".[32]

After five and a half hours on the mountains, following paths marked by a series of stone cairns, closely placed so as to be visible from one cairn to the next even in the fog, Imboden and his three climbers reached a rickety old hut on a narrow, rock-strewn ridge connecting two peaks. There they spent a sleepless night. The steep roof of the hut was low, at its highest point perhaps only seven feet high. Its walls were made of stones haphazardly held together with wattle.[33] On a hook outside the wooden door, coiled mountaineering ropes were hung. Inside, each of the climbers lay atop two six-inch-wide wooden planks placed side by side, covered with threadbare blankets, the only other furniture in the room a broken kettle and three small, filthy cups.

The next morning at 8.30 in gale-force winds, with the rain lashing down on them and the peaks hidden in the low storm clouds, they started up the rocks behind the hut, ascending the final portion of the murderously difficult 2,405-metre-high Skagastølstind. For Lottie Dod, already suffering bouts of the severe sciatica that would eventually hobble her, the climb must have been a huge test of her limits. Each step up the steep, rocky, muddy path would have pushed against her ankles, then contracted her calf muscles; each step would have radiated pressure around her knees, and then pushed that pressure up into her thigh muscles and hips. Each pace downhill, as she tensed her muscles to prevent her legs from running away from under her on the icy, slippery terrain, would have pushed burning pain into those thighs. Dod never faltered.

From the little hut in which they had spent the night, they climbed for more than three hours, through a glacial wilderness as spectacular, as otherworldly, as any on earth: surrounding them were many of Europe's largest individual glaciers, soaring up out of the Hurrungane plateau – a barren, icy limestone-and-granite landscape, bereft of all trees, what green there was either moss or clusters of wild grasses. There was nothing in this region to break the force of the wind, nowhere to shelter from the elements. Far below where they now were, lakes speckled the plateau, snow limning the edges. In the shallower sections, light-blue glacial ice could be seen under the surface. On all sides were jagged mountains rising up in fury towards the cloud-heavy sky. This was the land of Norse mythology, a wild place one could easily imagine the gods having fought over.

The four climbers eventually reached the narrow, near-vertical rock face leading to the summit. It looked, they thought, like a chimney, the top reachable through climbing up the rocks, assisted by holding on to a rope left by earlier climbers. Back in 1876, before there were ropes attached to the rocks, Slingbsy had looked at them and come as close to fear as he'd ever experienced near a summit. The rocks were "smoothly polished and almost vertical". Making matters worse, the ridges were all covered in a thin layer of rime, the ice making it almost impossible to attain a firm grip. "I scraped away the ice," Slingsby recalled, "and bit by bit got higher and higher . . . For the first time, I had to trust to an overhanging and rather a loose rocky ledge."[34]

Main stopped to take a few photographs, and then they embarked on the final ascent. "The Novice went like a bird," Dod's more experienced friend noted approvingly, "and gazed into space with the steady eye and untrembling nerve of an eagle."[35]

A few minutes more and, with the clouds swirling around the little party, the climbers were atop Skagastølstind. They perched on a flat rock, not much more than four feet by three feet, and one that only a handful of other people had ever touched before.

It was, by any measure, another truly extraordinary accomplishment. In desperately harsh weather, Lottie Dod, who had only begun mountaineering a year or two earlier, had made it to the top of one of Europe's most notorious peaks. In silence, as the clouds parted and reformed and parted again in the winds, they contemplated the vast landscape that unfolded in front of them. They felt, as their friend Slingsby had all those years before, a sense of "silent worship and reverence" at the majesty of what their eyes now saw.[36]

The adventures continued.

Some days later, they journeyed via boat to Marifjøra, near the Jostedalsbreen, a vast glacier, Europe's largest, some

350 square miles in size, with ice in places packed more than a quarter of a mile deep.

Main and the Dods had trekked glaciers in the Alps and on the approaches to Skagastølstind. They were familiar with putting on spiked grips, crampons around their boots, with slipping into safety harnesses through the metal carabiners of which were looped thick ropes connecting one ice trekker to the next. They knew how to read the rope by touch, to feel if it was suddenly going taut in their gloved hands, signifying that the person next to them had slowed down, or worse, had stumbled on the ice. They knew that if the taut rope started to pull them backward, the person behind them was falling, maybe into one of the deep crevasses or translucently blue water holes that lethally dot the glaciers. They had learned from their guides how to pull a person back up if they were dangling over the edge of an abyss.

From the "indifferent" inn that they stayed at, a steep-roofed affair with gabled eaves over the top windows, and balconies wrapping around the three storeys,[37] they set out, at 5.00 the next morning, under clouds that only grew blacker as the day advanced. They walked for four and a half hours, non-stop, to the foot of the glacier, a huge monster of compacted ice with soaring pinnacles that dwarfed the humans and steep, slippery ridges, its crevasses filled with the aqua-blue ice melt of summer. The top layer of ice was speckled with black particulates, a mix of fine-grained erosion from the nearby cliffs. Underneath were strata of crystal white and deep, almost phosphorescent shades of blue. They used the wedge ends of the ice axes that they were carrying to hack footholds into the ice, the sharp, pointed ends as walking sticks to help them up the steepest parts.

Imboden's brow grew increasingly furrowed as he glanced skyward periodically with growing alarm; the weather was worsening by the minute. "The pass was appallingly desolate," Tony noted somewhat fearfully.[38] Only the assurances of the local guide they had hired, that he could lead them around the edge of the glacier, through the mountain passes in the fog, kept them going. They ploughed through great snowfields, each tied by rope to the person in front of them.[39] Then, fourteen hours into their walk, they descended an almost vertical glacial ridge, the spikes ringing their boots allowing them to stay upright on the ice, the ropes they held on to giving them extra support. In places they would have had to swing their axes into the ice to hold their weight as they inched their way downward. Finally, with the clouds lifting and the late-afternoon sun illuminating their way, they found themselves at a lakeshore, where they hired a boatman to row them across to the hamlet of Hjelle, which Main wrote down in her notebooks as "Hjale". It was a tiny little lakeshore village, set against more magnificent mountain peaks. There, fortuitously, they found a most excellent hotel into the beds of which they could, and did, collapse.

The next day, the members of the expedition trekked along the edge of a salmon-filled river. Across the river was slung, at a downward angle, a thick wire rope, under which hung an armchair. It was being used, much like a zip line in later times would be, to propel travellers across the fast-flowing river. The only problem was that it had become stuck. Hanging over the middle of the river, looking somewhat bemused by the predicament he found himself in, was an old man, sitting in the armchair, which rocked back and forth over the cold waters. Main stopped – not, apparently, to help him but instead to take a photograph.

They continued on their way, traversing the huge wilderness areas of central Norway, their goal now the little town of Nes, which they hoped to use over the coming weeks as a base from which they would travel outward on a series of expeditions, the goal being to summit a number of other particularly challenging mountains. Their targets included Romsdalshorn, first summited in 1828; Vengetind, conquered by their friend William Slingsby only in 1881; and Mjölnir, a hefty nearby peak named after the Norse god Thor's hammer.

At Nes, they took a room in a four-storey hotel with a large Norwegian flag fluttering from the roof of the rear building. Its gardens were spacious and filled with trees. It was the sort of place one could easily relax in between physically exhausting expeditions. They would, it soon became clear, need that recovery time. For the challenges they now set themselves were formidable.

Over the next days, their treks were marred by more ferocious weather, with winds so high that one afternoon Lottie Dod's hat was carried off, falling at the foot of the cliffs a couple of thousand feet below the climbers.

On 16 August, near the summit of Romsdalshorn – which no woman had ever reached previously – the band of mountaineers looked for the metal chain which, they had been assured by Slingsby and other climbers, had been left hanging to help them climb the final, vertical portion. It was missing. Instead, with the wind blowing so hard it threatened to knock them off the rocks, they found a cleft in the cliff and managed to wriggle themselves up it, gripping the sides with their hands and feet, all their muscles straining. When they finally reached the top, they sat, breathless, next to a high cairn of rocks left by previous summiteers. Lottie pored over a guidebook, perhaps reading to mask her exhaustion, her back resting against the cairn.

As it turned out, that brush with disaster – the absent climbing chain on Romsdalshorn – was by no means their worst. Approaching the end of their five-hour climb up Vengetind, a landscape described by Slingsby as having "grisly summits",[40] the party only narrowly avoided death when an avalanche dislodged huge chunks of rock above their heads. They heard an initial boom, followed in quick succession by what Main described as "bang after bang, as if the spirits of the mountain were opening a campaign with very unspirit-like heavy artillery". In horror, they looked up to see falling towards them a cascade of rock fragments, shattering into smaller pieces as they bounced against the cliffs above. The hikers hugged the rock face, making themselves as small as possible, watching as the shards and boulders fell through the air in front of them. They waited until the avalanche stopped, their nostrils flared against the smell of gunpowder that always seemed to accompany such slides.[41] And then, explained Main with considerable British understatement, hoping to avoid further drama, they continued upward, towards panoramic views the like of which they hadn't yet encountered in their travels, "with all speed".[42]

For the Mjölnir ascent, they left their hotel in Nes at 2.45 one morning. In the far north's early-dawn light, the four of them walked to a nearby farm, Kolflot's, that they knew from recent experience would serve them hearty breakfast fare, likely including the eponymous *flatbrød* baked up in country homes throughout Norway during that period, as well as a variety of smoked and salted fish. And then, their hunger sated, they proceeded to set off walking again, mile after endless mile, on a route that resembled a huge S, up the sides of the mountain. Finally reaching the approach to the summit – from which they could see the nearby Vengetind rising above five glaciers – they found an unpleasant, ill-tended route, the rocks desperately steep, the handholds few and far between, loose stones in cracks a catastrophe waiting to be grabbed on to.

It was little more than a needle-sharp rock shelf atop the world. "There was barely room for the five of us, and we had to dispose of ourselves with circumspection on suitable projections," Main wrote proudly.[43] They stood, one in front of the other, on that tiny rock shelf, tied to each other by ropes, Imboden staying off to the rear in case, during the descent, one of them fell and had to be pulled back up.

On the way down, for the second time that week, they were almost caught in a rockslide, a huge boulder bouncing down the steep cliffs towards them. Imboden tried to protect the women with his body; it was a chivalric gesture, but it wouldn't have really helped any of them had the boulder actually landed on the party. Instead, as they held their breath in terror, it crashed on to a rocky ledge above their heads, and broke up into fragments that harmlessly flew past them on their way to the valley floor below.

"With Mjolnir ended our climbing for 1897 in Norway," Main wrote matter-of-factly, putting a bookend to the months of planning and weeks of adventure the team had lived through together.

SIX

Golfing Triumph and Transatlantic Fame

Lottie Dod (seated) with three competitors after winning the championships at Troon, Scotland, 1904. Courtesy of Sally-Ann Dod, Dod family archives.

The following summer, in 1898, Tony, Lottie, Imboden and Main headed back to Norway. Main had decided to explore the far north of the country, the Arctic area that made up part of the wild territory of Lapland. She was planning to camp for days at a time on the mountains, to explore wilderness areas largely uncharted, where reindeer were more plentiful than people; she was, in her planning for the trip, adding whole new levels of difficulty compared to their earlier expedition.

But the four didn't end up climbing together that year. Instead, as Main made her way north beyond the Arctic Circle, into the sparsely populated mountains of Lapland, the Dods abruptly returned to England, heading home to Margaret's gloom-filled Edgeworth House once more.

After nearly half a decade in which they had been inseparable, Lottie had had a dramatic falling-out with her dear friend Elizabeth Main. The exact reasons are now lost to time. Perhaps it involved some sort of romantic falling-out between one and another of the various members of Main's inner circle – Harold Topham; the Dods; Main herself; Joseph Imboden; Joseph's youngest son, Emil; William Cecil Slingsby. A falling-out that had necessitated each one choosing sides. Or maybe Lottie had read an advance copy of Main's essay on their 1897 mountaineering adventures in Norway, in which she dismissively, even if affectionately, nicknamed Dod "the Novice". Ever the proud sportswoman, Lottie had perhaps taken umbrage.

The break was serious enough that in her later autobiographical writings about the period, in which she documented more than two dozen first ascents she had achieved in the years following her first trip to Norway, Main all but erased Dod from her life. Perhaps she felt spurned. Whatever the exact reasons, the woman who had been at the centre of one of Main's photographs after another for close to five years, who had travelled around Europe with her during months of bicycle touring, who was described in such careful, intimate, even loving detail in Main's handwritten notes accompanying those photos, vanished. In the public telling, while the famous mountaineer dropped names of numerous other celebrity figures she spent time with, Dod would be, from now on, a *persona non grata*.

Just once, Main may have obliquely written about Lottie and Tony again: in her 1904 book *Adventures on the Roof of the World*, she wrote of a lady friend of hers who, later that summer of 1898, spent time with her brother climbing in the Italian Dolomites. The unnamed woman had taken off her cumbersome skirt once out of public view and replaced her heavy hobnailed boots with rubber-soled tennis shoes to navigate the smooth, slippery rock faces. She had kept a climbing diary, detailing her experiences on the trip, explaining how she, her brother and the guides had pulled themselves up a chimney in the rock face, "a grab, a hoist, a foot tucked into a crevice on either side of the *camino*, a long reach with my arm, a steady pull . . . The rock wall was abominably straight and holeless." The woman had called herself a "novice", and had written of losing her grip when she had to exit the chimney to make the final ascent, and of dangling helplessly from her mountaineering rope, the other end of which was held by her guide on the rocks above, "an abyss of 2,000 feet" below her. She was, she noted ruefully, "ignominiously pulled, kicking, up the precipice".[1]

But even if the tennis shoe–wearing climber was Lottie Dod, the storey served, at best, as a coda to a fractured friendship. In her numerous other writings in the decades following their split, Main was careful to airbrush the Bebingtonian from her life.

Exiled from Main's circle of celebrities, adventurers and eccentrics, presumably desperate to find ways to spend as much time as possible at a remove from the demands of her ageing, ailing mother, the Little Wonder threw herself into new sporting challenges. Anything would have been better than being secluded for months on end in the large Cheshire estate with her two brothers, Margaret and a teenage housemaid named Alice Jane Williams.

As Victoria's long reign drew to a close, England was both at the apex of its powers and also, increasingly, riven by social protests. There were frequent demonstrations on the streets of London, Liverpool, Birmingham and the other large cities, in favour of Irish independence. Labour disputes were on the increase, with unions increasingly willing to strike, and with political agitators campaigning for a socialist Labour Party to replace the more genteel Liberals as the party of progress. There were social-reform campaigns – against slum housing, against child labour, in favour of unemployment insurance and affordable access to doctors and to hospitals. And, from 1897, when Millicent Fawcett founded the National Union of Women's Suffrage Societies, there was the women's movement, determined to push for female suffrage and, as the years went by, willing to resort to more militant methods to secure their goals. In 1903, six years after Fawcett's group was formed, Emmeline Pankhurst and her two daughters established the Women's Social and Political Union – which would come to be known as the Suffragettes.

During these years, late Victorian assumptions about the order of society, and the role of women in particular, began to disintegrate. In 1869, Arabella Mansfield had become the first female lawyer in the United States when she was admitted to the Iowa bar. In 1872, Elizabeth Garrett Anderson, who a few years earlier had achieved notoriety as the first Englishwoman to qualify as a doctor – receiving her medical degree in Paris after British universities refused her admission – opened the New Hospital for Women in London. In 1893, New Zealand became the first country on earth to enfranchise women. In 1898, Marie Curie shot to fame after discovering two new elements. That same year, Utah began allowing women to sit on juries.

Slowly but surely, women were demanding, and starting to receive, respect in the public arena.

Under fierce attack from suffragists, growing numbers of whom turned towards civil disobedience, the old order tried at first to crush dissent; and then, gradually, started to look for ways to accommodate it, opening doors to women that previously had been firmly closed. Still, though, in almost every country on earth, as the old century gave way to the new, women remained without the right to vote. But they continued to express themselves, to make their presence felt, and break down age-old limits in other ways.

In 1899 and 1900, Dod played forward for the English national hockey team. The sport was picking up considerable attention in the media, as well as a large and enthusiastic following among sports aficionados. In a sign of its newfound visibility, Queen Victoria's grandson, His Royal Highness the Duke of York, who would later become King George V, had recently been made president of the English Hockey Union. Within the United Kingdom, each of the constituent countries was now fielding its own teams, and the meetings between them were wildly anticipated.

For turn-of-the-century women, barred from competitive football and rugby, it was the one rough-and-tumble sport in which they were permitted to play like men. Physically. Aggressively. Even sometimes drawing blood. "It is no mere child's play, this ladies' hockey," wrote a female sports columnist in Bristol, who signed her columns simply "Brenda". "They enter into it with an earnestness and a determination which men might envy, and bruises and nasty kicks are born without a murmur." It was all very different from the garden party frivolities of only a few years earlier. Or, as Brenda happily put it, these hockey games were "thoroughly real".[2]

Lottie Dod took to the new sport like a fish to water. She founded a hockey club at Spital, not far from her family home at Edgeworth; sat on the first committee of the Northern Counties Women's Hockey Association, later becoming its president; and represented the north of England on the executive of the All England Women's Hockey Association. By the century's end, she was playing for her country.[3]

In a home match against the Irish, held at the Richmond Athletic Ground in south-west London in 1899, the English ladies, Dod among them, sporting plain skirts that came down to just above their ankles and loose blouses, won 3–1.[4]

Early the following year, the Irish team went on a tear, slaughtering their Welsh opponents in a 9–0 shutout.[5] Their confidence soaring, they waited for revenge against the English. The chance wasn't long in coming.

Soon after the Ireland-Wales game, the eleven members of the English ladies' team headed to the west coast to embark on a ship across the Irish Sea. It couldn't have been a pleasant voyage. The weather in the waters surrounding the British Isles had been foul that month. In mid February, in the North Sea, a windstorm more powerful than any in living memory had capsized at least five boats and resulted in many deaths around the Shetland Islands.[6]

Lottie Dod and her teammates headed to Dublin. Two of them, including one of the team's backs, Alice Pickering, eleven years Dod's senior, were also successful tennis players. Mrs. Pickering, a late bloomer, had begun playing Wimbledon only in 1895, when she was already in her mid thirties. That summer of 1900 would be her sixth consecutive year at the event.

The rains continued to pelt down. Each day, it seemed, was wetter than the last. Hoping against hope that the weather would cooperate, the ladies went to the grounds at Milltown for their scheduled game on Monday, 27 February. There were, after all, thousands of spectators waiting to see them play. But the rains didn't stop and the officials realised they had no choice but to postpone. They tried again the next day; once more, the storms drove them back inside. If anything, the weather was even worse that Tuesday than it had been the day before. Finally, on Thursday, the downpours stopped. But now, the journalists assigned to cover the much-hyped game reported in consternation, another problem arose: the grounds were so waterlogged that it would prove an impossibility to play hockey on them.[7]

The organisers desperately cast around for an alternative venue. At last, the groundsmen of the Donnybrook and Dublin University Harriers' Clubs, in the Ballsbridge suburb, informed them that conditions at their stadium on Anglesea Road were playable. With the sunshine of the morning giving way to more ominous early-afternoon clouds, players and fans alike began heading across town.

Ballsbridge was an elegant locale, home to an annual horse show, a showground and an ornate white pavilion, around which was a well-manicured circular walkway for promenaders to take their stroll. Now, it would become the scene of another of Dod's singular athletic triumphs.

As the match got underway shortly after 3.30 p.m., the Irish women, their long skirts billowing in the winds, the ties they wore on the outside of their white blouses flying upward as they ran, more than held their own.[8] They parried Dod's runs towards their goal, launched effective counter-attacks and a few minutes before half-time, managed to score the only goal of the half. It was, alas, to be their last success. When the whistle blew to start the second period, Lottie Dod, her competitive instincts aroused, and the other English forwards attacked relentlessly. "A shot from Miss Dod looked a certain goal. But it struck Miss Ashlin's foot, and resulted in a fruitless corner," the *Freeman Journal* reported. Soon afterwards, however, the scoring began. "The visitors came again, and this time they made no mistake, Miss Dod shooting a grand goal, and thus equalising the score." From then on in, the result didn't look in doubt; as the English pressed forward, it was just a matter of time before they scored again. "The Irishwomen weakened a little, and played a trifle loose after this," the newsman forlornly continued. "And again Miss Dod scored, putting the Rose one goal ahead."[9]

Once more, however, having reached the pinnacle of another sport, Dod grew bored. She would, after her heroics in Ballsbridge, never again play for the national hockey team. Instead, dilettante-like, she flitted from one game to the next. She trained in horse riding and rowing – to such an extent that, decades later, one of her close friends who had known her since the 1890s termed her an "expert" in both.[10] She returned episodically to St Moritz, where in January 1903 she was elected a member of the Skating Association's committee.[11] She put heart and soul into golf and archery. During those *fin de siècle* years the Wimbledon champion was, by some accounts, among the best billiard players in England – although her older sister, Ann, laid a stronger claim to that particular hat, being profiled in a glossy magazine in March 1908 as "the amateur lady champion of billiards", with "an excellent billiard-room at her house"; and Ann's children would, decades later, say that they didn't think Lottie herself played that particular game.[12]

Whichever Dod sister was in fact the best, it must have irritated to no end the men of the smoking clubs, who had long thought of the old game of English three-ball billiards – the balls made of ivory from elephants' tusks, the tables covered in expensive green felt – as a sport solely to be played by whisky-sipping gentlemen in their male-only environs.

There wasn't, it appeared, a sport invented that the Little Wonder wouldn't try.

In early 1901, as Dod dabbled in one new sport after the next, Britain was rocked by the death of the octogenarian Queen Victoria.

Surrounded by her extended family – many members of whom, including her grandson, the German emperor Wilhelm, had rushed to England from their royal dwellings overseas at word of the empress's imminent death – Victoria breathed her last at Osborne House, on the Isle of Wight, on the evening of 22 January. While not unexpected, her passing sparked an outpouring both of national grief and also of carefully choreographed mourning pageantry.

Newspapers, which had been headlining the daily medical bulletins released by the queen's doctors over the past several days, rushed into print with special editions. "From Whitechapel to Mayfair, streets that had been filled with the usual throngs of the capital in nighttime suddenly turned deserted and desolate," the historian Jerrold Packard wrote of the moment the Victorian era ended. "Blinds on the huge West End mansions came down so that not a glimmer of light shone through them. The metropolis almost literally stopped."[13] Theatres closed, restaurants and pubs shuttered. Soon, pretty much the only noise that could be heard in these usually frenetic streets was the tolling of church bells. In the heart of the old city of London, the huge bells of St Paul's Cathedral solemnly rang out eighty-one times, once a minute, for each of the eighty-one years of Victoria's life. Silently, thousands gathered along the great thoroughfare of the Strand and in Trafalgar Square, to pay tribute.

Over the coming days luminaries from around the world made their way to England for the church services and public tributes, for the swearing of allegiance to the new king and, of course, for the processions that would accompany Victoria's body to its final resting place in Windsor Castle.

An eight-mile-long flotilla of navy ships, both British and foreign, accompanied the royal yacht *Alberta*, bearing the queen's coffin, from the Isle of Wight to the naval town of Portsmouth. Thousands of people lined the rail route that then took her body north to London's Victoria Station, named after the queen some forty-plus years earlier. From there, untold numbers of Londoners clogged the streets that the horse-drawn hearse carrying her body took, accompanied by 32,000 infantrymen, as it slowly, circuitously, made its way to Paddington Station. Some had paid scores of pounds, the equivalent of months of a worker's wages, to secure good seating along Buckingham Palace Road, Piccadilly and the other more desirable streets along the route. And thousands more stood by the tracks along Victoria's final journey to Windsor. From the station to the castle, huge numbers of additional mourners stood, heads bare, in solemn grief.

St James's Palace, the bureaucratic heart of the British monarchy, released official mourning schedules. For the ladies and gentlemen of the court, there was to be a year of mourning: for the first six months, the ladies would wear black dresses trimmed with crepe, black shoes and gloves, black fans, feathers and ornaments. The gentlemen would be expected to wear black court dress, adorned with black swords and black buckles. For the next six months, the men would keep wearing the same mourning garb, but the ladies would now be allowed to add coloured ribbons, flowers and feathers to their black attire.[14]

Outside of the court, the choreographed grief percolated through all levels of society. Women of wealth would, without exception, have been expected to partake in the mourning rituals. They would have donned black clothing, made of the dullest, most lustreless materials, their dresses and blouses twilled and ribbed to eliminate any possible shine. Carriages and doorways and indoor furniture – all would have been covered with crepe, heat-treated to make it stiff and lifeless. To the servant class, black cotton uniforms would have been issued.[15]

Church services throughout the land paid tribute to the queen's extraordinary sixty-four-year reign.

Almost certainly Edgeworth would have played its part, its windows and doors draped in mourning colours, its residents caught up in the national gloom. For its denizens were, by this point, firmly part of the local elite; when grand weddings and coming-of-age festivities occurred, the Dod children would be found among the guests, their presence, and the gifts they bore, recorded on the society pages of the Liverpool newspapers. And as part of that elite, they would have been expected to abide by the carefully calibrated rituals of grief that accompanied Victoria's passing.

Later that year, the Dods experienced another death, this one far more personal.

In early August, Margaret Dod, the matriarch of the family, died at the age of sixty-one. She had outlived her husband Joseph by nearly a quarter of a century. Now, she would be buried next to him and their infant son Philip in Bebington Cemetery.

Cruel though it sounds, in some ways Margaret's death

seems to have liberated her children, giving them belated permission to leave the Cheshire home that all four of them had long sought to escape but that only Ann had managed to actually leave.

Within a few years, Edgeworth House, along with its capacious grounds, had been sold off – to the nearby Lever soap manufacturing company, which wanted to use the house as temporary accommodations for visiting businessmen to the area to meet up with company executives. And by the middle of the decade, Tony, Lottie and William had relocated to the outskirts of Newbury, a commuter town forty miles west of London, to be somewhat nearer their sister Ann and her husband, Ernest, who were living in north London with their three children: Doris Winifred and her much younger brothers, Ray and Geoffrey.

Lottie and her two brothers lived together in a sprawling brick house on the outskirts of town, up a hill two miles east of the old town centre – it had been given the royal charter in 1596 – and fifteen miles west of the village of Andover. Their street was lined with large two-storey homes, kept in a deliberate state of slight disrepair, the front gardens overgrown and hidden behind high brick walls. There was something quintessentially English about the place. Most of the houses were quaintly named, with monikers such as Kit's Cottage, Laurel House and Oak Cottage, all intended to give off a country air. In the suburban silence, one could hear the birds chirping, and on a clear night see the sky above filled with stars.

The Dods quickly fell into the rhythm of the place. They named their new home, like Edgeworth before, after their fifteenth-century ancestor Sir Anthony Dod of Edge: from now on, their abode would be Edgecombe, on the Andover Road. Further along the road to Andover were a couple of little pubs, and just beyond them an imposing stone obelisk, erected in 1878 in memory of Royalist soldiers from the town who had died more than two centuries previously in an early Civil War battle against Cromwell's Parliamentarian army.[16] On the sides of the high base were inscribed words in Latin from Livy, in ancient Greek from Thucydides, and in English from the political philosopher Edmund Burke. "The blood of man is well shed for our family, for our friends, for our God, for our country, for our kind," Burke had written. "The rest is vanity, the rest is crime."

To keep the household going, the three unmarried siblings employed a cook, listed in the 1911 census as being twenty-nine-year-old Frances Flitter – although friends noted that Lottie herself was also a talented chef; a nineteen-year-old housemaid, Emily Harrison; and another teenage serving girl, from the village of Pangbourne, named Emma Sparks. On and off, a friend from London, the land agent Walter Edgington, also called Edgecombe home.[17]

The three siblings, tight as could be, and freed from their mother's whims, lived together and trained in sports together. William and Lottie in particular would golf at the local course, and later on join a nearby archery club, on the grounds of the Welford Park estate, about ten miles away along country lanes from their home, at which they would train to Olympic-level standards.

Welford Park was a spectacular locale, with 4,800 acres of forest, brilliant white snowdrop gardens, dappled streams and manicured grounds. In the huge brick manorial estate lived a family whose ancestors had occupied the premises since 1601, when they had bought it from the descendants of one of Henry VIII's courtiers – who had, back in the early sixteenth century, been awarded the grounds after the king, who frequently sojourned there, grew bored of using them as a hunting lodge from which to chase game. Before Henry's time, before the conversion to Protestantism and the seizing of Catholic religious sites, it had been a monastery.

To there, the two siblings would decamp with their long wooden boxes filled with arrows, one end of each feathered, the wood underneath the feathers painted red and monikered with their names.[18] The other ends were capped with a sharp metal point. Day after day they would practise their marksmanship.

As the new century got underway, Lottie Dod was one of the most famous women in England. Like few females of her era, she was dancing to her own tune, unmarried, seemingly with no desire to marry, financially independent, beholden to no one. What she thought of the idea of settling down into a conventional marriage can be glimpsed in a few pages of tiny old newsprint that she carefully saved from her childhood – in all likelihood these pages had been among Margaret's possessions, found by her children after her death. At the very back of Lottie's scrapbook, in which she carefully glued hundreds of newspaper articles on her and her siblings' sporting accomplishments during these years, she stuffed, unglued, a handful of news articles collected by someone when Lottie was still a child in Edgeworth. One was a long series of critical letters on "The Marriage Question", and another, from the *Liverpool Mercury* in 1877, was titled "The Property of Married Women". In it, the author lambasted as "unjust and degrading" the laws that handed over control of a married woman's property to her husband.[19]

Better to excel as an athlete than fade into obscurity as a wife. After all, Lottie was unbeatable, it seemed, in whatever sport she turned her hand to. That hand was now turned firmly in the direction of golf, a sport that had only reluctantly opened itself up to women competitors over the past decades. The Little

Wonder, who had apprenticed herself to the Scottish golf pro Jack Morris at the Royal Liverpool Club on the grounds of the Royal Hotel in 1886,[20] the year before she won her first Wimbledon tennis championship, promptly went on a winning tear.

Morris, whose father and uncle were both storied golfers, among the first generation of superstars in the sport, had been hired as the Royal Liverpool's first in-house pro in the early 1870s.[21] A short, heavyset man, he set up shop out back of the main hotel, in the stables – with the horses ridden by members of the local hunt club – designing the expanded golf course, and then, for more than fifty years, coaching up-and-coming young golfers.[22] As his reputation spread, so talent from the surrounding counties came to the club hoping that some of his skills, his teaching of aggressive, accurate techniques, would rub off on them. In Dod's case, his advice worked only too well. Throughout the 1880s and early 1890s, as she solidified her reputation as the country's best female tennis player, the Bebington girl also built up her skills on the links. By the mid 1890s, she was winning tournaments and had secured a place for herself among the top ranks of English golfers. And as one century wound down and a new one began, Dod was in the ethereal zone atop the sport that only a handful of competitors could occupy at any moment in time. Crowds would mob her at every tournament she entered.

By 1904, Dod's reputation as a golfer and an all-round athlete had crossed the Atlantic. Her accomplishments were being celebrated by American sportswriters as breathlessly as by their British counterparts. When she won the British ladies' amateur championships in Troon, Scotland, the newspapers in the United States published long pieces explaining her win – and her powerful technique – to readers back home. In an

Iconic photograph of fifteen-year-old Wimbledon champion Lottie Dod. *The International Tennis Hall of Fame, Inc., is the source and owner of the photograph used in this production.*

Photographs of the family home at Edgeworth, kept by Lottie Dod in her family scrapbook.
©AELTC. Reproduced by kind permission of the Wimbledon Lawn Tennis Museum.

Family photograph taken at Edgeworth in the early 1890s. Lottie Dod is front center.
Courtesy of Sally-Ann Dod, Dod family archives.

Lottie's grandfather John Aspinall and her brother William on a family vacation in northern England. ©*AELTC. Reproduced by kind permission of the Wimbledon Lawn Tennis Museum.*

Lottie Dod playing doubles at a tournament in the 1880s.
©*AELTC. Reproduced by kind permission of the Wimbledon Lawn Tennis Museum.*

LAWN-TENNIS CHAMPIONSHIP MATCHES AT WIMBLEDON

Top: cartoon of the lead players from Wimbledon, 1887. *©AELTC. Reproduced by kind permission of the Wimbledon Lawn Tennis Museum.*

Right: William and Ernest Renshaw, Lottie Dod's close friends and tennis rivals. *The International Tennis Hall of Fame, Inc., is the source and owner of the photograph used in this production.*

Anonymous poem about Lottie Dod in 1888, kept by Dod in her scrapbook.
©AELTC. Reproduced by kind permission of the Wimbledon Lawn Tennis Museum.

Above: Lottie and Anthony Dod playing tennis at Edgeworth, from her family scrapbook.
Below: Lottie and Anthony Dod playing mixed doubles. *Both photographs ©AELTC.*
Reproduced by kind permission of the Wimbledon Lawn Tennis Museum.

Above: Lottie Dod taking the skating test at St. Moritz.
Below: Dod playing an exhibition match at the Kulm Hotel in St. Moritz.
Both photographs courtesy of the Kulm Hotel archives, St. Moritz.

Photograph of Lake Sils taken by Lottie Dod's friend Elizabeth Main.
Courtesy of the Kulm Hotel archives, St. Moritz.

Scrapbook of mountaineering photos featuring Lottie Dod, taken by Elizabeth Main. *Courtesy of the Martin and Osa Johnson Safari Museum.*

Above: the glacial expedition. The woman in the middle is likely Lottie Dod. *Below:* two of Elizabeth Main's friends on the edge of a glacial crevasse. The woman is likely Dod. *Both photographs by Elizabeth Main, courtesy of the archives at the Badrutt's Palace Hotel, St. Moritz.*

Lottie Dod with the bicycle she used to cycle hundreds of miles across six European countries in 1896. *Courtesy of the Martin and Osa Johnson Safari Museum.*

From left: Harold Topham, Elizabeth Main, Lottie Dod, and Anthony Dod, during the European tour. *Courtesy of the Martin and Osa Johnson Safari Museum.*

Lottie Dod's impressive swing.
Photographer unknown.

THE FINAL BETWEEN MISS DOD AND MISS MAY HEZLET.

Crowd watches Lottie Dod during a golf tournament final. From *Golf* magazine, July 1904.

Above: Lottie Dod takes a full swing at the British ladies' golf championship in 1904.

Below: newspaper clipping about Dod after her championship win.

Both photographs courtesy of Sally-Ann Dod, Dod family archives.

MISS LOTTIE DOD, LADY CHAMPION, 1904.

after a stiff match with Miss B. Thompson, won on the 17th green.

By the afternoon of the 12th only eight players remained to play off in the final stages. Of these the closest fight was provided by Miss Dod and Miss Whigham. Miss Dod turned 3 up. On the home half Miss Whigham only secured the 10th and the 16th, and the 17th saw the fall of the Prestwick favourite by 2 and 1. In this round Miss D. Campbell and her sister, Mrs. Swanston (Miss

victory for Miss L. Dod and Miss Hezlet, the former particularly playing an extremely strong game in wind. Of the four now left in Miss D. Campbell was the only one who had not previously secured either a gold, silver, or bronze medal at a previous Open Championship, but at the Scottish Championship of 1903 she won a bronze medal.

Both matches on Friday morning drew a large number of specta-

Lottie Dod (front row, first from left) and the other members of the archery club with which she trained before winning the silver medal in the 1908 London Olympics.
Courtesy of Sally-Ann Dod, Dod family archives.

The Jubilee Medallists of 1926. Reading from left to right, *Back Row*: R. T. Richardson, J. T. Hartley, P. F. Hadow, M. J. G. Ritchie, C. P. Dixon, S. H. Smith, F. L. Riseley, R. Lycett, A. W. Gore, H. Roper Barrett. *Middle Row*: Sir H. W. W. Wilberforce, Hon P. Bowes-Lyon, W. Baddeley, H. Baddeley, L. A. Godfree, M. Woosnam, C. E. Weldon, J. Pim, W. J. Hamilton, F. O. Stoker. *Front Row*: Miss M. Watson, Mrs G. W. Hillyard, Miss L. Dod, Mrs A. Sterry, Mrs R. Lambert Chambers, Mrs A. C. Geen, Mrs D. R. Larcombe, Mrs L. A. Godfree

Photograph taken of past Wimbledon champions at the tournament's jubilee celebrations in 1926. Dod is in the front row, third from left. *The International Tennis Hall of Fame, Inc., is the source and owner of the photograph used in this production.*

William Dod in his Local Defence Volunteers uniform at the beginning of the Second World War. *Courtesy of Sally-Ann Dod, Dod family archives.*

Last known photo of William Dod, probably taken in the early 1950s. *Courtesy of Sally-Ann Dod, Dod family archives.*

Miss Ramsay, Mrs. Sterry, Miss Ransome, and Miss Lottie Dod, who took part in an "exhibition" game during the Roehampton Tournament.

(See page 65)

Champion of Forty-Two Years Ago.

SPECTATORS at the Roehampton autumn tournament were provided with a pleasant surprise when on the Friday two famous past champions, Miss Lottie Dod and Mrs. Sterry, happening to meet on the ground, agreed to take part in an "exhibition" doubles.

No fewer than forty-two years have elapsed since Miss Dod, in 1887, won the women's championship at Wimbledon when only fifteen years of age. Subsequently she earned renown at golf, in which she also became the champion, while at archery she was one of the leading experts. Mrs. Sterry, mother of Miss Gwen Sterry, the present prominent player, won the women's lawn tennis championship five times (twice as Miss Cooper) her first success being achieved in 1895, and her last in 1908. It says much for her unabated enthusiasm for the game that she was playing in handicap events at the recent Eastbourne tournament. In the game at Roehampton Miss Dod was partnered by Miss A. G. Ransome, and Mrs. Sterry by Miss J. F. Ramsey.

To the Editor of TENNIS ILLUSTRATED Mrs. Sterry expressed the opinion that Miss Dod has far better all-round strokes than girls of the present.

Last known published photograph of Lottie Dod, taken at an exhibition tournament in 1929 when she was fifty-eight years old. Dod is on the far right. *©AELTC. Reproduced by kind permission of the Wimbledon Lawn Tennis Museum.*

Studio portrait of Lottie Dod, taken when she was in her early twenties.
Courtesy of Sally-Ann Dod, Dod family archives.

article bylined from London on 18 May, the *New York Times* noted, "Ireland and England were represented in the final to-day of the Ladies' Golf Championship contest, with the result that Miss Lottie Dod of Morton [*sic*], England, won the title, defeating the former champion, Miss May Hazlet [*sic*], by one hole."

The crowd at the prestigious golf course at Troon was huge, numbering some 6,000 people, many of them dockworkers from the nearby Clydeside; and so enthusiastic were they that the course officials had to repeatedly shout out, "Let the players through!" to secure enough space through the dense throng for the ladies to progress from one hole to the next. On the slopes surrounding the green, men and women stood dozens deep, watching Hezlet and Dod face off, Dod using a wooden club recently designed by Andrew Scott, who marketed himself as being "golf club maker to HRH the Prince of Wales".[23] One journalist on the scene felt that in the audience's density, and in the raucous, noisy cheering of the fans, it resembled a horse race more than a normal golfing crowd.[24] Others were less charitable, viewing the enthralled working-class fans as little more than a rioting mob. "It is a matter of considerable regret that the first time the ladies should select the Troon links for their meeting," the reporter for the *Manchester Courier and Lancashire General Advertiser* sniffed, "the crowd let loose from the works and shops should have behaved so badly. The final was deprived of much of its interest by the disgraceful conduct of many of the spectators."[25]

Most of the observers, however, begged to differ. Interest in Dod soared, went truly transcontinental.

In America's leading magazine on the sport, *Golf*, published monthly in New York and available to readers for twenty-five cents an issue, Mrs R. Boys wrote of Dod's technique that "every stroke is perfect, the club held in the correct method, the ball hit with a perfect, circular swing and the follow through straight and thorough". The newly minted national champion was, Boys continued breathily, "faultlessly" demonstrating how the game should be played.[26]

At a photo shoot after her victory, Lottie Dod sat off to the side of a wooden table, atop which rested the polished trophy. She was wearing a heavy tweed cap, a buttoned-up jacket and a long skirt. Arrayed around the table, standing off to the side and each wearing modish "motoring caps", were the three other semi-finalists. Dod looked extraordinarily self-confident, a woman who could do no wrong.[27]

From around the world, congratulatory telegrams, the messages carefully copied out in thick pencil by the telegram operators; letters, delicately folded on lilac and blue and yellow and white papers; and postcards with halfpenny stamps on their top right corners, poured in. They were delivered to her in her hotel at Troon, at her home in Bebington, at every stopping point she found herself in over the coming weeks and months. Hundreds upon hundreds of pages of congratulations. There were handwritten missives from friends, from relatives, from erstwhile rivals in other sports, from golf club secretaries wishing to offer her lifelong honorary membership, from vendors of golf paraphernalia seeking her endorsement for their products.

Blanche Hillyard sent a brief to-the-point telegram: "Miss Dod. Bebington. Well done. Best congratulations." Her friends the Spences wrote, "How splendid. Three cheers. Congratulations." Budleigh Salterton penned a somewhat mischievous "More power to your elbow." From the president of the Royal St George's Golf Club in Sandwich came a long note expressing joy that an English lady had managed to put the Scots and Irish in their place. "You have now taken the Cup in every way for England. Long may you hold it, so that the Scotch and Irish ladies may know that there are as good even better golfers in dear old England as in the other lands. I cannot tell you how glad I am you have won." Her friend M. Warossop wrote, "My wife and I were so pleased to see you make your way to the top of the tree. You seem to be able to get to the top of everything you go in for." From Highgate, her cousin Tom sent her an ecstatic letter: "Dear Lottie, at last! Hooray! I was delighted when I searched my paper this morning and found you really had pulled it off." Her friend Lizzie Wilson declared, "Dear Lottie, you must let me give you (in spirit at least) a hearty kiss and a hug to express my great delight."

The new British ladies' golf champion was flush with pleasure at the attention. She kept every single letter, every telegram. She would, when things slowed down and she had a few moments to herself, glue all of them into the huge, heavy album of photographs, newspaper clippings and personal correspondence that she was putting together to commemorate her golfing career.

"I was so delighted, Lottie dear . . . I could have jumped for joy when I heard the news. How pleased your brother must have been too. Get him to give you a good hug from me," wrote her friend Mabel Steadman, from Barnes. A correspondent in Dublin, signing off only as "your companion", told Dod that she had "conquered the world in the great games. So what more have you to wish for?" Another female acquaintance, sojourning in a spa in Falkenstein, Germany, on a long recovery from a lingering illness, asked Lottie to "please accept my heartiest congratulations", and then second-guessed herself: "That sounds so awfully stilted. And I mean something a great deal stronger, but I can't find the words. It was grand!" From Loughborough came a letter announcing, "You are a Brick! We are *so* delighted, it is splendid." And from her friend Bagnall, the six-word telegram, "Simply splendid. You are a dream."[28]

In the wake of all of the hoopla following Lottie Dod's victory at Troon, American readers and sports enthusiasts became somewhat obsessed with the English sensation. Papers across the country published newswire stories on her triumphs, and many commissioned their own reporters to write up profiles of the tall, poised lady from across the pond who, somehow, didn't seem to know how to lose. Society ladies who had befriended Dod during their sojourns in Switzerland and England over the past years clamoured for her to come visit them in the United States.

Dod vacillated. Having conquered yet another sport, she was tempted to return to her roots in competitive tennis, she confided to several friends – and she sought their advice as to whether to play Wimbledon again that summer, eleven years after her last victory there. Several were enthusiastic, believing that she could pick up where she had left off and resume her string of triumphs. From Brussels, Charles Voigt wrote to "express the hope that you will do as well at Wimbledon in a fortnight's time. I regret I shall not be able to be there this year to see you play." Others, however, cautioned her not to do it. Her cousin Alfred Higgins sat down at his desk in his Belsize Crescent house in north London, and wrote a long, thoughtful letter, in which he concluded, "As regards Lawn Tennis, if I were you I would rest on my laurels, which are ample. I would not like you to lose, and on the other hand I see nothing to be gained by winning, as everyone knows you could have gone on for year after year winning the C'ship if you had cared to."[29]

Finally, she listened to the voices of caution. And so, having won everything that could be won in golf in Britain, the Little

Wonder accepted the invite of her American friends and set her compass westward, to try her hand on the golf courses of the Eastern Seaboard of the United States.

At the end of September, four months after her victory in Troon, her golfing reputation now international, Dod travelled to Liverpool and boarded the American-owned liner *Merion*. It was a modern, fast vessel, 530 feet long, with a twin-screw propulsion system and a top speed of fourteen knots.[30] The *Merion* had been launched in Scotland only three years earlier,[31] and despite two mishaps already in its brief history, the most recent of which had involved colliding with another steamer off the coast of Ireland that spring,[32] it was generally considered to be a comfortable and safe ship. On this vessel, she steamed across the Atlantic to compete in a month of tournaments in the United States. These were to include the women's national championship, which began in the second week of October in the town of Haverford, Pennsylvania.

The ship was a little more than half full, with 110 cabin passengers – of which the British golfing champion was one – and another 819 who had paid just under $8 apiece to travel in steerage. It arrived in Philadelphia on 2 October. Dod had arranged ahead of time that while in the Philadelphia area she would stay with the parents of Frances C. Griscom, a leading American golfer whose father, Clement, was a well-known financier and one of the country's leading shipping magnates – his company had an ownership stake in the *Merion* – and whose mother, Frances, came from a family long counted among Philadelphia's Quaker elite.

After a couple of hours' delay, as the passengers prepared to disembark, Dod skipped down the ramps leading to the wharf. There at the gate were Griscom and her friend Mrs A.J. Cassatt, the wife of the president of the Pennsylvania

Railroad Company, standing beside a red chauffeur-driven car, "a mammoth machine", the *Philadelphia Inquirer*'s reporter on the spot noted approvingly. It was a scene guaranteed to attract attention. After all, at the time there were in the whole of the United States only 55,000 privately owned motor vehicles;[33] in Philadelphia, probably only a few hundred. Dod, who had been heavily lobbying her two older brothers in recent months to buy a motorcar in which they could all tool around the British Isles together, and who had enlisted a number of her friends to argue the case,[34] waved at the two ladies and let out a merry little laugh. It "won the auditor's heart completely", the reporter told his readers.[35] Then, with two other friends, sisters to Cassatt, by her side, she continued down the gangway towards the Griscoms' car.[36]

As customs officials perfunctorily looked through the famous athlete's travel trunks, Dod talked with the journalists who had been sent from newspapers up and down the East Coast to catch a glimpse of her. She told them that her American golfing competitors were "formidable", but, she added with a twinkle in her eyes, she had every intention of winning the events in which she played.

For the next six weeks, Dod combined a whirlwind of social engagements with a brutally full schedule of golf tournaments and matches. So many people wanted to see her; and everybody who felt they had something to prove on the links wanted to tee off against her. Newsmen dogged her wherever she went, waiting to take her photograph, hoping she would spend a few minutes answering their questions.

In a one-day warm-up tournament in New Jersey, held just after her ship docked, and when she was presumably still getting her land legs back, "she completely outclassed the 30 or more other women who competed, and captured the cup with ease", according to a journalist from upstate New York who was assigned to cover her trip.[37]

As the days went by, however, Dod, who had never before shown any signs of fatigue during her sporting conquests, began to flag. She was rushing between events in Pennsylvania, New Jersey and New York. In a qualifying round to the nationals, she lost a fierce contest to one Miss Vanderhoef in a sudden-death playoff after tying for eighteen holes.[38] By the time she got to Haverford to play the nationals, her mood had soured, and her focus seemed to have waned.

Playing with a hickory club, which lost much of its spring in the hot, heavy weather, with rain showers episodically breaking out from the threatening skies above,[39] Dod didn't win the big American tournament. In fact, she underperformed rather spectacularly on the hard Pennsylvania turf, so different from the lush British greens she was used to, and went out in the opening round.[40] For perhaps the first time in her sporting life, she had sputtered instead of roared.

Facing a young American golfer, Pauline Mackay, in that first round, Dod just about held her own as they navigated the course. But uncharacteristically, she found it impossible to pull ahead. By the seventeenth hole, she was beginning to fade. A rumour spread through the crowd: the great English golfing sensation was about to lose. Huge numbers of people flooded in to watch them play the hole. Mackay opened with a long and accurate drive. Dod prepared her response. But incredibly, when she swung, the English ladies' champion made a rookie's error; she sclaffed her tee shot, the club scraping the ground awkwardly before making contact with the ball, its core rubber, its outside gutta-percha (a tough resin harvested from trees in Malaysia), of a kind patented by the American inventor Coburn Haskell only five years previously. As a result, the ball landed on the far edge of the bank, far from the hole. Two shots later, Mackay sank her own ball into the hole and won the match.[41]

The story was sent out by telephone and telegraph all the way across the country. Within hours, papers as far afield as San Francisco were trumpeting Dod's shocking loss.

In defeat, it seemed, Dod held the attention of the American media as much as she had earlier in victory, becoming something of a foil as the newspapermen reported on the exploits of the up-and-coming youngster who had improbably brought her to heel in the opening round. "Miss Pauline Mackay, a young golfer barely out of her teens and hailing from the Oakley Country Club Boston, was the heroine of yesterday's play in the championship tournament of the United States Golf Association over the links of the Merion Cricket Club at Haverford," wrote a reporter for the *Trenton Times* in New Jersey, somewhat gleefully. "She defeated Miss Lottie Dod, the British title holder, in a match replete with sensational incidents by 2 up and 1 to play and thus secured to a home golfer this year's American title, for the first time assailed by a visitor from the British Isles."[42] The *Topeka State Journal* out of Kansas attempted to smooth out the wrinkles, charitably putting Dod's loss down to the foul weather; but even in this, the author managed to make Dod look mediocre, a vulnerable English girl unable to adjust to the vicissitudes of the American clime. It was, the journalist noted, "one of those warm autumn days that enervate even Americans who are used to them. Miss Dod, dressed for the cool weather she would have encountered at home in autumn, was oppressed by the heat and rendered languid and nerveless." Had it been a "cool, bracing day", he continued, "she would have made a better fight".[43]

The loss didn't seem to dent Dod's cheer for long, however. Whenever she was abroad, she appeared to flourish, the somewhat sombre personality she wore among her family members in England replaced by something more carefree. She laughed a lot, danced at soirees, delighted the reporters – who noted her "democratic" charms.[44] When she wasn't playing, she caddied, later in the month carrying the bags for her friend and host Frances C. Griscom, who had won the prestigious US national title in 1900, in the championship tournament of the Women's Golf Association of Philadelphia.[45]

A few days after Lottie Dod's shocking loss, on Tuesday, 18 October, Griscom's socialite mother took a team of golfers, Dod among them, by train up through New York State, across the Canadian border and north to Toronto. They had been invited to attend by the wealthy businessman and golfer Albert William Austin.

There, two days later, the women golfers played a United States vs. Canada match at the Lambton Golf and Country Club.[46] Dod was made the honorary captain of the Canadian team. Yet again, it proved an unhappy experience. She lost, the New York Times reported, in a subsequent overview of her American trip, by two holes.[47]

The whirlwind continued. In the last days of October, the English champion played in one event after the next in golf clubs around Massachusetts.[48]

Then, in early November, Dod teamed up with the British men's champion, Walter J. Travis, to play a foursome contest in Garden City, New York, against her host, Frances Griscom, and Devereux Emmet. The latter pair won.[49] The next day, exhausted beyond all measure, practically propping herself up on her club between shots, perhaps in response to the sciatica pain that would come to plague her over the next years, the Little Wonder played her last event in America. It was a small tournament at the Baltusrol Golf Club in Springfield, New

Jersey. Dod and her partner, E.F. Sanford, barely managed to eke out a win.

Over the previous week the English champion, risking the displeasure of her hosts, had already cancelled her upcoming matches in Atlantic City. She had also contacted the people in Chicago, who were expecting her there a few days hence at what was billed as the start of a swing through the Midwest, to make her apologies.[50] "She has been greatly fatigued by steady play and entertainment," a sympathetic journalist wrote. "And nothing but determination has kept her from collapse."[51] Now, desperately needing some downtime, she booked her return trip and, a few days later, headed back to England.

Although Dod would remain a keen club golfer for the rest of her life, her days as an international competitor were at an end. The next year, she suffered a string of embarrassing losses in tournaments in England, including to May Hezlet, whom she had bested at Troon to win her national championship. "Her appetite for the game virtually evaporated overnight," the author Liz Pook noted.[52] Thirty-four years old, the tennis and golf champion, the hockey star, mountaineer and tobogganist was ready, once again, to reinvent herself.

SEVEN

Bull's-Eye at the London Olympics

Dod training with teammates in the run-up to the 1908 London Olympics. Courtesy of Sally-Ann Dod, Dod family archives.

Lottie Dod was by now increasingly hobbled by sciatica. And yet, despite the pain, after she retired from top-level golf there would be one more sporting turn in the Little Wonder's two decades in the spotlight.

Two years after she returned from America, impatient as ever for new conquests, Lottie Dod, living with her brothers in Newbury, a fifty-minute train journey from London's Paddington Station, more fully embraced a hobby in which she had partaken, on and off, since childhood: archery. In

1906, she joined the Welford Park Archers and began entering competitions. She was, as she had been in so many other sports, an instant success; shortly after she began serious training in archery, Dod won the grandiosely named Royal Toxophilite Society Ladies' Day Gold Medal, beating nearly 100 other competitors.[1]

In the esoteric world of archery, Dod had truly hit her bull's-eye. For the Royal Toxophilites, founded in 1781, with the then Prince of Wales and future King George IV as its patron, was the preeminent archery club in the country. In early tournaments, the king stamped his imprimatur on the events by personally handing out prizes.

For the few years that remained of Dod's sporting career, it was archery that commanded her attention.

The final act in that extraordinary public sporting career took place in 1908. That year, the thirty-six-year-old turned up as a member of England's Olympic team at the summer games in London.

By 1908, Edwardian-era England was a political tinderbox: Suffragettes were becoming more vocal, Irish independence movements were pushing Ireland towards full-blown civil conflict, and socialists and liberals in Britain were campaigning for important social reforms such as unemployment insurance, the eight-hour workday and pensions. Many of these proposals would be implemented in the 1909/10 budget, a hugely important document in British political history known as "the people's budget".

Dod, who seems to have remained scrupulously above – or outside – the political protests, simply continued doing what she did best: proving, through her sports accomplishments, that women were every bit the equal of men. Yet, political or not, as Britain's most acclaimed female athlete, Lottie Dod could hardly help but be caught up in the controversy about whether or not to let women compete in London's Olympic Games. She also couldn't help but become even more of an advertisement for those seeking to expand athletic possibilities for young women around the world. Indeed, in early August, following the conclusion of the Games, the *Pittsburgh Press* would report that the grande dame of society figures, Mrs John Jacob Astor herself, had been avidly following the women's archery contest, of which Dod was a part, and had now pledged to bring the sport to Newport, Rhode Island, summer vacation spot of the East Coast's rich and famous.[2]

For the female athletes of the 1908 Olympics, it had been a long and difficult journey. The first of the modern Olympiads, in 1896 in Athens, had featured not a single female competitor. In 1900 and 1904, a handful of women had made Olympic appearances, in golf, tennis and archery – the three sports for which Dod was most renowned – as well as in croquet, equestrian events and yachting. But they had done so in the face of overwhelming official hostility. Pierre de Coubertin, the president of the International Olympic Committee (IOC), and the man most responsible for the modern rebirth of the Games, hated the idea of women athletes. He believed they would only ever serve as sources of titillation for their audiences, and would later write that the competition ought to be an "exaltation of male athleticism", with one of the non-monetary prizes afforded athletes being "female applause".[3] Women's sports, Coubertin averred, were "against the laws of nature".[4] In this, he was echoing the warnings of late nineteenth- and early twentieth-century psychologists that competitive sports helped turn women into "inverts" or lesbians, and of medical doctors and religious leaders who claimed that too much strenuous physical activity would damage women's pelvises, vaginas and uteri, thus rendering them incapable of childbearing.

The historian Stephen Halliday, in *History Today*, reported that there were only thirty-seven female competitors at the 1908 Games, out of more than 2,000 athletes,[5] although an additional eight women informally participated in yachting, motorboat racing and other officially male-only competitions, making for a grand total of forty-five.[6] They competed formally only in tennis, archery, and figure skating – with the female archers making up twenty-five of those thirty-seven competitors[7] – and were allowed additional exhibition events in swimming, diving and gymnastics, sports that the IOC felt were suitably "ladylike activities".[8]

Until 1906, planning had been underway for the fourth of the modern Olympic Games to be held in Rome. But by late winter of that year, it was apparent that the Eternal City would be eternally unable to get the modern stadiums built and the facilities for the athletes arranged in time for a summer 1908 spectacle. Somewhat at the last minute, London was chosen as an alternative venue. With only two years on hand, thousands of labourers began working at breakneck pace on an enormous new stadium in White City, just outside of the Shepherd's Bush district of west London. It would be designed as a part of a huge complex, 140 acres in extent, that would host the Franco-British Exhibition, a sort of world's fair intended to showcase cutting-edge technological and cultural achievements in a world dominated by the two vast European empires.[9]

White City was the brainchild of a Hungarian businessman-cum-impresario named Imre Kiralfy, whose nose for a good deal had led him to seek an agreement with the organisers of the London Olympics to host the event at his sparkling new venue. The grounds themselves were magnificent, filled with artificial lakes, faux-Renaissance-era palaces, a smorgasbord of domes, steeples, columns and turrets. Kiralfy had conjured up a fantasyland, a whimsical world of dreams, in the heart of west London suburbia. On the eastern edge of this dreamscape, south of the Indian Arena, the Tunis, Algeria and French Colonies Hall, and a faux Senegalese village, was the Olympic stadium. It would be built to seat 70,000 spectators – though when people crammed into the stands, additional tens of thousands could watch the marquee events – making it far and away the biggest sports stadium on earth at the time. Eleven other smaller venues, dotted around the metropolis, in places far from White City, would also be co-opted by the Olympic organisers to host various contests that summer.

On 13 July, tens of thousands of spectators jammed on to tube trains, railway trains and city omnibuses, into horse-drawn hansom cabs, the electric cabs knowns as Berseys and the just-introduced petrol-consuming taximeter cars. All were heading towards the grand new stadium in White City for the opening ceremony of the fourth modern Olympics. The crush was tremendous.

Inside the stadium that afternoon, ambassadors and sports officials, royalty and cultural celebrities, joined with ordinary Londoners in celebration. For weeks, the country's prestige publications had been playing up the historical significance of the Games, stressing to an initially sceptical public the huge cultural, indeed imperial, importance of putting on a good show before the world's assembled dignitaries. This was billed as being the largest sports gathering in history, dwarfing in importance the games that had run, for hundreds of years, in the ancient Greek world. But they were also painted as representing a continuum between the high culture and political sophistication of the Greeks millennia earlier and the British Empire of the early twentieth century. "There can be no greater testimonial, however, to the enduring fascination and the permanent value of athletic sports than this continued existence of the ancient Olympic Games through good fortune and evil fortune, through famines and wars and pestilences, through changes of Governments and Empires," wrote an essayist in *The Times* six days before the opening ceremony. "It is not surprising that within a few years after the modern revival of athletics an effort should have been successfully made to bring about their resuscitation so far as modern conditions permitted."[10] Not to be outdone, *The Observer* declared that the Games would be "the greatest gathering of athletes the world has ever known". And missing no opportunity to make the event reflect imperial glory, it noted that "the British Empire, placed upon its mantle in an emergency, exceeded the most sanguine expectations in regards to thoroughness of organization". The London Games would, the paper stated, "stand for all the principles of purity" that the empire embodied.[11]

That 13 July afternoon, the noisy crowd waited for King Edward VII and his guest Lord Desborough, president of the British Olympic Council, to arrive. The weather was dull, the clouds from morning storms still hanging over the city; and the roads around the exhibition grounds were filled with pools of muddy water.[12] None of this, however, had dampened the enthusiasm of the tens of thousands of spectators. It was the first time the stadium had been filled, and the sight was overwhelming: huge tiers of seating, with tickets at the start of the competition selling for one shilling on upward,[13] surrounded the field, the two one-third-mile running tracks, and a 110-yard "swimming tank". Around the edge of the arena were dotted Venetian masts, from which "fluttered the flags of all nations".[14]

At 3 p.m., more than 2,000 athletes paraded in, Lottie and William Dod among them, cheered on their way by multitudes of spectators ranged around three-quarters of the stadium – the areas behind the competitors left temporarily empty. The athletes were dressed in formal clothes, some in white sports attire and tailored jackets, others in dark ones, with flag bearers from the competing countries leading each phalanx of competitors. All but forty-five of them were men; and of the forty-five women, forty were athletes from Great Britain.[15] They marched across the field, ranged themselves along the edge of the swimming tank and stood at attention while the cheers reverberated around White City.[16] Above them, a flock of doves, symbolising peace between nations, was released.[17]

Now it was the turn of the royals to make their appearance.

The entrances to the stadium were marked by letters, and at the end of the avenue that went between the stadium and the nearby Imperial Sports Club was a special entrance, marked "M", at which was erected a petal-covered platform draped with crimson hangings. "M" was the royal entrance, connected via a covered way, also draped with crimson buntings, to a staircase that led up to the royal box. The rear, the side and the ceiling of that box were all plastered with heavy Persian rugs, and two large tables, surrounded by cane wicker chairs, were provided for the comfort of the royal guests. When the king and his companions sat down, they would have seen, directly across the stadium from their box, an elaborate decoration covering the stadium's ironwork; on it were the words "Edward VII, Rex, Imperator."[18]

Just before 3.30,[19] Edward VII and Lord Desborough entered the royal box, to the roars of the crowd. They took turns speaking, each one promising that the Olympic Games would strengthen the cordial relations between nations of the world. Given the primitive state of amplifier technology in 1908, it is doubtful if most of the 70,000 spectators could hear a word that they said. Be that as it may, the king, in ending his brief peroration, declared the fourth modern Olympics officially begun, and the tens of thousands of gathered spectators cheered wildly.

Over the coming weeks, the *Winston-Salem Journal*'s man on the spot pronounced, in one of the more flowery descriptions of the Games, "The pick and flower of the athletic world will strive with every effort to win glory and fame and the plaudits of the multitudes. Never before in the history of the world has an athletic event of greater importance been held or one in which a keener pitch of enthusiasm has been aroused. The Olympic contests of ancient Greece pale into insignificance in comparison with the present meet."[20]

The weather that week was beyond abysmal. Some mornings, officials would arrive at the stadium to find the track and grassy turf so saturated that they wondered if they would even be able to hold the competitions that day. Time and again, contests had to be suspended due to the drenching rain, the water pooling on the track and making races unrunnable. So miserable were the conditions that after the initial excitement of the Games had worn off, the crowds stayed away. Four days in, the organisers, after emergency meetings of the French and British Olympic committees, had to announce that they were halving the price of tickets, hoping that, in so doing, they could draw Londoners back to the soggy contests.

Gamely, Dod and the others soldiered on. But the weather went from bad to worse. On 18 July, while the archers that morning managed to get off their shots in between the squalls, by the afternoon it was pouring so hard that officials had to repeatedly call a halt to the races. Even the divers had to wait the storm out, not because they couldn't dive in the rain, but because the judges couldn't see enough of the action through the downpour to accurately judge the athletes.[21]

The rains and wind cast a gloom over the entire Games. Damp and cold, athletes and team coaches alike grew impatient. Small disagreements over judging morphed into unpleasant spats. The American delegation, in particular, felt that the British judges – unlike in later Olympics, in 1908 the host country provided all the officials – were cheating their athletes. There were allegations that some of the track races had been fixed; that the tug-of-war contest had been deliberately misjudged. When the Italian who seemed to have finished first in the marathon was disqualified for receiving assistance during the final in-stadium lap of the race, the Italian delegation also cried foul. Soon, newspapers around the world were giving equal attention to the international rows that were brewing around the Games as to the results of the various races and contests. Some blared headlines indicating that US-British relations had hit a new low as a result of the dastardly conduct of the Olympic judges.

When, two days after the worst of the weather, Dod faced off against her fellow Brit, Sybil "Queenie" Newall, in the final round of the women's archery tournament, at least some of the American newsmen present were poised to ridicule her event. "If Great Britain's plan works out, it will win this year's Olympics through superiority in archery, figure skating, rugby, tiddledewinks, and diabolo. Of course, such mollycoddle sports as weight throwing, pole vaulting, the runs, and sprints do not count for much," wrote the reporter for the *Butte Daily Post* in Montana. Dripping with sarcasm, the opinion piece continued, "And to think that Mrs. Pough-Bow-wowly's victory in the archery event will count as much as Flanagan's record hammer throw."[22] In a backhanded compliment, numerous newspapers mentioned how archery was becoming particularly popular among women, a "society fad" that would likely spread its tentacles from one side of the Atlantic to the other. "To the English girl is perhaps due the revival of archery in America. For her Yankee cousins accepted this sport only after she had made it a fad," the *Buffalo Times* reported. While ostensibly an ode to the skills of the English female archers, it was at least as much a subtle dig at the outsize influence of women in a sporting milieu the author clearly thought ought still to belong exclusively to men.[23] Archery might once, in the age of Lottie's ancestor Sir Anthony Dod of Edge, have been a vital military skill; but half a millennium later, in the era of machine guns and long-range artillery shells that could be fired scores of miles, it was now considered effete.

Dod and Newall – both of them benefiting from the absence at White City of Alice Legh, a childhood friend of Dod's who was widely judged the best archer of her era, but who had decided not to take part in the Olympic Games – managed to ignore the ridicule. A few seconds of old silent-film footage of Dod at White City Stadium shows a determined woman in a black dress, tightly belted around the waist, and a high hat, her face a picture of concentration, aiming her arrow at the target, time and again in quick succession. Over the course of the two-day competition, every entrant would fire off 144 arrows, some at sixty yards, the rest at fifty.[24] The footage shows her walking up to that straw, white, oilcloth-covered target, with her competitors, to see where her arrows, each one weighted by English silver coins to the value of three shillings and sixpence, had landed. She doesn't smile in the old film, doesn't show any sense of vulnerability. She is, instead, all business.[25]

It was one of the tightest contests of the Games. Over the course of the first day, Newall and Dod went back and forth for the lead. On day two, however, Dod's marksmanship fell off noticeably; meanwhile, her opponent seemed to improve as the day went on. When the last arrows had been fired, it was clear that Newall had won. Lottie Dod, so unused to finishing second, ended up with 126 hits to Newall's 132; and 642 points to Newall's 688.[26] In the next day's morning papers, however, more attention was focused on the tug-of-war event in which Britain ran away with all three medals, the gold going to the London police team, the silver to the Liverpool police team, and third place to members of the Metropolitan police.

Adding insult to injury, Lottie's brother William – with a thick moustache, wearing a cloth cap that seemed to cast his face in permanent shadow – won the gold in the men's archery contest. And in their reporting of this, some of the news reporters then casually misidentified the leading female athlete of the era, assuming that William was Lottie's father, and that the young daughter was there only on his coat-tails.[27]

The day that Lottie Dod won her silver medal, it wasn't only sports that were grabbing the headlines, however. To the north, in the city of Manchester, a huge Suffragette rally, organised by the Women's Social and Political Union and held in support of a number of hunger-striking women imprisoned at Holloway Prison, was underway on the 600-acre Heaton Park. It was the third Sunday in a row that Suffragettes had gathered in the park,[28] and this meet was by far the largest to date. In fact, so enormous was the crowd – some observers calculated upward of 50,000 people in attendance – that thirteen separate raised speaker platforms had to be erected.[29]

From the principal platform spoke Mrs Emmeline Pankhurst, the grande dame of the Suffragette movement, who had been addressing enormous gatherings all that week, including a meeting of some 20,000 people in Nottingham Forest the previous afternoon. "If women had sufficient intelligence to earn their own living, to pay their rent, and obey the laws which 7 1/2 millions of men in the country were making for them, surely in justice the vote should be given to them," *The Guardian* reported her as saying.[30] Pankhurst reflected her audience's angry, frustrated mood when she averred that women were tired of waiting: tired of being told there was other more important legislation to consider before parliamentarians could get around to considering suffrage; tired of being told that other social reforms, such as an old-age pensions measure, were of more vital national consequence.

The Liberal Party's prime minister, Henry Campbell-Bannerman, had fallen ill and died in late April, and had been succeeded by H.H. Asquith. The new, younger leader was committed to a raft of social reforms. In recent conversations, he had reportedly admitted that most of his cabinet were now in favour of giving women the right to vote. "Very well, then, Liberals who believed in majority rule ought to see that the majority in the party ruled," *The Guardian* reported Pankhurst as saying, challenging Asquith, to the loud applause of the gathered crowd, to live up to his ideals.[31]

It was the start of a massive summer of Suffragette protests, one that would culminate three months later, on the evening of 13 October, with close to 100,000 demonstrators ringing the Houses of Parliament. Many of those protesters, increasingly committed to the tactics of civil disobedience and direct action, would attempt to storm the hallowed legislative chambers to insist that the male MPs take up the issue of women's right to vote. They would be held back, if only barely, by cordons of police, some of them on horseback, by soldiers, and even by marines.[32]

* * *

Six days after Dod's archery face-off with Newall, the Games
– begun with a racquetball contest back in April, ten weeks
before the official opening ceremony – drew to a close. When
the medals were tallied, Britain had considerably more than any
other country: fifty-six golds, and a total of 146 medals; the
United States, its Olympians unhappy with the host country's
refereeing, came in a distant second with forty-seven. Two of
those British medals belonged to the Dods, the first brother-
sister combo ever to place at the same Olympics.

The medal ceremony, in which the Dods were to take part,
was scheduled for that afternoon, 25 July. Lottie, having finished
with a silver, received hers in the first part of the proceedings.
With all the other silver and bronze medal winners, she
stood on the far side of the stadium. The Grenadier Guards
played the national anthem of every country represented on
the medal platforms, then the drums and bugles of the Irish
Guards sounded the advance, and the second- and third-place
finishers marched along the cycle tracks to a series of tables set
up opposite the royal box. There, the silver medallists (with
the exception of those in the last two remaining contests of the
Games) were presented with their medals by the Duchess of
Rutland; and the bronze medallists by Catherine, Duchess of
Winchester. Lottie's, like those of the other runners-up, was
given to her in a dark-blue leather box. One side of the medal
featured an image of a muscular St George atop a rearing horse,
killing the dragon in front of a half-naked princess; the other
showed two women seated on elevated daises, dressed in ancient
Greek garb, crowning a naked male athlete standing between
them with laurels.[33]

Through the ceremonial covered way that led to the royal
box, in choreographed pageantry Queen Alexandra entered

the stadium, to the playing of the national anthem and the unfurling of the royal standard, as had her husband, Edward, twelve days earlier. She settled comfortably in her wicker chair, and her retinue arranged themselves around her; and then the final two races of the tournament – presumably held back so as to allow the queen to at least glimpse the spirit of competition during her Olympic visit – got underway: the finals of the 110-meteres hurdles and what was labelled the "1,600-metre team race," more commonly known today as the 4 x 400-metre relay.

On cue with the last races, the orchestra started playing George Frideric Handel's "See, the Conqu'ring Hero Comes", part of his massive work *Judas Maccabaeus*, composed in 1746. The chorus sang, "See, the conqu'ring hero comes! / Sound the trumpets! Beat the drums! / Sports prepare! The laurel bring! / Songs of triumph to him sing!"[34] The words echoed around the huge stadium.

At the sound of Handel's rousing oratorio, its great chorus, its French horns, all the gold medallists emerged out of their changing rooms. With near-military precision, they began the long march across the arena to the royal box, there to receive their gold medals from the queen herself, surrounded by members of the IOC and the British Olympic Council. Each rendition of the song lasted just over three minutes. The chorus sang it repeatedly, the words accompanying the parade of athletes on their journey across the stadium.[35] William Dod, winner of the men's gold in archery, was sandwiched between the javelin and the just-declared 1,600-metre relay race winners in front of him, and the fencing, gymnastics and lawn tennis victors behind him.[36]

As the scores of medallists bowed and, in the case of the handful of women, curtsied, they were also each given a large diploma – depicting a winged, laurel-wreathed, somewhat androgynous athlete in a pillared temple, surrounded by eight muscle-toned acolytes in various states of undress, Lord Desborough's signature on the bottom of the page. William would frame that diploma and keep it hanging on a wall of his home for the rest of his life.[37] Each, too, received a sprig of oak plucked from Windsor Forest, individually wrapped in a Union Jack, a personal gift from King Edward. Now Queen Alexandra, her Olympic role complete, rose to leave, and the entire crowd stood and cheered. The swelling verses of the national anthem filled the stadium one more time.[38]

For Dod, that wild applause, the delirium of the enormous Olympic gathering, must have sounded like a requiem mass to her athletic triumphs. Her sciatica was getting worse. Almost certainly she knew that, at the age of thirty-six, her sporting glory days were now behind her.

EIGHT

From Sporting Legend to Wartime Nurse

Surname *Dod*	Rec'd 2 9 MAR 1919
Christian Names *Charlotte*	(Mr., Mrs. or Miss)

Permanent Address: *c/o Lloyds Bank. Bideford. N. Devon. late of Chircombe, Bideford. N. Devon.*

Date of Engagement *Nov. 1916*   Rank   Pay *Nil*

Date of Termination *April 1918*   Rank   Pay *Nil*

Particulars of Duties *Pantry & House maids work in hospitals*

Whether whole or part time, and if latter No. of hours served *about 600*

Previous Engagements under Joint War Committee, if any, and where *as a Member of London 72 Chelsea V A D Hospital*

Honours awarded *Passed 1st Aid & Home Nursing (St. John's) 1912*

Lottie Dod's Red Cross card, detailing her First World War service.

Lottie Dod would never again compete at an international level. Instead, like so many women of her social class in those years, including the future literary luminaries Agatha Christie, Vera Brittain and Enid Bagnold, as the international situation grew more tense, and as the storm clouds of war grew darker, the champion athlete moved into medicine. Not as a doctor, but as something akin to a hospital assistant. "I have always thought it is such a mistake to think too much about games and sports," she told a friend, perhaps explaining the twists and turns her life took in the years after she won the Olympic silver.[1]

The political protests around women's suffrage were, in these years, gaining in intensity, with Suffragettes moving from civil disobedience to violence. Some had firebombed the homes of prominent politicians, others had set fire to sports venues, even trying to burn down the stands at the All England Lawn Tennis and Croquet Club. By the hundreds, women were being sent to the notorious Holloway Prison; many of them would go on hunger strike there, and many would, as a result, be agonisingly force-fed by their guards.

Dod continued to stay shy of political involvement – although her erstwhile friend Elizabeth Main did tell others that she considered herself a "suffragist". But as the new century wore on, the ageing athlete continued to live a life that showed her belief that women had an important place outside of the home. She continued dancing to her own tune.

The tight-knit world of Edgecombe had by now unravelled. In 1912, Tony peeled off, when he met and married Evelyn, moved to the southern English county of Somerset, and, well into his forties, started having children. And sometime that same year, William decided to invest in a property on the north coast of Devon, near one of the country's most spectacular golf courses. The house that he bought was a narrow, five-storeyed brick edifice in the village of Westward Ho! It was named The Divot – all of the houses on that stretch of road boasted names, such as Cairncross, de la Zouch, and The Den, rather than street numbers – and its elegant, unpainted brick front entrance on Kingsley Road afforded the occupants unobstructed views of the coast below, and, curling around the edge of the estuary, the spectacular grounds of the Royal North Devon Golf Club. Just up the street was the oldest house in town, Culloden House, built in 1865, and just a little bit further up still was the old Holy Trinity Church.

For Lottie, her brothers' departures must have been a shock. She was, for the first time in her life, alone, charged with maintaining the huge house in Edgecombe without her brothers' presence. Her immediate response was to spend as much time as possible in Westward Ho! with William, travelling down to the town and its prestigious golf course often enough that, in early December 1912, she was nominated by her friends Mrs Cooper and Miss Boyd to become a member of the club.[2] On some of her official documentation, she now listed north Devon as her home. Over the following two years, as the international situation worsened and war became more likely, Dod attended several meetings a year at the ladies' branch of the Royal North Devon Golf Club, finally, six weeks after the outbreak of war, being elected on to its executive committee. Perhaps she felt the environment calming, the incessant crashing of the surf against the shore hypnotic, the low, feathery summer clouds enveloping the landscape like a down comforter. Perhaps the tide pools – the boulders slippery with seaweed, the rocks pocked with the shells of molluscs, seagulls squawking low overhead – that limned the shoreline south of where the open sand stretches began, in some ways reminded her of the freedom she felt when mountaineering. Maybe the lights of the Hartland Point lighthouse, at the end of a thin slip of land jutting out into the Atlantic south-west of Westward Ho!, reminded her of the lines of cairns high up in the Norwegian glacial regions, which in her youth had helped guide her from one spot to the next along her journey. Conceivably, the rugged cliffs, speckled with wildflowers, that stretched south of the village, along which hikers could walk for hours, their clothes snagging on the brambles as they went, served as something of a surrogate for the epic vistas of her younger days.

Yet however great the allure of Westward Ho!, sport was

no longer the be-all and end-all for her, and she soon grew tired of the club's endless, often-mundane meetings. She did, in the run-up to the war, continue to attend some of the Royal North Devon's bigger events, and she made a point of going to meetings to nominate other women to be admitted as new members. But while she remained an enthusiast, golf and the other sports of her past were no longer quite the epicentre of her life. In her forties now, Dod began adjusting to life without her brothers, and started spending more time by herself in Newbury and London. She was looking for fresh ways to express herself, new ways of proving her independence. She was playing the piano again, and singing, both skills she had cultivated in her childhood, and starting to engage more fully with the London cultural scene.

Four years after the London Olympics, Lottie Dod trained in first aid; her cardboard Voluntary Aid Detachment (VAD) card, filled in with her careful, looping script, states that she passed the first aid and home-nursing certification at St John's Hospital in 1912.[3] She learned how to apply dressings and bandages to wounds, how to inject vaccinations for tetanus and other common diseases into the shoulders of patients – and then how to wash out those syringes for reuse. She learned how to keep a hospital room tidy and clean, how to carry prone soldiers to their beds, and then how to bathe them while they were lying in those beds. She learned the bedside manner needed in talking to people who had been operated on and were just emerging from the anaesthesia.[4]

"In London the training was very strenuous. A three year training course was provided with lectures, drill, and camp life," wrote Katharine Furse, the commandant-in-chief of the British Red Cross Society, Women's Voluntary Aid Detachments. "We learnt the theory of nursing and our examination papers compared pretty favourably with those of hospitals . . . Further we learnt discipline. Drill pounded into us the art of holding our tongues and obeying orders, grading and observance of etiquette taught us self-control and obedience."[5]

As part of Dod's training, she would have had to read medical textbooks, attend a minimum of six lectures on nursing, spend two days a week during her training shadowing fully qualified nurses at a local hospital outpatient ward, and finally doing home visits with a district nurse. In addition to preparing for an influx of the war wounded, she would also have encountered patients suffering everything from the effects of venereal disease to ulcers. "We passed our exams and got a small printed card to prove our success," wrote the detective novelist Agatha Christie of her years as a VAD. "So great was female enthusiasm at this time that if any man had an accident he was in mortal terror of ministering women closing in on him. 'Don't let those First Aiders come near me!' the cry would rise."[6]

And yet, despite it all, for most of the women it seemed still a dream. Yes, anyone who was reading the newspapers, or paying attention to the political discussions held in Parliament and the great political clubs of London, anyone who travelled in Europe and saw the ever-larger public displays of military hardware, knew that all wasn't well between the great powers. Hence the War Office's rationale for creating a "territorial scheme" a few years earlier, which would set up VAD around the country and, hopefully, plug gaps in medical services should fighting break out.[7] But there was a world of difference between inflammatory rhetoric and actual conflict. "No civilised nations went to war," Christie remembered thinking. "There hadn't been any war in years; there probably never would be again."

Meanwhile, tensions mounted. When Archduke Franz Ferdinand, heir to the Austrian throne, was assassinated in

Sarajevo in late June 1914, a global conflagration became all but inevitable. "And then suddenly one morning it had happened," Christie wrote. "England was at war."[8]

For Sylvia Pankhurst, daughter of the formidable Suffragette leader Emmeline Pankhurst, the opening of hostilities was a catastrophe, one that, as she travelled back to England from Ireland on a ship full of drunken soldiers, she conceived as being hell-like in what it would inflict on her world. "Throughout Europe would be a vast widowhood, the cries of fatherless children, the groans of injured men; a gigantic arrest of human progress; a huge vanquishing of the higher life of culture, and the finer process of thought; a triumph, sadly immense, of the annihilating power of violence," she wrote.[9]

When the fighting did indeed break out a month after the assassination, at the end of July 1914, Lottie Dod was ready. Having completed her training, she was by now a full member of the Other Empire Force, Voluntary Aid Detachment, qualified to be posted to a hospital, preferably, she indicated, across the English Channel in France, to work as a nursing auxiliary and to help in their convalescence soldiers injured in the first battles of the conflict. The VADs overseas were doing everything from triage work at railway stations where the injured soldiers congregated through to ambulance driving.

While Dod waited to be assigned a hospital, she returned to Westward Ho! to play golf and to attend meetings. The attention of the ladies of the Royal North Devon Golf Club was divided between an all-out concern for the war and a sense that the whole thing was somehow an illusion, that they would blink and it would be over. In late August, they decided to hold a competition, the entrance fees to which would be used to make a War Distress Fund donation, and debated whether to cancel the next few meetings until the end of the war – which they blithely assumed would come swiftly, probably by the end of the year; a few weeks later, however, their concern was much more parochial. While the first battles of the war were being fought, the ladies in Westward Ho! were spending hours debating what handicap to allot players who couldn't obtain an official handicap certification from the Ladies' Golf Union.[10]

The Little Wonder's motivation for requesting France for her VAD assignment may well have been personal. For, a few weeks after the war was declared, forty-seven-year-old William – the other unmarried Dod sibling, the one with whom she had so recently shared Olympic glory, with whom she still lived on and off in Newbury and in Westward Ho! – had volunteered to join a very particular branch of the army.

On the last day of summer, 20 September 1914, an intriguing recruiting advertisement was published in bold print in the Sunday newspaper *The Observer*. "A special battalion for active service sanctioned by Lord Kitchener [the newly appointed Secretary of State for War] is now being recruited from sportsmen up to 45 years of age. Only those used to shooting, hunting, and outdoor sport, who are thoroughly sound and fit, need apply. Now is the opportunity for the RIGHT MAN to join a sportsman's corps."[11]

The corps in question was the brainchild of a rather eccentric, fiercely patriotic society lady, Emma Cunliffe-Owen. In her youth, Cunliffe-Owen, who was rumoured to be related in some way to the royal family, had played a variety of sports; in more recent years, however, she had been crippled by arthritis. Some days, the pain was so intense that she was reduced to using a wheelchair.[12] Despite her inability to play sports anymore, the fifty-one-year-old had remained friendly with many of the country's top athletes; and when war broke out she had the idea of recruiting and funding a battalion made up entirely of sportsmen. Cunliffe-Owen sent a telegram to Lord Kitchener detailing her idea, and rapidly got the thumbs-up. "Lord Kitchener gratefully accepts complete battalion."[13]

Soon, Emma Cunliffe-Owen had set up a recruiting station in the Indian Room of the fashionable Hotel Cecil, reputed to be Europe's largest hotel, on the Strand, in the heart of London. There, twelve retired soldiers set to work processing the hundreds, and then thousands, of athletes who responded to the call. It was, as Cunliffe-Owen's ads made clear, to be an elite club in every sense of the word. "Sportsmen, aged 19 to 45, upper and middle class only. Wanted at Once. Entrance fee 3 guineas, or kit," one ad stated.[14] Another further clarified the type of man being sought: "Too Old at Forty? Not at all! The Sportsman Battalions of the Royal Fusiliers accept the right men up to 45. The Right Men? Yes, the physically fit Sportsman, be he cricketer, golfer, country gentlemen – all are welcome."[15]

Over the months that followed, variants on this ad were published in all the papers of record in the United Kingdom. Across the Atlantic, a barrage of coverage soon followed suit. It was, after all, the only battalion, among all the nations at war, put together by a woman. Early the following year, romantic, swashbuckling references to the battalion would even make it into a fictional story by Keble Howard, published in newspapers across the United States on Valentine's Day.[16] In it, the protagonist wants to surprise his wife by joining the battalion. His friend asks him how she'll take the news. "She'll be as keen as mustard! My little wife is a fine plucked 'un, I tell you! She'd be off to the front herself tomorrow if she could get there by hook or by crook!" Once he gets accepted into the Sportsman's Battalion, the protagonist proudly announces that it will be a virtual aphrodisiac for his war-enthused wife. "There'll be no holding her," he boldly predicts.

Week in and week out, the newspapers reported the fighting unit's latest news. Soon, many of the best sportsmen in England and Canada were parading up and down Savoy Street and drilling on the Strand, to the annoyance of drivers caught in traffic jams because of their antics.[17] Others were doing jumping jacks and similar exercises in the ballroom at the Cecil. Afterwards, they would decamp and head to the fabled basement tavern on the Strand known as the Coal Hole, there to replenish their spent energies with meat pies and libations. The British and American press lapped it all up, following the battalion's every move with something akin to breathless anticipation. After all, in addition to Emma Cunliffe-Owen's curious role, it was made up of men who for years, in some cases decades, had already been heroes in the popular imagination. Taller than the average recruit, and physically toned by years of athletics – recruiters mandated that the battalion members be at least five feet, six inches tall, and with a chest measuring at least thirty-five and a half inches round – the soldiers were soon known by a nickname, the "Hard as Nails Corps".[18] Each was given a silver good luck medallion on joining, on one side of which were the crests of the Royal Fusiliers and the Cunliffe-Owen family; on the other side were the words "From Mrs. Cunliffe-Owen, October 1914, God guard you."[19]

These Sportsman's Battalion members included cricketers, boxers, footballers – within months the first battalion sported eight complete football teams[20] – polo players, Canadian baseballers, rowers, rugby players, runners, champion walkers, golfers and, of course, archers.

Sometime in the early autumn of that first war year, William Dod enlisted in the Royal Fusiliers Sportsman's Battalion.

Regimental records list him as the 690th man to join. He was by then forty-seven, slightly above the official cut-off age for recruitment – but the recruiters didn't seem to mind; indeed, in some of their later recruiting pleas they raised the age of admission to fifty-five.[21] One of Dod's comrades in arms was even older: Frederick Courteney Selous, a larger-than-life big game hunter and friend of ex–US President Teddy Roosevelt, was sixty-four when he enrolled.[22]

Parading around the centre of London with his battalion, and then moving on to a more suitable training camp in Hornchurch, Essex, in those first months of the war Lottie Dod's older brother reinvented himself as a soldier.

Over the next few years, the unofficial anthem of Emma Cunliffe-Owen's battalion would be a poem, aptly titled "The Sportsmen". Its first stanza set the tone: "Sportsmen of every kind, / God! we have paid the score / Who left green English fields behind / For the sweat and stink of war! / New to the soldier's trade, / Into the scrum we came, / But we didn't care much what game we played / So long as we played the game."[23] The members of the Sportsman's Battalion would, in these years, experience all of the toughest conditions of that game. Thrown into trench warfare on the western front, the athletes-cum-soldiers would go through a baptism by fire.

"When the Battalion was in its infancy," later remembered Major General R.O. Kellett, who joined the battalion in December 1914, it was "deficient of arms and equipment, but full of men whose physique, zeal, and spirit were magnificent . . . Many hundreds of their best and bravest made the last sacrifice, but the splendid gallantry and dogged and cheerful endurance of the Battalion never lessened."[24]

In those early days, the Sportsman's Battalion, commanded

by Colonel Viscount Maitland, had thirty-one officers and 1,006 other ranks, for a total of 1,037 soldiers. In the years that followed, as the war dragged on another 3,950 were posted to it when it was already overseas. Four hundred and fifty-three battalion members were known to have been killed in action, and an additional 130 died subsequently of their wounds; 2,297 were wounded, and 350 were declared missing in action, their bodies never recovered. Barely one-third of the athlete-soldiers made it through physically unscathed.

For the first fifteen months of the war, the athlete-soldiers trained in London; then in Hornchurch; at Clipstone Camp, near the town of Nottingham; and finally at Tidworth, in southern England. They dug trenches, both for training purposes and also to help secure the routes into London should the Germans attempt a land invasion. They learned sharpshooting, hand-to-hand combat with bayonets and artillery firing. They spent endless hours on marches, and hours more in informal sports contests arranged on the barracks grounds after the final marches and inspections of the day were over. There were football and rugby games, boxing matches, wrestling contests.[25]

In mid November 1915, the sportsmen journeyed from Tidworth to the port of Folkestone, crossed the English Channel to Boulogne, and marched through the evening to Ostrohove K Rest Camp. The next day, they boarded trains and headed to Steenbecque, in the Bethune sector, where they were initially billeted in requisitioned farmhouses and barns. Over the next months, they would take part in the brutal trench warfare around the town of Cambrin, living in trenches filled with several feet of water and mud – where even if one could sleep through the thunderous barrage, one had to do so standing up – surrounded by rampaging rats, and facing near-continuous shelling. To train for the horrors of gas war, which had over the past weeks become a part of the fighting on the western front, they would, according to the military historian Michael Foley, put on their gas helmets and pass "through a hut full of chlorine gas".[26]

At some point during these dog days of war, William Dod put a black ink pen to paper and, in elegant, confident script, wrote a poem about the war that he titled "St Dunstan's Times".

It is sad, makes you mad
To rush and scurry the whole day long;
There's not a soldier chappie,
Can make the matron happy,
He's up there, anywhere,
To make his bed, so they all declare,
He's lost his quilt and sheet,
And he's too slow on his feet.

And then the chorus kicked in:

From the hour the bell for breakfast rings
St Dunstan's Times
They keep you on the jump;
And if you're late
You curse your fate,
Your bason's freezing in the plate,
And VADs yelling in frantic state,
"St Dunstan's Times."

Later on in the four-page poem, William wrote forlornly of "casualty lists, until you're next. / Then come a whistle blow, To the ship we sadly go".[27]

By early the following year, they were in the Festubert and

then Givenchy sectors. Some of the battalion was in Souchez, just north of Arras. Finally, in July, they were sent to the slaughterhouse that was the Somme, taking part in bloody battles in Delville Wood. The life expectancy for a soldier in this hellish battle zone was, Foley reported, "just three weeks, and many men died within a week of arriving from England".[28]

By then, however, William Dod had transferred to the Royal Navy's volunteer reserves, based in France, performing what his military documents described as "intelligence duties No. 1 Aeroplane Wing"[29] in the newly constituted Royal Naval Air Service (RNAS). Like almost all of those over the age of forty who had enrolled in the Sportsman's Battalion in those heady early days of the war, he had spent only a relatively brief time in the trenches before being either invalided out of the army or given an officer's commission and moved over to other duties. On 4 May 1915, the *London Gazette* noted Dod's transfer, listing him as a newly commissioned lieutenant.[30]

William Dod would serve with the RNAS until late November 1916, when the military accepted his "request to be allowed to resign, on account of age and failing health", and sent him a letter of appreciation for services rendered.[31]

For the remainder of the war, he would watch from the sidelines. What had gone wrong with him health-wise is no longer known. Military records do not indicate that he was seriously injured, or that he spent time in a convalescent hospital. It is entirely possible that he was burned out, that he experienced what would later come to be known as shell shock, and that his nerves were, quite simply, shattered. Certainly, in the years and decades following the war, William became more reclusive, more withdrawn from society. The big game hunter's confidence seems somehow to have been lost, extinguished, in the nightmarish conditions on the western front.

* * *

Lottie never got her wish to serve in France. In her mid forties now, her sciatica was serious enough to disqualify her from overseas service. Red Cross records show that she instead spent the early part of the war bouncing between hospitals, before ending up at the Chelsea VAD hospital as part of London unit 72 of the volunteer force.

"Let our mottos be 'Willing to do anything' and 'The People give gladly'. If we live up to these, the VAD members will come out of this world war triumphant," Katharine Furse, the VAD's commandant-in-chief, wrote in a message given to all unit members. "Do your duty loyally, Fear God, Honour the King."[32]

A converted five-storey town house, the Chelsea, on loan from Lady Morrison-Bell, which opened in March 1915, seven months into the fighting, was an elegant stone building boasting one of London's most desirable addresses: 13 Grosvenor Crescent, in the upmarket neighbourhood of Belgravia.[33] (One hundred years later, Lloyds Bank would list Grosvenor Crescent as the single most expensive street in London.) As recently as the previous summer, it had been the London residence in which Lady Morrison-Bell, her husband Sir Charles and a younger female relative had sojourned for what men and women of their standing called "the season", the endless round of parties and teas, dances and marquee sports events, that occupied the aristocracy come summertime. When they arrived in mid-June of 1914, eleven days before the assassination of Austrian archduke Franz Ferdinand in Sarajevo, *The Times* noted their return in its society pages.[34] But Sir Charles had died later that year at the age of eighty-one, and his grieving widow had decided to turn the sprawling town house over to the war effort. She was, perhaps, influenced in her decision by her neighbour Lady

Northcliffe, who owned the house at number 14, having also decided to convert her property into a hospital for convalescing officers.

Within a two minutes' walk of the elegant Grosvenor Crescent residence were the great stone gateways leading into Hyde Park; the grandiose stone mansion, known simply as No. 1 London, in which lived the descendants of the Duke of Wellington; the ornate arch mounted with a massive carved four-horse chariot ridden by a winged goddess, to commemorate Wellington's military victories; and, most importantly, Buckingham Palace, London residence of the king and queen. It was a landscape of imperial monuments and embassies, the curved crescents and mews of which had been designed by Sir Robert Grosvenor, first Marquess of Westminster, in the early decades of the nineteenth century. Like Lottie Dod, Sir Robert was also Cheshire-born; perhaps homesick for his family's estate 197 miles to the north-west, he had named his new district after Belgrave, one of the villages on his ancestral land.[35]

The Chelsea Hospital fully lived up to its majestic locale. The thick wooden door, adorned with a heavy brass knob, was tall, perhaps fifteen feet, with ornate stone columns on either side. The floor of the hallway leading off the ground floor entrance was an expensive dark marble. Each storey, with the exception of the second, had its own bathroom – a rare luxury in those days. Delicate wrought-iron railings protected balconies that went along the exterior of the street from one house to the next on the first floors above the high, colonnaded doorways. Above them, each window going up the remaining storeys had its own carefully cut metal balustrade, on which were hung flowerpots filled with geraniums. And the conservatory, which in happier days would have hosted guests mingling at the Morrison-Bells' soirees, had been converted into a small operating theatre, its floors tiled to keep conditions as sterile as possible, where a Mr. Gillespie would operate on the wounded soldiers.[36]

On any given day, there would have been three fully trained nurses on hand, their hair confined under white caps, their official positions sanctified by the uniform scarlet capes; there would also have been eight full-time and twenty-four part-time members of the VAD, each wearing a white apron with a red cross on the chest, each also wearing a peaked white cap and comfortable shoes with rubber heels.[37] Not only were these women unpaid, but they also donated funds, over and above the War Office grant to the hospital, to provide needed medical services.[38] These VADs were from London units 156 and 72; Dod was among the latter. As Agatha Christie, herself a young woman at the time, noted, it was the middle-aged VADs, women like Dod, who seemed to be posted more quickly to the hospitals to care for the war wounded; rightly or wrongly, it was generally believed that the older women would show more fortitude when faced with horrendous wounds to treat.[39]

During the more than four years of the war, just over 2,000 patients were treated at the Chelsea. For the volunteer workers, few of whom had previous experience dealing with war wounds, life would have been one continual adjustment, an ongoing battle to cope with images that previously would have been unthinkable. Many of the soldiers evacuated to hospitals in England for treatment had had limbs blown off, or internal organs devastated by machine-gun bullets; some had third-degree burns, others had been blinded by shrapnel. The nurses, mostly of a genteel background, people more acquainted with tea parties than violent combat, would have seen things that mere months earlier they couldn't have even known existed: the gangrene that came with trench foot, for example, and often led to amputations. The author Vera Brittain would later write, about her work at Camberwell Hospital during the war years, of "the prevailing odour of wounds and stinking sheets" that "lingered perpetually in our nostrils". She recalled having to "fight the queer, frightening sensation – to which, throughout my years of nursing, I never became accustomed – of seeing the covered stretchers come in, one after another, without knowing, until I ran with pounding heart to look, what fearful sight or sound or stench, what problem of agony or imminent death, each brown blanket concealed".[40]

The volunteers would have experienced the horrors of watching men, injured by metal shell fragments, succumb to tetanus. They would have had to swab down the bloody floors of the operating theatres. Agatha Christie remembered being asked once to take an amputated leg and throw it in the furnace at the hospital in which she was stationed.[41]

The author Enid Bagnold, writing of her experiences as a wartime VAD, focused on the awfulness of the dimly lit corridors in her hospital, the monotony of laying out endless trays of plates and cutlery for endless meals, the heartbreak at seeing patients writhing and crying out in pain and her discomfort at seeing the wounds themselves. "To see [soldiers] pass into Mess like ghosts," she shuddered. "Gentleman, tinker, and tailor; each having shuffled home from death; each having known his life rock on its base."[42] Wandering through her hospital one day, the recently trained Bagnold was horrified to see a man whose nose had been blown away. "He breathes through two pieces of red rubber tubing: it gave a more horrible look to his face than I have ever seen."[43]

The Red Cross subsequently reported that Dod and her fellow VAD nurses at the Chelsea spent those months after the hospital first opened doing "altogether splendid" work. They had, the anonymous chronicler reported, often to journey from homes far away – in Lottie Dod's case, the far-off suburban town of Newbury, or the even further-off village of Westward Ho! in Devon, where, during the early part of the war, she still spent much of her time. Yet, once they were at the hospital, "their one and only thought was to do their work efficiently and make the patients as comfortable and happy as possible".[44]

As the second year of the war dragged on, Dod temporarily stopped returning to Devon, and as a result was asked to resign her committee position at the golf club. It didn't matter too much anyway; the golf club was a shadow of its former self, the grounds largely untended since all the groundskeepers were off fighting, the money brought in by membership dues largely tied up in war loans upon which the government paid 4.5 or sometimes 5 per cent interest. For more than six months of the year, from October to May, the untended grounds simply had to be closed down.[45]

By the end of 1916, having spent more than thirteen months in the service, Dod would have qualified to wear a white bar on her uniform, signifying seniority among the volunteer ranks.[46] The records aren't clear as to why she stopped working at other hospitals in late 1916, or why she began working more exclusively for the Chelsea. But since she scaled back her work at almost the same time William was invalided out of the service, it's possible that she decided to spend more time looking after him in Westward Ho! – she did resume attending meetings at the Royal North Devon Golf Club the following year. It's also entirely possible that, exhausted by the war, she wanted to spend more time with her older sister, Ann, who was living in a comfortable Hampstead home in north London and had been widowed that spring. Working solely at the Chelsea in central London would have made it easier for her at day's end to travel north a few stops on the Underground to Hampstead to see Ann.

For most of the rest of the war, until April 1918, when the German spring offensive in Flanders was at its height, Lottie worked part-time at Grosvenor Crescent for the Red Cross – presumably returning to the hospital during times of particularly heavy casualty counts – eventually putting in 600 hours of what was described as "pantry and housemaid's work".[47] The exact details of where she was and when have not, apparently, survived in the Red Cross records.

Whatever the precise names and locations of the hospitals that she was assigned to from early in the war through to April 1918, she clearly saw her work as important, as contributing in the best way she knew how to Britain's fighting strength.

Treating the wounded, convalescing soldiers wasn't glamorous; but for the tens of thousands of VADs now enrolled in the war effort, slopping out bedpans, washing dirty dishes, clearing up piles of vomit, sterilising bandages that stank of the pus from festering wounds and trying to provide cheer to the wounded, damaged men who were brought in on a dispiritingly regular basis on stretchers, was one way they could feel that they were doing their part. "Again and again I realise, 'A nation in arms',", wrote Bagnold. "Watchmakers, jewelers, station-masters, dress-designers, actors, travellers in underwear [travelling salesmen selling undergarments], bank clerks . . . they come here in uniforms and we put them into pajamas and nurse them."[48] When trains would chug up to the local station with large numbers of casualties, the VADs would spring into action. "Reflection ends, my feet begin to move, my hands to undo bootlaces, flick down thermometers, wash and fetch and carry."[49]

The Red Cross and the National Archives have no records explaining why Lottie Dod stopped her hospital work months before the Great War ended.[50] Dod's letters, which would likely have shed light on this decision, have not survived. Possibly, she had just worn herself out with long commutes on crowded trains from Newbury to London, and endless hours on her feet rushing around the hospitals, cleaning up after patients and delivering food to the bedbound; after all, for years now, Dod had suffered deeply from sciatica. Possibly her unmarried and unwell brother William, and her widowed older sister, were now making enough demands upon her time and energies that she had nothing left over afterwards.

Throughout the war, women had served vital roles: as nurses, ambulance drivers, munitions factory workers, and so on. By 1918, as many as one million female workers in the United Kingdom had worked as "munitionettes", filling shells with TNT and other hazardous chemicals, many of which seriously impacted the health of the workers.[51] Millions of other women had stepped into traditionally male roles, delivering the post, driving omnibuses, seeking employment as clerical workers, helping farmers desperately short of hands at harvest season.

The Suffragettes had won some victories in the years leading up to the war, including, in 1907, the right for women to be elected on to city and county councils. But they had had no luck in convincing the country's leaders to let women vote in parliamentary elections. In 1910, the House of Commons had passed a very limited franchise bill; but the House of Lords had failed to follow suit and the bill had languished. When 300 Suffragettes marched on Parliament in protest, they were beaten by the police; in Suffragette lore, the incident rapidly became known as "Black Friday". In 1911, another, broader franchise bill was narrowly defeated in Parliament.

As a result of these repeated parliamentary defeats, the

Suffragettes became increasingly militant. Indeed, until the eve of the Great War, members had been lobbing bombs, smashing windows and setting fire to public buildings and sports arenas – including two failed efforts to set ablaze the stands of the All England Lawn Tennis and Croquet Club. At the end of February 1913, a woman was arrested at Wimbledon after she attempted to use paraffin oil and bundles of wood and shavings to set fire to the stands around Centre Court. In her possession was a piece of paper, on which was written, "No peace till women have the Vote."[52] That July, the nightwatchman at Wimbledon interrupted another arson attempt. And at the Gosforth Golf Club, near the town of Newcastle, police discovered an unexploded bomb outside of the clubhouse.[53] Three months later, the *Suffragette* newspaper reported that in the space of a week, both Yarmouth Pier and the Wrigley Head Mill in Failsworth had been set on fire. A number of pillar boxes, in which mail was deposited, had been set ablaze by the dropping of test tubes filled with phosphorus into the letter slots; and the tennis pavilion in Dudley had similarly suffered an arson attack. In each instance, the *Suffragette* didn't directly claim credit for the fires, not wanting to put the arrested women in more legal peril, but did point out that, in the case of the pavilion fire, "a quantity of Suffrage literature was found near the spot".[54]

Hundreds had been arrested as the conflict intensified, and many women were now serving long prison terms.

During the war, however, the Suffragette leaders had agreed to suspend their agitation for the vote; but they had done so only on condition that the coalition government agree to at least a partial enfranchisement of women immediately after hostilities ceased. Ministers had signed on to the truce. And in March 1916, in the same period that male conscription was finally introduced in Britain, the then Prime Minister Asquith had belatedly, and somewhat grudgingly, added his imprimatur to the deal, publicly announcing his conversion to the cause of women's suffrage.[55] Assuming Britain won the war, it was now only a matter of time before at least the wealthier part of the female population would be able to vote in national elections.

The Representation of the People Act of February 1918 allowed women from the age of thirty to vote if they, or their husbands, met a property qualification. And on 21 November 1918, ten days after the 11 November armistice brought the years of war to a close, Parliament passed the Qualification of Women Act. It allowed women from the age of twenty-one to serve as Members of Parliament.

It would take another ten years for all women over the age of twenty-one (at that time the age of majority for men in Britain) to win the franchise. But there was now no doubt as to which way the winds of history were blowing.

Two months after the war ended, Lottie Dod made her own personal demand for women to be accorded equal treatment. At an "extraordinary general meeting" called by the ladies of the Royal North Devon Golf Club to reopen their greens, which had been closed in the latter part of the war, Dod pointed out that the weather and the lack of upkeep rendered the course unusable for much of the year. Unwilling to accept this state of affairs any longer – the segregation of the sexes seemed increasingly ludicrous in the new, chaotic modern age they found themselves in – she and her friend Miss Dessing pushed a resolution, unthinkable only a few years earlier, urging the men's club to allow ladies to use their facilities from October through May of each year. The resolution passed unanimously.

NINE

Singing Her Way into Old Age

Charles B. Cochran
presents

ARGENTINA

in her
Dance Creations.

MATINEES at 3.
WED., MAY 27. FRI., MAY 29. TUES., JUNE 2.

Prices: Stalls, 16s. 6d., 12s., 8s. 6d. Dress Circle,
8s. 6d., 3s. 9d. Upper Circle, 5s. 6d., includ. Tax. At
all Agencies and Adelphi Box Office. (Temple Bar 7611.)

ORIANA MADRIGAL SOCIETY.
Patron, H.R.H. the DUCHESS OF YORK.
Conductor, CHARLES KENNEDY SCOTT.
AEOLIAN HALL. TUESDAY, JUNE 2, at 8.15 p.m.
TUDOR MADRICALS. Part-songs and Folk-songs by
Liszt, Grieg, Warlock, Coleridge Taylor, Harvey Grace,
Harold Phillips, and Whittaker.
Assisted by MURRAY LAMBERT (violin),
All seats unnumbered, 5s. 9d., 3s. 6d., 2s. 4d. Mr.
Adams' Box-office, 159, New Bond-st. (Mayfair 4775),
or Hon. Sec., Miss Lottie Dod, 5, Trebovir-road, S.W.5
(Frobisher 2715).

SALZBURG MUSIC FESTIVAL.
25th JULY—30th AUGUST.
VIENNA OPERA COMPANY.

EMPIRE. Dec. 24. 10 a.m.—Midnight
Dorothy Brandon's Drama
Huth, Joan Barry, Frank

KENSINGTON.—To-nig
to 11. The Office
Utah Kid. Next Monday
(Tom Walls), "He Knew

LEICESTER-sq. THE
Astor, with Robert
DOORS. Also "PRESS

LONDON PAVILION.—
successor to "PITZ
VIRTUE. A Brit. Intn'l

MARBLE ARCH PAVII
tinuous. 6-11.
Thrill Supreme ! ED
6.20, 8.55. Also Gaumo

NEW GALLERY, Gert.
ARLISS. David Mar
Berry in "THE MILLIO

NEW VICTORIA. (Vic
.5 p.m.) Lily Har
"THE SPECKLED BA
British Movietone News.

PALACE THEATRE. S
To-day, 6 and 8.30,
in glorious sound. 5.00

PHOENIX THEATRE.

Observer *newspaper advertisement for the Oriana Madrigal Society concert with Lottie
Dod's contact information, 24 May 1931.*

In the strange calm of the post-war years, Lottie Dod looked
for new ways to pass her time. She didn't have a traditional
career and, given her age and her social status, likely never
would. Her youth had been spent triumphing in one sport after
the next. The first years of her middle age had been defined by
the war and her work as a volunteer in the military hospitals of
London. Now, bored, she needed other outlets.

Miss Charlotte Dod, who had been classically educated by
her governesses and tutors in Edgeworth House back in the
high Victorian era, turned to music. She had always been a

skilled pianist, and had always had a wonderful singing voice. As far back as July 1892, a long profile of her in *Queen* had told readers that "if she had not been the Lady Champion, she might have become a fine singer, for she has a good voice and is extremely musical".[1] Now, as the 1920s got underway, she picked up her stakes again, finally moving away from the big, empty house in Newbury and into the London metropolis, where she bought a property at 5 Trebovir Road in Earl's Court, living in unit one and, when the need merited it, renting out the other floors. She installed a phone, WESTERN 2715 – later it would change to FROBISHER 2715 – and set about furnishing her flat. As a property owner, Dod could now, according to the 1918 reform, register to vote.[2] And according to the electoral register, she promptly did so. She also joined the prestigious Oriana Madrigal Society, the country's premier choral group, and reinvented herself as a concert singer, filling her days with vocal exercises and concert practices. She would eventually rise to become the society's secretary. Perhaps she was intrigued, as William had been regarding the ads for the Sportsman's Battalion at the outset of the war, by the society's appeal both to talent and to class. At the back of its programmes in those early post-war years, the society announced that "singers of special ability are invited to join the choir. Practices are held at Leighton House on Mondays – Ladies 5.15 to 6.45, Gentlemen 5.45 to 7.15, or as otherwise arranged." And then the kicker: "The annual subscription for singing members is one guinea."[3] In other words, no matter how talented you were, if you couldn't find the cash to join the club, well, that club probably didn't want you as a member.

Friends encouraged her move. One of them, Sophie M. Stubbs, wrote to her from the southern beach town of Torquay to compliment her on her "real contralto voice". She urged Dod to take singing lessons so as to make best use of her vocal chords, and told her that if she did, there was no reason she couldn't perform solos, or sing oratorios, at choral performances. "I missed you very much. So you must come back to town and study," Sophie pleaded. "I'll look out for a nice little flat for you. You have been very much missed at the services at St. Matthews." The letter continued, "Do come back to town for a bit. I have thought of no end of nice things to do together, and perhaps I can be some use to you with your singing." It was one of the few personal letters that the fading athletic superstar kept in her scrapbooks.[4]

Over the next decade, Lottie Dod participated in regular concert performances, many of them of Bach's music, at the fabled Aeolian Hall. The brick building, with arched windows and an interior concert space storied among London's musicians, was one of the capital city's most august musical venues. It could be found down an alleyway off New Bond Street, an elegant shopping-and-gallery locale that, since the mid-eighteenth century, had played home to some of London's finest jewellers. There was an effortlessly superior quality to these environs, a timeless atmosphere to the streets and colonnaded arcades that took for granted that they were at the centre of the most bustling, dynamic, imperial, powerful place on earth.

Dod would, in these years, form a fast friendship with the conductor and composer Charles Kennedy Scott, who had founded the Oriana Madrigal Society in the first years of the new century and launched its concert series at the Portman Rooms on 4 July 1905.[5] She would, throughout the 1920s and early 1930s, play under his direction, not only with the Madrigal Society, but also the prestigious Bach Cantata Club, performing at contemporary music festivals as well as in traditional church venues and concert halls in London and beyond.[6]

Scott was by now a legend in the music world. A lean man, with a ramrod straight posture, cropped hair and a patrician's face, he had parlayed his obsession with Tudor music into a unique position within the world of British concertmasters. Largely because of his efforts, performing madrigals had become something of a national obsession. By the mid twentieth century, the *Musical Times* estimated that in the capital city alone some 400 groups were meeting to sing the Tudor compositions. But the Oriana Madrigal Society, which attracted a huge range of high-society figures – "people of leisure, drawn from the cultured, university class, of social standing", as the *Musical Times* put it[7] – and musical superstars, from the conductor Thomas Beecham to the celebrated organist Harvey Grace, into its ranks, remained in a league of its own.

Charles Kennedy Scott was a taskmaster. If he wasn't satisfied with how a madrigal sounded, he made his choir sing it and sing it and sing it again, until they got the timbre just right. He wanted, he said, to make the Oriana Madrigal Society sound like a "collective" rather than simply a collection of individuals. He prescribed breathing and tongue exercises, as well as enunciation tasks, demanding from his amateur musicians "private study, enthusiastically undertaken by the singers". And in his insistence that they demonstrate an "almost spell-bound concentration", that they learn how to sight-read scores so well that they could glance at the sheet music and then memorise it almost instantly so as to free up their attention to look at the conductor, he would frequently reduce his choir members to states of complete exhaustion. Scott wanted each and every singer to be "like a bird hovering with outstretched wings, stirring to the slightest breath of wind".[8] In his private notebooks, little lined volumes bound in black leather, he penned notes to himself on teaching methods, on the interactions that he needed to have with his singers in order to coax the best out of them. "All good conductors should, before beginning the practice of a new choral composition, analyse its spirit and character in a speech addressed to the choir," he noted.[9]

When Scott felt that his musicians weren't putting in their all, he would berate them mercilessly. Madrigalists referred to his "wrath" and his "chiding". One disgruntled singer wrote that he risked killing "the plant which your own hands did rear".[10] Yet in the main his choir stuck with him through the bullying tirades, because at the end of the day, what he coaxed out of them was magnificent, and, as importantly, it was fresh and different. Scott was extraordinarily eclectic in his musical choices. He would often pair 400-year-old madrigals with works by contemporary composers such as the Yorkshireman Frederick Delius, who spent much of his life in France, and the Frenchman Gabriel Fauré, always searching for new modes of expression, new ways of testing the waters. "Kennedy Scott's attitude to contemporary music may be summed up in the words of St. Paul, 'try all things and hold fast to that which is good'," wrote the music critic Ronald Peck.[11]

Delius, an intense, rake-thin figure whose music could be lyrically beautiful at times, jarringly discordant at others, was a particular favourite of Scott. Blind in his old age – the years in which Dod was singing with the Madrigal Society, and the period in which, largely thanks to Scott's championing of his work, he finally became well known in Britain – he straddled, critics wrote, past and present. His great compositions, such as *A Mass of Life*, represented what the writer Philip Heseltine considered "the sunset of that great period of music which is called Romantic". But, Heseltine continued, "it is neighbour to night: it looks before and after, seeing the day that is past mirrored upon the darkness that is approaching".[12]

Many of Delius's choral works, including "To Be Sung of a Summer Night on the Water", were premiered in London by Dod and the other singers from the Oriana Madrigal Society.[13] Scott found the difficulty of his music, the challenge of playing well what many critics found to be impossibly complex themes, an irresistible lure. It was an attitude that his friend Lottie Dod, who had spent decades skipping from one sport to the next in her endless quest for new adventure, would have found intoxicating. She became an indispensable sidekick to Scott, helping to keep the choir on track as demands on its time grew more extreme.

The Oriana's schedule in particular was frenetic, one concert after the next being announced in small advertisements published in London's broadsheets. "Seats can be bought at Box-office, 139 New Bond Street (Mayfair 4775)," one such ad in *The Observer* informed readers. "Or Hon. Sec. Miss Lottie Dod, 5 Trebovir Road, SW5 (Frobisher 2715)."[14]

At first, the reviewers were underwhelmed. "There was not much to congratulate them upon," one particularly scathing critic noted in April 1921, after a performance that included pieces by Byrd, Holst, Gardiner and other composers spanning the centuries. "The choir is not what it used to be; it needs weeding. There are too many untrained voices."[15] Gradually, however, the strict regimen of rehearsals bore fruit. Dod played no small role in this; her friends would later recall her extraordinary dedication to practice, her willingness to put in as many hours as it took with her fellow singers to ensure they could bring the best out of the music. After all, lacking a family of her own, with no career to fall back on, and with her extraordinary sports accomplishments now but memories, she was hardly short of spare time.

In March 1922, the society's singers performed the French composer Clément Janequin's "La Guerre: Bataille de

Marignan", a fast, staccato piece, the men's and women's voices playing off each other, a martial drum in the background, the sum intended to conjure the noises and atmosphere, the building chaos, of war. *The Observer* found it compellingly "vivid".[16] When they performed the poet-cum-composer Arnold Bax's "Of a Rose I Sing a Song", a piece in which a cello and harp accompanied the chorus, it was received so well that they took the performance on the road, playing Bax's tunes in a number of concerts in suburban venues around London. The voices, layered one atop the other in a complex tapestry, the cello blending in almost as a deep-voiced member of the choir, the harp contributing the occasional celestial burst, all contributed to a swelling crescendo.

One could listen to the polyphonic tones of the Madrigal Society musicians and be transported back in time hundreds of years, to dark, echoing stone churches filled with pious congregations. It was an extraordinary sleight of hand, a modern musical company playing in state-of-the-art concert venues, and in doing so recalling the sounds and timbres of a distant past. One could, at other times, however, be riveted by the bold, modernist tones they managed to slip in between the madrigals. By the latter part of the decade, they were receiving one rave write-up after another. Their Christmas concert in 1928, *The Guardian*'s critic purred, showed "vitality and intelligence"; the three Bach choral pieces were "refreshingly sung"; and the carols composed by Byrd were "glorious".[17] Of their rendition of Bach's Mass in B Minor and his *St Matthew Passion*, another wrote that it was "the most perfect one can remember ever to have heard or need wish ever to hear".[18]

Sealing her reputation as one of London's best choral singers, on 16 March 1927, Dod was one of a select group of Bach Cantata Club singers "commanded" to perform before the king and queen in a private concert in one of Buckingham Palace's chapels.

To fill in more of her time, with some of the other ladies from her church she also began volunteering with Girl Scouts and youth groups in the impoverished East End of London, teaching the children, most of whom were from desperately underprivileged backgrounds, music and singing, and doing other activities with them. It may well have been, for many of these children, their first exposure to the arts.

Dod, who had moved to Newbury at the turn of the century to be nearer her sister Ann's young children, was now spending much of her time, as middle age began to give way to old age, working with boys and girls young enough to be her grandchildren. She was also teaching Tony's younger children, in particular his son Philip, whom she adored, how to play tennis. The game itself didn't stick – none of the younger generation took up competitive, tournament-level tennis – but the life lessons did. Lottie encouraged the children, but she also expected results. "Do it right, or don't do it at all," was the no-nonsense attitude that family members recalled her having.[19] She wasn't one to suffer fools gladly.

Tennis had never entirely disappeared from Lottie Dod's life. She continued to play matches with friends and relatives. Every year, the Little Wonder would return to Wimbledon to watch the tournament unfold over its two weeks.

On 21 June 1926, now aged fifty-four, Charlotte Dod was part of a large group of surviving former champions, both male and female, who gathered together on Wimbledon's hallowed grounds on a blustery but sunny afternoon, to celebrate the jubilee anniversary of the tournament's existence.

For two hours, a band from the Royal Military School of

Music played the national anthem and other patriotic tunes, and the crowd continuously cheered. Then, at precisely 2.50 that afternoon, the erstwhile champions took up their positions along the east side of the court. Ten minutes later, King George V and Queen Mary arrived inside the stadium. (Another royal, the Duke of York – later to become King George VI – was likely already on the grounds. He would be competing later on in the men's doubles tournament; it would turn out to be a short-lived appearance, in which he and his partner would be swiftly dispatched by the ageing ex-champions A.W. Gore and H. Roper Barrett.)[20] Over the twenty minutes following the king and queen's arrival, the players paraded into the middle of the court, one at a time, their names and championship years announced in a "stentorian voice" from the royal box by Blanche Bingley Hillyard's husband, Commander Hillyard.[21]

First the men paraded before the monarch – a champion's roster diluted by the deaths, years earlier, of both Renshaw twins, and several of the other early tennis heroes. Ernest had died in 1899 after ingesting carbolic acid – whether deliberately or not was unclear; his twin brother had followed five years later, dying of epileptic convulsions at the age of forty-three. The Doherty brothers too, Reginald and Laurence, who had dominated the championships in the final years of the previous century, had also died some time before.

After the most recent male victor, the great Frenchman René Lacoste, had received his medal, it was the women's turn. Maud Watson, followed by Hillyard, followed by Dod. And onwards through the roster of champions. They took their silver medals from Queen Mary; curtsied to her as she stood before them, the plumage in her huge hat blowing in the wind; shook hands with the king, who doffed his grey bowler to each lady as she curtsied again; and walked off to the sides to watch the remaining champions parade forward. In old film footage from the event, a silent newsreel just under two minutes in length, Dod can be seen standing next to several of the other ladies, her long black coat caught in the breeze, as the younger champions step up to receive their royal medals. Around them, the packed Centre Court audience is, to a person, standing too.[22] A *Women's World* columnist going by the pen name of Corisande declared that "by far the most interesting of the women ex-champions was Miss Dod. In her day, she was one of the finest athletes, and although she won the Single's Championship as long ago as 1887, she looked as if she could still give a good account of herself on the courts." *The Times* simply observed that "she still looked young and fresh".[23]

In a photograph taken after the ceremony, and distributed to sports enthusiasts a few days later by a postcard company, twenty-eight champions are ranged in three rows, the eight women seated in the front row, the men, standing, in the two rows behind them. Dod sits third from the left, facing the camera, wearing a long white dress, a pearl necklace, and a rose over the right side of her chest. She is smiling, and her face does indeed still look remarkably youthful, the fifteen-year-old champion peeking out from under the middle-aged lady's big black hat. To her right is a somewhat dour-looking Blanche Hillyard, a white handbag resting on her left leg; and to Hillyard's right, at the edge of the row, is the grande dame of women's champions, Maud Watson, staring stolidly ahead, her face expressionless. To Dod's left is Charlotte Cooper Sterry, one of the great champions of the 1890s, sitting awkwardly in a somewhat shapeless, heavy pale dress. And behind her stand the Baddeley brothers, Wilfred and Herbert, identical twins who dominated both the singles and doubles events in the years following the Renshaws' retirement from the game. In their time, they had been strikingly handsome, their hair parted on the right, moustachioed, posing for photos with each wearing pressed white shirts, perfectly knotted ties, and cream-coloured slacks.[24] Now, thirty years after their glory days, in their high collars and starched suits, they looked somewhat shrunken, the men on each side of the twins towering over them by a full head, their hair receding, their faces, absent the moustaches, looking wizened.[25]

A year later, the oldest Dod sibling, Ann, died at the age of sixty-four, after a struggle with cancer. The Dods, once the greatest athletic family in England, celebrated by thousands for their accomplishments, were bumping up against mortality. Charlotte Dod, who had once hung on ropes from alpine ledges and rocketed on a steel-skeleton toboggan down the Cresta Run, was now entering her long journey into old age.

Although the youngest of Joseph and Margaret's four children still headed to the golf links on a regular basis, and even occasionally shocked tennis fans by turning up to play an exhibition match against other ageing stars, she was unmistakably hobbled. Her last tennis appearance took place in 1929, when she appeared in Roehampton to play a singles match against Charlotte Sterry, and also a doubles event against two other bygone figures.[26] She had now replaced her cumbersome Victorian-era dresses with a much shorter garment, a white, sleeveless V-neck dress that ended not far below the knees. Her heavy black shoes had been substituted for much lighter canvas sneakers. In her late fifties, Dod stood slightly taller than her friends, her hair tied back and parted severely down the middle.[27] The journalists on the scene were sympathetic, one even noting, a touch implausibly, that "she made many shots that few of our young and eager girls even attempt today". But in reality, Dod's was a fading glory. By now, she was becoming disillusioned with the tennis world she had helped to birth, writing a letter to the editor of *The Times* bemoaning "ill-mannered" modern players who had the temerity to try "taking the umpiring into their own hands".[28] They were, she felt, too mono-focused, too interested in the commercial potential of their talents. "While realizing that to get to the top of the tree nowadays players *have* to devote their lives to one game, the idea of it still strikes me as appalling," she wrote many years later, in the foreword to a book on tennis by the author Denis Foster. "I sometimes wonder if they manage to derive half the enjoyment out of sport that we used to get. I have always been against commercialisation of games because, regardless of the sporting spirit in which they may be played, continued advancement must inevitably be uppermost in mind to the exclusion of so much of the fun of it."[29]

Increasingly, Miss Charlotte Dod's favoured pastimes were non-physical: listening to or making music, playing bridge with friends and teaching the East End children. Her passion remained the madrigal Tudor-era songs that, after centuries of slumber, had come back into vogue in the early twentieth century. But her expertise was wide-ranging – from masses composed by Bach, through to works by Gustav Holst and Bax's growing opus of choral works.

On 4 July 1927, a warm but windy summer's day in the capital, the members of the Oriana Madrigal Society trooped into Kingsway Hall, London, the grandiose home of the West London Mission of the Methodist Church.[30] Built in 1912, the hall, complete with a huge organ, had originally been intended simply as a meeting place for sermons and worship; but so stunning were its acoustics that it soon began being used by recording companies and rapidly acquired a reputation as one of the best venues in the world to record classical music. By 1927, the HMV label was firmly ensconced in the building.

It was for that company that Scott's choir now came to Kingsway Hall to record, in mono, a series of old English folk songs on to 78 rpm vinyl records. Scott conducted, and the tenor Norman Stone was brought in to sing solo. The sound was hauntingly beautiful. In the song "Brigg Fair", the voices cascaded over each other, the soloists singing of repairing to Brigg Fair to find love and nature, the chorus in the background providing a constant hum, a rising and falling sound like waves ebbing and flowing gently on the shore. Occasionally those choir voices would burst out into discernible words, helping along the soloists in extolling the pastoral virtues of the scene. "Coventry Carol" was a mournful religious dirge about a girl who died too young, a medieval allegory about the innocents slaughtered by King Herod. The subject was tragic, but the sound of the choir was intended to bathe listeners in calm. In their timeless timbre, these songs were a world away from the modernist compositions of Stravinsky and the other young headline-making, cutting-edge composers of the age; so, too, in their sounds, conjuring up country fields and old stone churches, the rays of morning light hitting the stained glass windows, they were far removed from the mechanised mayhem of the world war that, just a handful of years earlier, had ripped the old order apart. Maybe their popularity was due to just that, to their ability to tap into an audience's yearning for a prelapsarian past.

A little under two years later, on 3 March 1929, the choir performed Handel's rapturous pastoral ode *L'Allegro, il Penseroso ed il Moderato* from 1740, a one-and-a-half-hour choral work, forty-six verses in length, based on two poems by John Milton. In the final verse of the first half of the work, the chorus, of which Lottie Dod would have been a part, sang:

And young and old come forth to play
On a sunshine holiday,
Till the livelong daylight fail.
Thus past the day, to bed they creep,
By whisp'ring winds soon lull'd asleep.

Perhaps, as she sang, Dod recalled her long-gone days sleeping in mountain huts, the wind howling outside, after an exhausting day of climbing.

At the Aeolian Hall and other concert venues dotted around London and its environs, she and her fellow choir members sang Christmas carols with titles like "Now Is the Time of Christmas"; they sang, too, folk songs, and also performed masses. They even took part in specialised concerts featuring Northumbrian and Cumbrian folk music, heavy on the haunting sounds of the bagpipes, from the far north of England.

These days, Lottie was spending less time with Tony, the sibling closest to her in age. He had married relatively late in life, his children were still young, he was increasingly involved in local church parish activities, and he had his own family duties to attend to. But William was unattached, a bachelor. Lottie and he became, in these later years, inseparable. Where once she had played tennis with Ann, or climbed mountains and bicycled around Europe with Tony, now Lottie turned to her other brother, with whom she had shared Olympic glory decades earlier, for company. The pair could be found together more and more often. Frequently William would join her at choral concerts – by the early 1930s he was taking advantage of a special offer for relatives of choir members to subscribe at a discount to the Oriana Madrigal Society's major concert series.[31] In all likelihood, he also accompanied her to the Philharmonic Choir performances for which she had also taken out an annual subscription.[32] Just as frequently, however, they would engage in bucolic pleasures, seeking out golf courses far from the metropolis on which they could play rounds of the one sport that both of them still excelled in.

As the infirmities of age began to affect them more regularly, they reduced many of their obligations and spent less time in the fast-paced capital. In May 1931, newspapers published a series of ads listing upcoming Oriana Madrigal Society performances of Tudor madrigals and folk songs, accompanied by the Stradivarius-playing female violinist Dorothy Mary Murray Lambert.[33] Patrons were, as had been the case for a number of years, advised to contact the "Hon. Sec. Miss Lottie Dod" for ticket information. It was, however, to be Dod's last hurrah with the musical group. That summer, just shy of her sixtieth birthday, Lottie became ill – with what is no longer known. It wasn't, however, simply a minor inconvenience. Sick to the point that she could neither sing nor maintain her administrative duties with the Oriana Madrigal Society, Dod reluctantly sent in a letter of resignation, informing her friends that she couldn't continue to serve as secretary.

On 14 October, the chairman of the society, Andrew Gibbon, sat down at his heavy desk at the society's headquarters, Leighton House – an elegant art-filled building, some of the rooms decorated with deep-blue Arab tiling and rugs, others festooned with high Victorian paintings – in the Holland Park district of west London, and penned a reply. "My dear Miss Dod," he wrote, "We had our first rehearsal of the Oriana last Monday evening and, during an interval, tributes were paid on behalf of every member of the choir concerning your excellent and valuable work as Honorary Secretary." And then Gibbon, who had known the ageing woman throughout her time with the society, got more personal. "We all feel very sorry that ill-health has been the cause of your resignation. We sincerely hope you will soon be restored to health and vigor, so that we may have you with us again. The Oriana without you is not the same!"[34]

Lottie did recover her health but didn't return to a full schedule of choral singing. Taking stock, she decided to decamp from the city more frequently. Some years, she would spend more time in London – as evidenced by her listing in the Oriana Madrigal Society's cream-coloured, thick-papered programmes as an honorary member, a status that allowed her to attend not only concerts but also choir practices with her erstwhile colleagues. But other times as the decade advanced, her name was absent; she had, in all likelihood, chosen to spend more months those years in the countryside with William, and, frugal as she was – *in copia cautus*, the Dod family motto, engrained into her consciousness – had decided that she couldn't justify the subscription cost if she wouldn't be able to attend all the concerts. The casual, free-spending days of her *fin de siècle* Kulm Hotel sojourns were now far, far in her past. Lottie and William, neither of whom had settled into money-earning careers after their sporting glories ended, were able to maintain their social status – but only just. Only by penny-pinching and careful accounting, only by settling for increasingly modest environs. As the years went by, they pared the number of employees hired to maintain their homes; they ceased travelling overseas and staying in fashionable hotels.

As she entered her seventh decade, Lottie and her brother William began spending more time in Westward Ho!, the picturesque seaside community on Devon's north coast that William had owned a house in since before the Great War –

and which Lottie had also, episodically, spent time in over the intervening quarter of a century. It was an extremely pleasant place to while away the time, and with several miles of dramatic sandy beaches nearby. Twelve miles offshore was Lundy Island, one of the most pristine bird-watching sites in all of Britain.

Perhaps the solitude, the quiet of the coastal hamlet, with a population of just over 800, appealed to the invalided, somewhat reclusive war veteran. Perhaps his friend Rudyard Kipling, whom he had met on an Atlantic liner early in the century, and who had attended the area's United Services College and worshipped at Westward Ho!'s Holy Trinity Church, just up the street from The Divot, in the 1880s, had talked to him of its charms.[35] Or maybe, as a Royal Naval Air Reserve intelligence unit man, he had been intrigued by the little community's role as a launching ground for anti-submarine aeroplanes, Short 184 seaplanes, Curtiss H12 Large America flying boat biplanes and de Havilland DH.6 patrol aircraft during the Great War.[36]

Everything about Westward Ho!, right down to its odd, exclamation-pointed name, was escapist. It was a high Victorian seaside retreat, on one of the most beautiful stretches of English coast, connected to the ancient town of Bideford by a regular omnibus service, yet suitably enough separated from it by pebbled ridges and windy grasslands – through which crossed a series of public footpaths known as the Pathfields – that it preserved a feeling of isolation. And it had been named, in a marketing gamble designed to secure its share of the fast-growing tourism industry of the 1860s, after a best-selling mid-nineteenth-century novel by Charles Kingsley that was set in the vicinity.

Westward Ho! or, The Voyages and Adventures of Sir Amyas Leigh, Knight told the story of an Elizabethan corsair from the north coast of Devon, and his adventures chasing after the Spanish Main in the Caribbean. Kingsley's book, written while he sojourned at the Royal Hotel in Bideford,[37] and more than 600 pages in length, had proven to be a sensation. Its poems and sea shanties, replete with references to the fortunes that could be made by adventurous young privateers willing to sail west in pursuit of silver from the New World, time and again referenced the book's title: "Westward ho! with a rumbelow / And hurra for the Spanish Main, O!"[38] was one such. Another, recounting an improbable yarn about how an earl's daughter would only agree to be married if the man wooing her secured locks of hair from six princesses, concluded with the earl's daughter herself being the last of the six heads to be sheared.

> He leap'd into the water,
> That rover young and bold;
> He grip'd Earl Haldan's daughter,
> He shore her locks of gold;
> "Go weep, go weep, proud maiden,
> The Tale is full to-day,
> Now hey bonny boat, and ho bonny boat!
> Sail Westward-ho and away!"[39]

The little village that the Dods now decided to call their primary home had been established – against the wishes of Kingsley, who wished to preserve the undeveloped, wild beauty of the coastline he loved so dearly[40] – a decade after the book's sensational debut. Originally, it had been little more than a series of hotels and spas, which advertised their proximity to the ocean, the special rates at local golf clubs that patrons were eligible for, their seafront tennis courts, and their state-of-the-art smoking rooms. Some boasted of the fine restaurants available on site and the vintage wines in their cellars; some even mentioned the Havana cigars that they provided guests.

By the century's end, however, a small but thriving permanent community had grown up around the area, protected from storm surges by a robust seawall, and with an impressive 550-feet wrought- and cast-iron pier extending out past the breaking point of the Atlantic's waves.[41] There was a boarding school for "gentlemen's daughters" and a number of small grocery stores and tea shops.[42] There were also several businesses selling golf supplies to the golf-obsessed tourists who descended on the village each year. A popular postcard from the time showed four beach scenes, along with the words "Greetings from Westward HO!" and a five-line poem:

No clothes to wash,
No room to dust,
No work at all to do,
Household chores are left behind,
"Good Luck" I send to you!

On the letters pages of the local newspaper, residents wrote about the issues roiling their community. Far from being engaged with the affairs of the world, they were firmly parochial in their outrage, protesting, for example, when one of the golf clubs allowed members to play rounds on a Sunday.[43] In 1937, three decades after the brouhaha around Sunday golf, and two years before Lottie Dod made a decision to move full-time to the region, a similar controversy was unleashed when the local town council debated whether to allow the public tennis courts to open on Sundays. The controversy must have rung a familiar, somewhat dispiriting bell for William and Lottie; decades earlier, a number of their more religious cousins had expressed their distaste for the Dod siblings and their proclivity for Sunday sports. As Lottie and her sporting exploits became more renowned, their cousins, descended from her grandfather William's siblings, had responded by shunning them for desecrating the Sabbath.[44]

In this picturesque, somewhat insular Devonshire retreat, Charlotte and William continued to play rounds of golf at the Royal North, one of the oldest and grandest courses in England, and a place that, over the decades, had hosted many of Britain's top players, from five-time British Open champion John H. Taylor to two-time British amateur champion Horace Hutchinson.[45] Lottie herself had played there as far back as 1900, when she was first becoming noted as one of the country's top female golfers. Fresh off a series of successes, and flush with the praise from a glowing write-up in the first-ever golf manual for ladies, she had entered a tournament there and reached the semi-finals, losing, in a tight match, only on the last green.[46]

It was an idiosyncratic, some would even say eccentric, golf course, the men's club founded in 1864, the women's four years later, and was located on common land on the Northam Burrows. In places the marshes intruded on the green, and where they did clusters of huge, sharp marshland reeds known as "great sea rushes" rose up out of the ground, threatening players who weren't paying attention with significant injury. Elsewhere, smaller reeds, fugs, speckled the land. Near the fourth hole, an intimidating bunker threatened to sabotage players' efforts. Rugged sand dunes came up off the windswept beach and limned the greens. A stream wound its way through much of the course. On a clear day, the Dods could look back from the top of the sand dunes and see their house about a mile off to the south-west.

Because no one owned the land, the club couldn't limit who or what would intrude on to the links. As a result, hundreds of sheep, ponies and horses, as well as countryside ramblers, would routinely make their way on to the course, adding a unique charm to the place, but also making it that much more difficult for the players to keep their concentration. Any "potwalloper" – an old term for a local who owned a fireplace over which he heated his pots of food – from the nearby borough of Northam had the right to graze his animals on the golf course.[47] The hundreds of sheep, it was widely believed, were the club's first-responder ground crews, helping to keep the length of the grass in check, albeit at the cost of depositing their droppings all over the course.

In all likelihood, Dod also continued with her singing. For a number of wassails and other popular songs had been written over the years about this stretch of the north Devon coast, and most likely some would have been sung by the church and choral groups of which Dod remained a member. "Ay, it's Westward Ho, where the sun doth go, To light up the night with its rud-dy glow," opened one song. "Bound once again, for the Spanish Main. Hurrah! For it's Westward-Ho!"[48]

Well into her sixties by now, Lottie Dod was largely a forgotten figure, a relic of a vanished past. In 1933, the American superstar Helen Wills Moody, the dominant female tennis player of that age – she was number one in the world an astonishing nine out of eleven years between 1927 and 1938 – wrote a long piece for *Nash's Pall Mall*. In it she asked readers if they remembered "the English girl player, Lottie Dod", and then went on to say that had she not abandoned tennis at her peak and "turned suddenly to golf", she would have been one of the true greats. As it was, Wills Moody noted somewhat condescendingly, she and Suzanne Lenglen, the star of ladies' tennis a generation later, had, in their own ways, helped advance the status of modern women. "I imagine that she was a strong bouncing girl," Wills Moody wrote of Lottie.[49]

Had she explored a little bit more, the dashing young American, in appearance a world apart from the laced-up players of the high Victorian era, might have found out that Dod was still very much alive, perhaps no longer quite so bouncy as she had been in her heyday, but still a forceful, engaging personality.

However much Lottie and William simply wanted to escape into a stress-free old age, they couldn't absent themselves entirely from what was going on in the broader world. Once more, the war clouds were darkening. The Dod siblings seem to have sought shelter from the storm. In 1939, months before the Second World War began, Charlotte decamped from her Earl's Court abode in London and joined William full-time in The Divot. They would live there together throughout the war, along with a widowed housekeeper, four years Lottie's junior, named Edith J. Johnson.

Together, they navigated all the privations that came with the global conflict, the rationing – each person received coupons for one shilling and twopence worth of meat per week; soon, coal, sugar, milk, eggs, clothing and other necessities were similarly restricted – the blackouts, the lack of petrol, the scarcity of fuel to keep homes heated. Even the removal, by cadres of young ladies from the Women's Voluntary Service, of the iron fencing from around the front of the property, taken early in the war to be melted down and used in armaments.[50] Perhaps they negotiated the purchase of fresh eggs occasionally from their neighbours, many of whom kept hens in their back gardens. Maybe, too, they were given extra milk by some of the local farmers, who, in the open areas outside of Bideford, kept sheds in which lived their milking cows, or vegetables grown in local victory gardens. They might have been befriended, as a fragile, elderly duo, by women workers with the Land Army, brought to the farms to make up for the disappearance of male labourers into the armed forces.

The Divot had a steep roof over the attic and a small, treeless yard fronting the street. The Dods could enter it either from a basement-level back door, accessed, via stairs from Cleveland Terrace, by a little wooden gate, its slats painted a dark green, or from Kingsley Street itself.

As the war intensified, so Devon's role in it became more pronounced. Within weeks of the outbreak of hostilities, thousands of evacuees had flooded in from the large cities and throughout the county, people opened up their homes to these displaced women and often-unaccompanied children. By virtue of its southern location, the county swarmed with air defences as well as encampments of soldiers and home guards, ready to form a front line of resistance if and when the expected German invasion got underway. Squadrons of aeroplanes sat on airfields, their pilots ready at a moment's notice to take to the skies to fight off incoming German raiders. On Dartmoor, soldiers bivouacked, training in the early years of the war to ward off invading armies; in the latter years of the war, after England, the United States and the Soviet Union turned the tide against the Nazis, to land on French beaches and roll back the German occupation of Continental Europe. Off the coast of Westward Ho! a series of metal spikes were planted underwater, designed to thwart any Nazi landing craft. On Northam Burrows, near the golf course, three enormous steel pylons, each 325 feet in height, were erected with sensors atop each one intended to detect submarines cruising in the nearby waters.[51] On the golf course itself – which, somewhat bizarrely, remained open throughout the war, its clientele reduced to a handful of local retirees and army brass – the green surrounding the eighth hole was, on certain days, used as a firing range. The clubhouse was requisitioned by the army.[52]

Both now slightly reclusive, reluctant to engage too closely with their neighbours and their golf club friends, William and Lottie sat in their small kitchen, in hard-backed wooden chairs, carefully reading their morning newspapers and absorbing the latest information about the conflict.[53]

There was a lot to absorb.

In May 1940, the "phony war" came to a dramatic end, with the German blitzkrieg against Holland and Belgium, followed in June by the rapid collapse of the French armies and the Nazi invasion of northern France. More than 100 Polish soldiers, who had been living in exile in France, fled to Devon to join the exiled Polish army. They were housed in a makeshift camp in Westward Ho![54] Wanting to do his part, William, now approaching his seventy-third birthday, signed up for the Local Defence Volunteers, later known as the Home Guard, or more prosaically, "Dad's Army"; they issued him a uniform, which he proudly donned shortly afterwards for a studio portrait. He looked rugged, tall, his thick brush moustache now a silky white, his eyes twinkling with glee, perhaps at being in the mix again, perhaps simply because he had always known how to project himself well in front of the camera. There were photos of him in the Archery Register from thirty years earlier, wearing a shirt with a stiff, high collar, his hair and moustache still black, in which he looked just as determined.[55] As like as not, while he had paraded up and down the Strand during his stint with the Sportsman's Battalion in the previous war, he had had that same glint in his eye.

At Dunkirk in early June, Britain's Continental fighting force was driven back into the sea, hundreds of thousands of soldiers saved from death or capture only by the extraordinary operations of a civilian rescue force of small boats that sailed back and forth across the English Channel, each one ferrying small numbers of men to safety. Many of those boats were, of course, from Devon. By 14 June, Paris was in the hands of the Nazis.

That summer, Britain found itself alone, fighting for its very survival; and the newly installed prime minister, Winston Churchill, was desperately trying to prop up morale, promising that, come what may, the country would never surrender. For the airmen of Devon, the moment of truth had arrived. In early July, in the skies over southern England, the Battle of Britain began. Huge numbers of German planes flew in, fighters and bombers with a mandate to destroy Britain's air and coast defences, to strip the country of the protections that would stand in the way of a naval invasion. Day after day, the planes swooped low over the southern counties; and day after day, the British pilots, operating with no margins for error, with almost no reserves left on the ground, took to the air to fight them off. On the streets and in the fields below, residents could watch the dogfights unfolding in the skies above. William and his ageing Dad's Army mates prepared to fight Nazi invaders along the coastline and in the city streets of Devon.

From the air bases outside of Exeter, a large town just inland from Devon's south coast, RAF squadrons 87 and 213, flying newly delivered Hurricane fighters with a top speed of 330 miles per hour, screamed into action. Over the course of August, those two squadrons would down over eighty Nazi aircraft.[56]

When Nazi planes did make it through the air defences, some sought out Exeter and other large towns in the area, dropping their bombs and strafing city streets with machine-gun fire. The intent seemed to be to sow as much terror as possible.

In those early raids, dozens were killed. In later, more

deadly German aerial assaults, which began in 1941 and continued on and off until the spring of 1944, thousands died in high explosive and incendiary attacks on Plymouth and Exeter, and the centre of both cities was largely reduced to rubble. Apart from the London blitz, which ran for fifty-seven straight nights in September and October of 1940, and the firebombing of Coventry, the attacks on Plymouth and Exeter were among the most destructive of any launched on British towns. In one raid alone, 336 Plymouth residents were killed. Witnesses reported that the heat from the fires was so intense that plate glass windows in buildings that hadn't been destroyed simply melted.[57] By the middle of 1941, nearly 4,000 homes in Plymouth had been reduced to rubble, another 18,000 had been seriously damaged, and nearly 50,000 more in the region had been somewhat damaged. When Prime Minister Churchill toured the devastated town with his wife, Clementine, driving through the streets in an open convertible and then walking around the bomb-damaged neighbourhoods, he was so shocked by what he saw that he was moved to tears. In Exeter that year, the destruction was also enormous: 1,500 homes were obliterated there in 1941 alone, and another nearly 3,000 were significantly bomb damaged.[58]

William kept up his parading and training with the local defence force. When he was off duty, he would work on his wood carvings; all his adult life, he had been fascinated by the art form, and had for decades subscribed to magazines such as *Work* that explained, in copious detail, the different approaches to woodworking. How to carve a perfectly shaped wooden cricket ball. How to render a large cabinet. When he had enough magazines saved, he would take them to a bookbinder and have them preserved as one huge volume. He also read books voraciously, building up a large collection over the years.

His taste leaned towards the classic: to Shakespeare, to Milton, to the great poets. The Divot's bookshelves were stacked with tomes.

Lottie kept herself busy doing volunteer work as well – feeding evacuees, helping out at soup lines for those whose homes had been destroyed by bombs. Come the evenings, she and William would hunker down in their little home and read poetry together. Perhaps, too, they sang and played music; Lottie was still a talented pianist, and in photos taken at Edgeworth in the long-ago days of their youth, she and her siblings could also be seen strumming ukuleles.[59]

In the first year of the war, the so-called "phony war" before the hard fighting on the western front got underway, the military bureaucracy had kicked into gear. All sorts of offices and preparation units were set up, many of them centred on those vital southern counties. Over the coming six years, they would play a central role in shaping the conflict and determining which battles would be fought, and where, and how. So, too, gas masks were distributed to every resident. They were heavy and cumbersome, held up by rubber straps that went around the wearer's head. Civilians were advised to carry these masks with them at all times.

In Devon, the Combined Operations Experimental Establishment (COEE) began testing a range of new devices. It was, wrote the historian Henry Buckton in his book *Devon at War Through Time*, "tasked with developing weapons that could be used to overcome German coastal defences", especially those heavily fortified concrete walls facing England along vulnerable points of the French coast.[60] In Westward Ho! residents would, some days, have heard huge explosions, as COEE operatives rolled a huge wheel, which they named the "Giant Panjandrum", at speeds of up to sixty miles per hour down the heavily fortified, mined beach, testing its reliability at releasing its payload of high explosives at the moment that it made contact with its concrete target.[61] Near Exeter, the Gunnery Research Unit tested new machine guns and turrets for use on aircraft.[62]

When German planes bombed Plymouth in 1940 and 1941, the glow from the fires, sixty-plus miles away, could be seen in the night sky from Westward Ho![63] A similarly eerie nightglow could be seen by Westward Ho! residents in April 1942, when the Luftwaffe launched a particularly massive onslaught against Exeter's ancient town centre, in a series of attacks on historically interesting and beautiful tourist destinations around England that became known as the "Baedeker raids", after the popular guidebook series. Occasionally, a wayward bomb, intended for one of the county's larger population centres, instead fell in the fields near the village. One day, a plane crashed nearby. And one night, at about two in the morning, locals were woken by the sound of a huge explosion; it turned out a mine had washed ashore and detonated.[64]

Up and down the north coast, navy bases and military training grounds proliferated. In Appledore, once the Americans entered the war, a massive moorage was built for new forms of landing craft needed in a future assault against Nazi-occupied Europe. Inland, up the River Torridge, more such craft were stored.[65] In Woolacombe Bay, Saunton Sands, Braunton Burrows, groups of soldiers trained in neutralising beach defences. In Westward Ho! itself, a special dock was built for landing craft.[66] American troops bivouacked in Bideford, Bowden Green and many other communities around the county.

The final words of Kingsley's picaresque novel from ninety years earlier had saluted the English explorers who had ventured west to settle new lands, "heroes who from that time forth sailed out to colonise another and a vaster England, to the heaven-prospered cry of Westward-Ho!"[67] Now the Americans were returning the favour, returning to the Old World to fight against the Nazis. By the tens of thousands, they camped out on the moors and in naval bases that were built, at speed, along the coast. As D-Day neared, huge numbers were concentrated in the county, waiting, waiting, for orders to embark. Some 36,000 troops left Plymouth for Normandy in the early hours of 5 June 1944, including 110 ships carrying members of the 4th Infantry Division of the American VII Corps. Thousands more embarked for Utah Beach from Salcombe, Dartmouth,and Brixham. From Turnchapel, the Americans of the 29th Division set sail.[68]

When the war's end came, Westward Ho! erupted in festivities. Red, white and blue bunting went up everywhere – on houses, shops, pubs, all along the fortified waterfront. Locals remembered one lady so joyful she ran up and down a village street in the nude. Children were given a victory feast, served on trestle tables in a nearby park.[69]

William could now, finally, retire his Dad's Army uniform. Lottie, still physically fit, could once again walk along the seafront. Maybe she spent time sitting on the rocks, looking out over the Atlantic. Maybe, when her sciatica wasn't playing up, she would still amble south along the cliffs; to her right, as she walked, she would have seen the endless ocean; to her left, the tidy fields and pasturelands of local farmers, each field separated from its neighbours by tall hedgerows, rising up the hillsides away from the oceanfront cliffs. It wasn't quite as beautiful, nor as dramatic, as Switzerland or Norway, but it was a tolerable approximation, as glorious a stretch of coastline as anything the battered United Kingdom had to offer.

And thus the siblings began their twilights.

William and Charlotte Dod, both now well into their seventies, retreated more fully into the genteel world of club golf. As a member whose connections to the club could be traced back to the first years of the century, William was elected to the ceremonial role of president of the Royal North Devon in 1948 – though he was by now too frail, likely too much of a recluse, to attend most of the meetings; instead, he routinely sent in letters of apology, and delegated his responsibilities, his attendances at gala dinners, his officiating over awards ceremonies, to other committee members. Those men, in turn, seemed more concerned with vital issues such as the shortage of whisky, and the need to restrict how much of the amber nectar each golfer could purchase on any given day – a problem that the minute taker carefully documented in his notes on the meetings held in 1948 – than they were with Dod's absence.

A year later, in 1949, William's younger sister was elected "lady president" of the ladies' club – and while she was more active than her brother, donating a prize trophy cup one month, and attending several of the meetings, by 1950 she too had largely absented herself from the venue, sending in written excuses and asking friends to take over her correspondence with club officials.[70]

Westward Ho! was changing. Its residents, starved for pleasure during the dog days of war, wanted to celebrate, to have fun, to look ahead and see better, more carefree times. In November 1946, a dance palace had opened in the village, the local tobacconists and stationers selling tickets to jazz-band dances for five shillings a person. Special buses were chartered to bring audience members in from Bideford.[71] The village, long celebrated for its coastal isolation, its quiet, timeless ambience, now looked and acted "modern", the writer S.P.B. Mais noted mournfully in his 1950 travel book about the south-western counties, *We Wander in the West*. Perhaps what he really meant was that the class boundaries had broken down; that what used to be a firmly middle- and upper-class enclave was now a holiday mecca for Britain's working classes. It was now a somewhat commercial clutter, filled with "hotels and boarding houses overlooking the wide open stretch of waters that form Barnstaple Bay".[72] The glorious open views of the coast and the sea that the Dods had once had from their upper-floor windows were replaced by a panorama of slipshod houses and hotels.

The Dods' coastal paradise, their getaway, had become tacky, gaudy. The romance of the high Victorian years, the homage to Charles Kingsley's imagined world, had been replaced by jukeboxes and cheap beer joints.

TEN

The Final Days

Lottie Dod

No 2 * Gave to Michael Dod
„ 14 * ... Rock Ferry L.T.C.

No	Prize	Partner	Where played	Year	Value
1	Tennis clock	open cou A.D.	M'chester	1883	£ 3 .. 3 .. 0
2	Silver watch	„ 2nd A.D.	L'pool	1884	3 .. 3 .. 0*
3	Sugar basin & sifter	„ 1st Gun ...	Waterloo	1885	6 .. 0 .. 0
4		„ 1st A.D.	„	„	3 .. 0 .. 0
5	dressing bag	„ 1st M.J.Edmunds	„	„	5 .. 0 .. 0
6	} Gave to caretakers	„ 2nd	M'chester	„	5 .. 5 .. 0
7		„ 1st A.D.	„	„	7 .. 7 .. 0
8	Gold watch & chain	„ 1st Gun ...	Bath	1886	25 .. 0 .. 0
9	Onyx clock	1st A.D.	„	„	5 .. 10 .. 0
10	Gold brooch	handicap 2nd	Cheltenham	„	1 .. 0 .. 0
11	} Jewel casket	open 1st A.D	L'pool	„	4 .. 4 .. 0
12		„ 1st	„	„	10 .. 10 .. 0
13	Hot water jug	„ 2nd H.Grove	„	„	3 .. 3 .. 0
14	Salt cellars	„ 1st May Langton	Buxton	„	5 .. 0 .. 0*
15	Silver card case	„ 3rd J.D.	„	„	1 .. 0 .. 0
16	Diamond & sapphire bracelet	„ 1st	Dublin	1887	20 .. 0 .. 0
17	Gold bracelet	„ 1st E.Renshaw	„	„	5 .. 0 .. 0
18	Diamond ring	„ 1st	Bath	„	25 .. 0 .. 0
19	Silver backed brushes	„ 1st J.Dwight	„	„	6 .. 0 .. 0
20	2 silver mounted bottles	„ 1st A.D.	„	„	5 .. 0 .. 0
21	Silver tea service	handicap 1st	M'chester	„	25 .. 0 .. 0
22	Case silver spoons	open 1st	„	„	10 .. 10 .. 0
23	Silver fruit dish	„ 1st A.D	„	„	7 .. 7 .. 0
24	Carriage clock	„ 2nd H.Grove	„	„	3 .. 3 .. 0
25	Silver cup & stand	„ 1st	Wimbledon	„	20 .. 0 .. 0
26	Championship gold bracelet	„ gave ...	„	„	5 .. 5 .. 0
27	Pearl brooch	handicap 1st	Taunton	„	5 .. 5 .. 0
28	Chinese vases & jug	open 1st May Langton	Buxton	„	5 .. 0 .. 0
29	Silver dessert knives &c	„ 1st J.Dwight	„	„	6 .. 0 .. 0
30	Silver fish eaters	„ 1st	Bath	1888	25 .. 0 .. 0
31	Breakfast dish	„ 1st A.D.	„	„	6 .. 0 .. 0
32	Salad bowl &c	„ 2nd J.D.	„	„	3 .. 0 .. 0
33	Silver tea caddy	handicap 1st	„	„	5 .. 0 .. 0
					£275 .. 15 .. 0

Excerpt from a list of tournament wins and trophies accumulated, compiled by Lottie Dod in her old age. Courtesy of Sally-Ann Dod, Dod family archives.

While William, long the recluse, might have been content, despite Westward Ho!'s changes for the worse, to remain in rural Devon for the rest of his days, his younger sister was restless. Inertia, for her, had never proven a particularly appealing law of nature. Temperamentally, the Little Wonder wasn't ready to slide gently into the night of old age. She had, after all, always loved attending concerts and gallery exhibits, had always, from the time she was a little girl, needed the thrill of the new. Westward Ho! must, those many decades, have been something of an awkward fit for her.

In 1950, maybe because maintaining the large house on Cleveland Terrace and walking the steep hills down to the oceanfront was becoming too difficult for her; maybe, more likely, because she was bored and Westward Ho! had lost much of its pre-war charm, Lottie left William behind in Devon and moved back to London, to the Earl's Court flat she had owned for the past thirty years, at 5 Trebovir Road.

It was a lively locale. Trebovir Road, a one-minute walk from the Underground station at Earl's Court, was lined with four-storey brick-terraced houses. Built in the 1870s, the architecture was as high Victorian as one could find. Even the streetlamps, with their narrow iron posts and their elongated glass lightbulb casings, looked like relics of the nineteenth century. Down the street a couple of hundred yards were the Kensington Mansions, a block-long expanse of elegant redbrick flats that looked straight out of central casting; not surprisingly, at least one period piece had been shot there.

Nearly eighty, Dod began writing letters about her life to old friends. She pondered how far removed everything, right down to the clothes women wore, was from the Victorian world of her youth. "I don't think that our old-fashioned dresses were as much of a handicap as people now suppose," she wrote to

Arnold Herschell, a lawn tennis association official whom she had known for nearly sixty years. "But," she then acknowledged slightly ruefully, "it was difficult to run backward to volley a high ball as one feared treading on one's skirt!"[1] She recounted how her tennis rival and friend Blanche Bingley Hillyard had, in her old age, bemoaned to her the fad for young women these days to paint their nails red. She worried that athletes had become too preoccupied with making money.

On Lottie Dod's end of the street, the front of each house in the post-war years was painted over in white, the outlines of the yellow bricks vaguely visible behind the paint. On each floor of each house, three tall, narrow windows fronted on to the street. The roofs were flat, surrounded by low, columned stone fencing, under which were ornate cornices. And each building had a basement flat, reachable via steps that were secreted behind delicately crafted wrought-iron street-level fencing.

Next door to the old lady's flat was a house that, neighbourhood gossip had it, had long ago been a "home for fallen women", providing an austere, regimented living arrangement for young unwed mothers and their infants. Across the street was a block of flats that, in 1905, had witnessed a terrible tragedy: a young Korean diplomat named Yi Han Yeung had killed himself there in protest at the British government's tacit approval of Japan's taking over of Korea.[2] Reports differed as to whether he had hung himself or imbibed poison. A couple of houses down from there was the building occupied, at the turn of the century, by Sir Roland Lomax Bowdler Vaughan Williams and his wife; Sir Roland served, from 1897 to 1914, as a lord justice of the Court of Appeal, one of the most senior legal figures in the land. His wife, locals recalled, would sit outside on her first-floor balcony, looking out at the goings-on in the street down below. Around the corner, on Cromwell Road, was where the young film actor and director Alfred Hitchcock and his wife had lived for several years in the late 1920s and early 1930s.

Like so much of London, Earl's Court in those years was terribly bomb scarred. At least thirty bombs had fallen in the immediate vicinity, including a high explosive device that detonated, to devastating effect, on Earl's Court Road itself during the blitz. Even on Trebovir Road there were holes where old brick buildings had once stood. The damage had been intense. Five years later, there were still craters, and piles of bricks and other rubble, dotting the neighbourhood.

But amid the damage, Earl's Court was also extremely vibrant. Many Polish refugees had moved in during the war; and in the years following, the Polish Air Force Club and other institutions catered to this large community of ex-pats. There were pubs like the Prince of Teck, on the corner of Earl's Court Road and Trebovir Road. There were some fish and chips shops. Nearby, too, was a small butcher's shop and several grocery stores. A few years later, there would even be a little Depression-era-themed hamburger shop, aptly named the Hungry Years.[3]

If you were willing to accept the eccentrics and the street noise, Earl's Court, in those often-grim years, was a fun, cosmopolitan place to be.

Apparently, for the Dods, or at least for the one-time Little Wonder, the recipe worked.

Lottie had rented out most of the floors of 5 Trebovir Road to lodgers – 1953 census numbers would report nine people living in the house – keeping only a flat for herself. Despite the fact that the investments that sustained her and her siblings had taken grievous hits during the First World War – much of their investments were in France and had been irretrievably lost during the fighting, and the Dods had, as they aged, gone from effortless affluence to precarious gentility – her careful, modest approach to spending had allowed her to keep enough income from her inheritance to negate the need to work. Lottie and her siblings had stopped travelling overseas after the Great War, and she and William spent the rest of their years living in relatively modest dwellings, their circumstances downsized by the changing times in which they lived. When they needed to raise money, they weren't above selling off furniture, lace, even clothing. And Tony had, as he grew older, taken to raising bees and selling their honey in the village market in Sway.[4]

But now, in the austere post-Second World War years, Lottie found her circumstances straitened yet again, and the rent money would have been immensely helpful in making ends meet.

William, now in his mid eighties and in poor health, packed up his heavy wooden travel trunks, the iron handles rusted with age, and joined his sister there in 1952.[5] For the next two years the elderly siblings would totter around the neighbourhood together, each sustaining the other as the travails of age hemmed them in. They had both journeyed a long, long way from the rural calm, and the capacious Edgeworth estate, of their mid Victorian-era Bebington childhoods.

Eventually, however, death closed in. William's end came first, in 1954 in Earl's Court.

Charlotte "Lottie" Dod, one of the last surviving grand Victorian adventurers, was finally alone. Gamely, she continued with her routines, visiting Wimbledon every summer for the tournament, going for groceries at the local shops. She would still take the London Underground, would still be seen walking around her neighbourhood. For most of her adult life she had lived with one or other sibling and their household help, or spent months on end travelling somewhere exotic with siblings and friends in tow. Now, well into her ninth decade, Lottie, childless, unmarried and having lost the brother with whom she had lived for most of her life, since the Dod siblings had first decamped as a group to Newbury half a century earlier, had no one to lean on. Ann's and Tony's children and grandchildren were spread around England and points further afield – including Australia, New Zealand, Morocco, Canada and the United States; none of her myriad younger relatives lived in her part of London.

When it came time to write her will, she had no nearby niece or nephew, no friend whom she could appoint as the executor of her estate. Instead, she opted to nominate the District Bank Limited in Manchester to perform that role, mandating them to sell off her estate so as to pay for her funeral. As witnesses, she pressed two of the other residents at 5 Trebovir Road into service, one of whom listed himself as a "surveyor", the other simply as a "married woman". She mulled about leaving her "personal chattels", presumably including her trophies and other mementos from her sporting past, to her elderly niece, Doris Winifred, Ann's oldest child. But in 1955, she abruptly changed her mind and instead left her possessions to be divided between two of Tony's four children, Barbara Margaret and Geoffrey Francis. Her signature in that 1955 codicil was a little bit less clear, the black-penned letters heavy, a tad ragged, suggesting not quite as steady a hand as she had shown in the will signed four years earlier. As for the money resulting from the sale of her property, she left a lump sum of £500 to one of her nephews, who was at that point living in New Zealand, and divided the rest into equal parts between the six other children of Ann and of Tony.[6]

During those same years, as she looked back on her long life, Dod wrote up a list of all the tennis tournaments, in singles, ladies' doubles and mixed doubles, that she had won in that first bloom of her youth – sixty-one in all that she could recall; the prize money that she had received and what she had bought with it. Her cache ranged from a tennis clock valued at three pounds and three shillings that she won in her first doubles victory, in 1883, with her sister Ann in Manchester, through to £25 from her wins at the contest in Bath. Sometimes the tournaments presented her with trophies, other times with cash or vouchers that she could spend on what she wanted. She had, as a result, collected an extraordinary array of artefacts: a silver fish platter worth £25 from her Bath victory in 1888; a silver toast rack from one of her Wimbledon wins, a silver flask from another. She had bought a diamond-and-sapphire basket with her £20 won at Dublin in 1887, and a gold watch chain valued at £25 from the proceeds of one of her wins at Bath. There were twelve dessert spoons from another tournament, candlesticks from yet another. Now, seeking to catalogue her life's possessions for her heirs, she annotated her list, explaining whom she would give which items to: a "jewel casket" – presumably a jewellery box – that she had bought after winning the tournament in Liverpool, was to go to her nephew and niece, Geoff and Barb, as well as a hot water jug and a salt cellar. A silver brush set had already been given away, to someone whom she didn't feel the need to list by name. To her sister Ann's daughter went a Wimbledon championship gold bracelet, and so on. One of her caretakers was to receive a dressing bag.[7]

Lottie Dod didn't leave any instructions in her will as to where she wanted to be buried. Perhaps, for her, it was an irrelevance. Maybe she recalled the Thucydides quote on the Civil War memorial in Newbury, a memorial that she would have walked past numerous times before and during the Great War: "The sacrifice which they collectively made was individually repaid to them, for they received again each one for himself a praise which grows not old and the noblest of sepulchers. I speak not of that in which their remains are laid but of that in which their glory survives for the whole earth is the sepulcher of illustrious men."

The old lady struggled on.

Into the mid 1950s, Dod could be seen at the Earl's Court station, clutching a basket of raspberries[8] and preparing to board the crowded District Line train to take her down to Southfields station, where the crowds would exit and walk the mile or so to the entrance of the All England grounds. Afterwards, when she could no longer endure the trip, she would still make her way to the shop to buy her raspberries, and then head home to the empty flat on Trebovir Road to sit surrounded by ghosts and to listen to the games on her radio.

Only in the very final years did she find herself too frail, too chronically sick, to live alone in Earl's Court. Now, with her one surviving sibling, Tony, living in Sway, a small village in the New Forest, just off the south coast, Charlotte decided to join him. She moved into the Birchy Hill nursing home. Her nephew Philip, for whom she had long had a particular soft spot, would sometimes come to visit her; but increasingly, in her little bedroom in the house on the edge of the New Forest, she was left alone with her thoughts and her memories. Sway would be the final stopping place for the restless woman whose life had taken her from Edgeworth to Switzerland, Norway, the United States and Canada; from homes in Newbury to London to Devon and then back to London again.

By 1960, the Victorian world into which Lottie Dod had been born was long vanished. In its place was a faster, more interconnected world, a world woven together by air travel and television, by information beamed down from satellites, and by computers that could process information at warp speed. The pony traps that delivered tennis-playing friends to Edgeworth House in the 1870s had long been replaced by cars, the steamers that took travellers across the Atlantic by the newly developed intercontinental jet planes.

In that new world, many of the global public's most feted heroes were those who had achieved sporting greatness: Pelé had already shot to fame in the world of soccer; Cassius Clay was about to ascend to the heights of boxing greatness; Roger Bannister had, some years earlier, broken the four-minute mile; and in 1953, Edmund Hillary and Tenzing Norgay had summited Mount Everest.

For decades, women athletes had performed extraordinary feats, and sports that in Dod's youth had been barred to the fairer sex were now routinely competed in by women. In the July 1932 Olympic try-outs in Evanston, Illinois, Babe Didrikson, as she was known before her marriage to the wrestler George Zaharias, won six gold medals, in everything from shot-put and javelin throwing to the eighty-metres hurdles, and broke four world records in the space of three hours. A United Press reporter on the scene declared it "the most amazing series of performances ever accomplished by any individual, male or female, in track and field history".[9] The following month, at the Los Angeles Olympics, in which the United States fielded 357 men and forty-three women, Didrikson dominated, coming away with two gold medals, one second-place finish and two more world records. In the decades that followed, before her premature death from cancer at the age of forty-five, she burnished her record, playing top-level basketball and baseball and dominating the field in ladies' golf.

If Didrikson Zaharias knew that Dod had notched up

similar achievements nearly a half century earlier, she didn't say. She probably had no idea that Dod was still alive, living in genteel retirement across the Atlantic. Throughout Didrickson Zaharias's too-brief life, the sporting heroine acknowledged no forebears, no equals along the road she trod.

Yet, acknowledged or not, Dod was a champion who had helped usher in that world.

That final afternoon, Monday, 27 June 1960, Dod lay in her bed, fading in and out of consciousness. She had suffered a serious fall at the nursing home, the bone breaks that resulted coming on top of pneumonia, anaemia and the other ailments of extreme old age; and there wasn't, at that point, much more that the doctors could do for her.

On the radio, the BBC commentators took their audience through the Neale Fraser match, the marquee event that day on Centre Court.

The old lady listened. Perhaps, in her head, and through the fog of her pain, she heard those enthusiastic Victorian crowds from more than seventy years earlier. Heard them as they chanted slowly, rhythmically, "Lot-tie! Lot-tie!" when their new-found teenage heroine pummelled the white melton cloth–covered tennis ball into the far corners of the court.

"Hers is no fitful brilliancy," wrote one of her admirers in the year of her fifth Wimbledon victory. "It is a steady glow, which seems to grow brighter and more intense as victory succeeds victory, and triumph follows triumph."[10]

Acknowledgements

I would first and foremost like to thank my family, once again, for putting up with my extreme writing habits and for tolerating, mostly with remarkably good grace, my never-ending conversations about the facts, the images and the wondrous, musty old tomes that I encountered while researching this book. To my wife, Julie Sze, to my daughter, Sofia, and to my son, Leo, thank you from the bottom of my heart. Thank you also to my parents, Jack and Lenore, to my brother, Kolya, and to my sister, Tanya, for being who you are, for all the unconditional love and for creating an environment when I was growing up that gave me the room to spread my wings.

A huge thank you is owed to my agent, Victoria Skurnick, and her colleagues at the Levine Greenberg Rostan Literary Agency in New York. At Akashic Books, similar salutations go to my editor, Dave Zirin, to my publisher, Johnny Temple, and to Aaron Petrovich for his sterling work with the photographs that appear in this book. Hearty thanks, too, to my UK publisher Birlinn, and to Peter Burns, my editor at that publishing house, for recognising early on the importance of this project, and the value of recovering this lost history, to a British readership.

Over the past several decades I have written for numerous publications in the United States and overseas. These include *The Nation*, *The Atlantic*, the *New Yorker*, *Rolling Stone*, *Salon*, the *New York Times*, the *LA Times*, *Haaretz*, *The Guardian*, the *New Statesman*, and many other first-rank newspapers and magazines. I am also the author of eight previous books. I have been invited on to many radio and television shows as a guest. And I have given speeches about my work on campuses, at think tanks, in libraries and in bookstores around the United States. To all those hundreds of editors and foundation programme officers, to the fact-checkers and the production crews, the critics and the radio and television hosts, who have supported my work over the decades, I owe one mighty yawp of gratitude. You have been the backbone to my efforts these many years.

Yet in writing *Little Wonder*, I found that, at the risk of mixing my metaphors, I was leaning on not just the usual suspects but also upon a largely new crew of wingmen and wingwomen as I swam in what were, for me, fresh waters.

What fuelled me as I recreated Dod's fascinating life was a very personal obsession: my lifelong passion for the game of tennis. And the people who have nurtured this obsession over the decades, and who over the past couple years have, more broadly, helped me bring this book to fruition are, in the main, a very different cast of characters from those who have worked with me on my more political books. They are fellow tennis enthusiasts, archivists, sports historians, genealogists, local history buffs and even musical scholars. They are people fascinated by the great outdoors, and enthralled by the cast of adventurous, eccentric late Victorian characters, men and women impatient of limits and willing to push every boundary they encountered, whom Dod surrounded herself by.

Forty years ago, my first explicitly thought-out career choice involved a decision, when I was about eight years old, that I would be a tennis pro and, one day, win Wimbledon. That dream died not because my interests shifted but because

I came up against the stone-cold reality that I simply wasn't good enough to compete in the rarefied atmosphere of top-level tennis. It was the first truly devastating personal realisation of my life. But despite this setback, tennis remained a staple of my life, both as a sport to play and also to watch, to study in minute, obsessive detail.

As an adult, I have hunted down televisions in some of the obscurest corners of the world, including high in the Himalayas, in the Buddhist retreat town of Dharamshala, in 1997, to watch matches that were of particular significance, contests that involved players whom I had mentally entered into my pantheon, or records on the line. I have driven hundreds of miles, on a whim, to see a match that looked particularly likely to spark drama, or, in the context of Dharamshala, to embody "dharma" – the underlying nature of reality taught by Buddha as an eternal truth. For me, a perfect tennis match does indeed seem to nudge me closer to some form of transcendental vision of the cosmos – to an understanding of its harmonies but also its tragedy, its capacity for destruction.

When Roger Federer lost the five-hour 2019 Wimbledon championship match to one of his two great rivals, Novak Djokovic, I mourned his shattering defeat – his inability to convert two championship points, deep in the fifth set – with something approaching madness. The impossibly small margins between triumph and catastrophe, the clipped net cord, the serve just a few miles too slow to be a winner – all got infinitely magnified in the moment. I, a somewhat cynical, hard-bitten forty-seven-year-old journalist, felt personally bereaved, as if I needed to keen and wail, to rend my shirt and tear my hair. The next morning when I awoke, I felt as deflated as I have on days after an election in which the party and candidate I supported were defeated. I felt somewhere deep in my soul as if I had watched a form of vandalism unfold before my eyes: as if I had been privileged to sit and observe Leonardo da Vinci paint the *Mona Lisa* right in front of me, only for his hand to slip at the very last instant and to impossibly disfigure, beyond repair, the model's enigmatic smile. Everything that morning felt fragile, less solid – as if the roads and buildings had buckled and cracked during an earthquake, and now all one could do was to wait for more tremors. The earth had been knocked just slightly off its axis.

I also started to imagine that, somehow, if I just concentrated hard enough, I could alter the outcome; after all, if Djokovic's passing shot on Federer's match point had gone just a few millimetres further to the right, it would have landed out and the championship would have been Federer's. In those milliseconds that Djokovic's ball arced downward towards the right sideline, Federer existed as a quantum paradox. In those fractions of time before the ball landed, he both was nine-time champion and he wasn't. He both had sealed the deal and secured for himself the title of Greatest of All Time, and he hadn't – he had left a question mark hanging over the acronym. For, in air, the projectile's path back down towards the court was too close to call, subject to the merest fluctuation in the air currents, conceivably even to the concerted willpower of a few thousand spectators all holding their breath simultaneously.

That loss of proportion, that emotional response outside of the bounds of reason, that flirtation even with temporary madness, is, of course, what makes for a true obsession with sport. And for indulging and cultivating that obsession over nearly half a century, I have many people to thank.

My earliest tennis partners were my dad and his cousin Pete Hillel, both of whom showed infinite patience in teaching me the basics of the game. For introducing me to what has been a lifelong love affair with tennis, I thank you both from the very bottom of my heart. Of course, over the years I have played tennis with dozens, maybe hundreds, of people. It is, unfortunately, impossible to list them all by name. But a few who stand out over the years: in school, I played tennis most every weekend with Laurence Glynn or Clive Swillman. In college, with Hugh Mallinson, Christina Boswell and a handful of others. Since I moved to America, my court partners have included Eyal Press, Eric Klinenberg, Danny Postel, Kari Lydersen, Omar Jadwat, Darrene Hackler, Chris Hoene, Clarence Ting, Doug Heller, Jen Laflam, John Hill, Darrell Steinberg, Rowan Phillips and, over the past few years, my son, Leo, who is if anything even *more* obsessed with tennis than am I. To all of you, and to all the others whom I have hit with over the years, let me express my gratitude for all the fun times, the frenetic competition and the wonderful physical and mental exercise.

For helping me navigate all of the arcane history of tennis; for letting me into their wondrous archives and tennis memorabilia collections; for allowing me, however temporarily, to feel like Charlie when he found the golden ticket that would permit him to tour Willy Wonka's chocolate factory; and finally, for allowing me to reproduce the incredible photographs and other images held in their collections, I owe profound thanks to the archivists at the All England Lawn Tennis Club in Wimbledon, and at the Newport, Rhode Island, International Tennis Hall of Fame. At Wimbledon, particular credit is due to head librarian Robert McNicol, to assistant librarian Janet Baylis and to picture researcher Sarah Frandsen. In Newport, my thanks are aimed squarely at librarian Meredith Miller Richards, who spent months fielding my emails and phone calls, and, time and again, came up with the goods when I requested copies of obscure articles or needed access to early histories of the sport of tennis. My visit to the Hall of Fame, over several days in early January 2019, was one of the highlights of this literary adventure.

As my fascination with Lottie Dod's story took off, so my research folders became improbably balanced, spiralling piles of notes and photocopied articles, old books and delicate sepia photos. And so the list of people drawn into the orbit of this project – many of them far removed from the world of tennis that I had initially, and wrongly, assumed would occupy the bulk of the book – grew.

At the Martin and Osa Johnson Safari Museum in Chanute, Kansas, the curator, Jacquelyn Borgeson Zimmer, and the director, Conrad Froehlich, spent untold hours working to identify relevant images from their collection of photos by Dod's friend Elizabeth Main. They then spent many more hours helping me line up additional sources. And when it came time to choose photographs to include in the book, their generosity in sending images my way was extraordinary. Their enthusiasm for *Little Wonder* was, from the get-go, one of my great motivators.

Soon, dozens of people were scouring old records, looking for snippets of information that would add to my understanding of who Dod was and of the changing milieu in which she lived her nearly nine decades. Tennis historian Robert Everitt and the Tennis Bookshop owner Alan Chalmers indulged me in some of my early, perhaps naive, questions about Lottie Dod and the great tennis players in the infancy of the sport. Librarians and archivists at the Red Cross, the Imperial War Museum, the Liverpool Record Office, the Museum of Liverpool, the London Metropolitan Archives, the British Library, the Trinity Laban Conservatoire of Music and Dance, the Westminster Music Library, the UK's Probate Office, the University of East

London, the British Film Institute, the New-York Historical Society, the Royal North Devon Golf Club, the All England Women's Hockey Association, the University of Bath, the Royal Toxophilite Society, and the Alpine Club all dived into their records to see if they could find relevant material. Sometimes they came up empty; other times, they rose to the surface with nuggets of gold. Particular thanks here to Helen Mason, of the Jerwood Library of the Performing Arts at the Trinity Laban Conservatoire, for the information she found on Oriana Madrigal Society performances; to Lizzie Richmond, at the University of Bath, for her discovery of old photos of, and writings about, women's hockey in the last years of the nineteenth century; to Robert Fowler, honorary curator and club historian at the Royal North Devon Golf Club, for letting me explore its archives; and to Mehzebin Adam, curator of the Red Cross archives in London, for managing to find what little documentation exists about Lottie Dod's volunteer work during the First World War. Immense thanks as well to Katja Schneider, Evelyne Lühti, Antonia Meier and Claudia Jann, who delved into the archives of the Kulm and Badrutt's Palace Hotels in St Moritz, toured me around the public and private rooms of the buildings, and subsequently gave me access, over a marvellous three-day stay, to do my own digging around their trove of papers and photographs for information on the St Moritz scene in the 1890s. I doubt I shall ever again play tennis while looking at a wraparound view as beautiful as that from the courts at the Kulm Hotel.

So, too, a number of local history buffs in Westward Ho!, whom I contacted through Facebook's Westward Ho! History Group, helped me locate information about Lottie and William Dod during their latter years, as well as details about Westward Ho! during the Second World War.

To Jeffrey Pearson, who wrote a short book about Lottie Dod a generation ago, and who was kind enough to share with me his recollections about interviews with deceased family members, I raise a glass to toast your early realisation of Dod's historical significance. To sports historian and researcher Madie Armstrong, and to Stephen Bartley, honorary archivist at the St Moritz Tobogganing Club, many thanks to both of you for generously providing me access to some of your research materials.

To the librarians and archivists at the University of California at Davis, who for many years now have helped me locate books and articles across my range of writerly interests, I salute you. So, too, I thank Sally Dod, a distant cousin, several generations removed, of Lottie's, who dived into her family records to come up with useful details about the Dod family over the centuries. And I offer my deepest gratitude to two of Anthony Dod's grandchildren, Sally-Ann and Bill, both of whom opened up their extensive family archives to me and welcomed me into their homes to talk with them about their grandfather and their great-aunt. To my extraordinarily talented genealogist friends Teven Laxer and Jeremy Frankel, a million thanks for at times directly finding vital but obscure pieces of this puzzle, and at other moments giving me the research tools to embark on my own voyages of discovery. And to my old comrade Pete Sarris, whom I have known since we were both undergraduates at Balliol College, Oxford, thanks once again for helping access some of the more hidden archival materials.

Beyond those who helped with specific parts of this writing project, or focused my mind by walloping tennis balls my way, there are so many other friends and mentors, relatives and colleagues, who have, over the years, volunteered to read early drafts of my various works, or who have simply been there to lend an ear or to shoot the breeze. Those who have particularly helped me navigate both the stormy waters and the welcome calms in recent years include (in no particular order) Jon Wedderburn, Adam Shatz, Carolyn Juris, Jason Zeidenberg, Holly Cooper, A.G. Block, Jessica Bartholow, Robert Rooks, Theo Emery, Audie Cornish, George Lerner, Jenny Abramsky, Lauren Pollack, Larry and Shirley Kedes, Ofelia Cuevas, Glenn Backes, Steve Magagnini, Maura McDermott, Peter and Suzanne Greenberg, Andrew Cooper, Kim Gilmore, Anders Krab-Johansen, Joy and Jerry Singleton, Jesse Moss, Ben Caplin, Sam Freedman, Michael Shapiro, Jon Nichols, Joe Rubin, Kitty Ussher, Dave Colburn, Kate Raworth, Roman Krznaric, Carl Harms, Dottie Guerrero, Lena Sze, Nakeeb Siddique, Betty Sze, Brad Kagawa, and Lily Sze. There are, of course, so many, many more friends out there, all of whom help fill my days with joy.

My friends and colleagues in the University Writing Program at the University of California at Davis have consistently proven to be bulwarks of strength, decency and common sense. And my editors at *The Nation*, where I publish so much of my freelance writing, in particular Roane Carey, Katrina vanden Heuvel and Don Guttenplan, continue to radiate the beacon light of social justice.

It goes without saying that in a project of this kind, at times the historical detective work produces ambiguous information. I have tried, wherever possible, to double-check all of my claims and all of my sources. If, despite these efforts, readers discover that my feet have at times slipped as I have climbed this mountain, the fault is, of course, entirely mine. I can only be thankful that there have been so many people at the other end of the rope willing to haul me up the steep and treacherous rock face.

Select Bibliography

Arengo-Jones, Peter. *Queen Victoria in Switzerland*. London, England. Robert Hale, 1995.

Aronson, Theo. *Prince Eddy and the Homosexual Underworld*. London, England. John Murray, 1994.

Backman, Jules and Gainsbrugh, M.R. *Economics of the Cotton Textile Industry*. New York, United States. National Industrial Conference Board, 1946.

Bagnold, Enid. *A Diary Without Dates*. New York, United States. William Morrow, 1935.

Baker, Keith. *The 1908 Olympics: The First London Games*. Cheltenham, England. SportsBooks, 2008.

Barrett, John. *Wimbledon: The Official History of the Championships*. London, England. HarperCollins, 2001.

Barrett, John and Little, Alan. *Wimbledon: Gentlemen's Singles Champions 1877–2015*. London, England. Wimbledon Lawn Tennis Museum, 1986. Revised fourth edition, 2015.

Beaufort, Duke of (ed.). *The Badminton Library*. London, England. Longmans, Green, 1890.

Beecham, Sir Thomas. *Frederick Delius*. London, England. Hutchinson, 1959.

Brittain, Vera. *Testament of Youth: An Autobiographical Study of the Years 1900–1925*. London, England. First published 1933. Republished by Victor Gollancz, 1980.

Brownlee, W. Methven. *Lawn-Tennis: Its Rise and Progress. The Championship Meetings. Eminent Players. A Treatise on the Game*. London, England. J.W. Arrowsmith, 1889.

Buckle, George Earle (ed.). *The Letters of Queen Victoria, Third Series: A Selection from Her Majesty's Correspondence and Journal Between The Years 1886 and 1901*. London, England. John Murray, 1930.

Buckton, Henry. *Devon at War Through Time*. Stroud, England. Amberley Publishing, 2012.

Burke, Bernard. *A Genealogical and Heraldic History of the Landed Gentry of Great Britain*. London, England. Harrison, Pall Mall, 1879.

Burrow, F.R. *The Centre Court and Others*. London, England. Eyre & Spottiswoode, 1937.

Carley, Lionel. *Delius: A Life in Letters*. Volume 2, 1909–1934. Aldershot, England. Scolar Press, Gower Publishing, 1988.

Carley, Lionel and Threlfall, Robert. *Delius: A Life in Pictures*. Oxford, England. Oxford University Press, 1977.

Cayleff, Susan E. *Babe: The Life and Legend of Babe Didrikson Zaharias*. Urbana and Chicago, United States. University of Illinois Press, 1995.

Christie, Agatha. *Agatha Christie: An Autobiography*. New York, United States. Dodd, Meade, 1977.

Collins, Bud. *The Bud Collins History of Tennis*. New York, United States. New Chapter Press, 2008.

Conner, Floyd. *Tennis's Most Wanted: The Top 10 Book of Baseline Blunders, Clay Court Wonders, and Lucky Lobs*. Lincoln, United States. Potomac Books, 2002.

Cook, Sir Theodore Andrea. *Notes on Tobogganing at St. Moritz*. New York, United States. Charles Scribner's Sons, 1894.

Dole, William Peters. "Carmen Acadium: Ode for the Jubilee Year of the Reign of Queen Victoria." Canada. 1887. Text archived by the Electronic Text Centre at the University of New Brunswick Libraries.

Ellison, Thomas. *The Cotton Trade of Great Britain: Including a History of the Liverpool Cotton Market and of the Liverpool Cotton Brokers Association*. London, England. First published by E. Wilson, 1886. Republished by Frank Cass, 1968.

Everitt, Robert T. and Hillway, Richard A. *The Birth of Lawn Tennis: From the Origins of the Game to the First Championship at Wimbledon*. Surrey, England. Vision Sports Publishing, 2018.

Foley, Michael. *Hard as Nails: The Sportsmen's Battalion of World War One*. Stroud, England. Spellmount, 2007.

Foster, Denis. *Improve Your Tennis*. London, England. Findon Publications, 1950.

Fowler, Robert. *The Royal North Devon Golf Club, 1864–2014*. Westward Ho!,

England. Royal North Devon Golf Club, 2014.

Hargreaves, Jennifer; and Anderson, Eric (eds). *Routledge Handbook of Sport, Gender and Sexuality*. London, England and New York, United States. Routledge, 2014.

Harris, Clive and Whippy, Julian. *The Greater Game: Sporting Icons Who Fell in the Great War*. Barnsley, England. Pen & Sword Books, 2008.

Heseltine, Philip. *Frederick Delius*. London, England. John Lane, Bodley Head, 1923.

Howe, Anthony. *The Cotton Master, 1830–1860*. Oxford, England. Clarendon Press, 1984.

Jenkins, Rebecca. *The First London Olympics: 1908. The Definitive Story of London's Most Sensational Olympics to Date*. London, England. Piatkus Books, 2008.

King, Billie Jean; with writing assistance from Starr, Cynthia. *We Have Come a Long Way: The Story of Women's Tennis*. New York, United States. McGraw-Hill, 1988.

Kingsley, Charles. *Westward Ho! or, The Voyages and Adventures of Sir Amyas Leigh, Knight*. First published 1855. Republished in New York, United States. A.L. Burt, no date listed.

Lambert, David. *Jubilee-ation! A History of Royal Jubilees in Public Parks*. London, England. English Heritage, 2012.

Le Blond, Elizabeth Alice. *Adventures on the Roof of the World*. London, England. T. Fisher Unwin, 1904.[*]

Le Blond, Elizabeth Alice. *Day In, Day Out*. London, England. J. Lane, 1928.

Le Blond, Elizabeth Alice. *High Life and Towers of Silence*. London, England. Sampson Low, Marston, Searle and Rivington, 1886.

Le Blond, Elizabeth Alice. *Mountaineering in the Land of the Midnight Sun*. London, England and Philadelphia, United States. T. Fisher Unwin, J.B. Lippincott, 1908.

Le Blond, Elizabeth Alice. *The High Alps in Winter; or, Mountaineering in*

---

[*] Le Blond wrote under many names, reflective of the fact that she was married three times. Sometimes she used her own first name, sometimes she went by "Mrs" followed by the first and last name of her husband. Different editions of her books use different ways of identifying her. She wrote as Elizabeth Main; Elizabeth or Lizzie Le Blond, Mrs Aubrey Le Blond, Mrs Fred Burnaby and Elizabeth Hawkins-Whitshed. For the sake of convenience, all of her books in the bibliography are attributed to Elizabeth Alice Le Blond, which seems to have been her most popular literary nomenclature.

Search of Health. London, England. Sampson Low, Marston, Searle and Rivington, 1883.

Le Blond, Elizabeth Alice. *True Tales of Mountain Adventure: For Non-climbers Young and Old*. American edition. New York, United States. E.P. Dutton, 1903.

Little, Alan. *Lottie Dod: Wimbledon Champion and All-Rounder Extraordinary*. London, England. Wimbledon Lawn Tennis Museum, 1983.

Little, Alan. *Wimbledon Compendium, 21st edition*. London, England. All England Lawn Tennis and Croquet Club, 2011.

Maas, Jeremy. *This Brilliant Year: Queen Victoria's Jubilee, 1887*. London, England. Royal Academy of Arts, 1977.

Mackern, Louie and Boys, M. *Our Lady of the Green*. London, England. Lawrence and Bullen, 1899.

Mais, S.P.B. *We Wander in the West*. London, England and Melbourne, Australia. Ward, Lock, 1950.

Marshall, Nancy and Warner, Malcolm. *James Tissot: Victorian Life/Modern Love*. London, England; and New Haven, United States. Yale University Press, 1999.

Mazak, Karoly. *The Concise History of Tennis*. Self-published, 2017.

McCrone, Kathleen. *Sport and the Physical Emancipation of English Women 1870–1914*. London, England. Routledge, 1988.

Medlycott, James. *100 Years of the Wimbledon Tennis Championships*. London, England; and New York, United States. Hamlyn Publishing Group, 1977.

Miscellaneous authors. *Hymns for Use During 1887, the Year of the Jubilee of Queen Victoria*. London, England. Skeffington & Son, 1887.

Myers, A. Wallis. *Lawn Tennis: At Home and Abroad*. London, England. George Newnes, 1903.

Myers, A. Wallis. *Twenty Years of Lawn Tennis: Some Personal Memories*. London, England. Methuen, 1921.

O'Neill, Bill. *The Great Book of Tennis: Interesting Facts and Sports Stories*. United States. LAK Publishing, 2018.

Packard, Jerrold M. *Farewell in Splendor: The Passing of Queen Victoria and Her Age*. New York, United States. Dutton, 1995.

Pankhurst, E. Sylvia. *The Home Front: A Mirror to Life in England During the World War*. London, England. Hutchinson, 1932.

Paret, J. Parmly. *Lawn Tennis: Its Past, Present and Future*. New York, United

States. MacMillan, 1904.

Pearson, Jeffrey. *Lottie Dod: Champion of Champions – the Story of an Athlete.* Cheshire, England. Countyvise, 1988.

Robyns, Gwen. *Wimbledon: The Hidden Drama.* Newton Abbot, England. David & Charles, 1973.

Scott, Charles Kennedy. *Madrigal Singing: A Few Remarks on the Study of Madrigal Music with an Explanation of the Modes and a Note on their Relation to Polyphony.* London, England. Oxford University Press and Humphrey Millford, 1931.

Slingsby, William Cecil. *Norway: The Northern Playground.* First published 1903. Republished, with introduction by Geoffrey Winthrop Young, in Oxford, England. Basil Blackwell, 1941.

Smith, Graham. *Devon and Cornwall Airfields in the Second World War.* Newbury, England. Countryside Books, 2000.

Suffolk and Berkshire, Earl of; Peek, Hedley and Aflalo, F.G. (eds). *The Encyclopaedia of Sport.* Volume 1. London, England. Lawrence and Bullen, 1897.

Suffolk and Berkshire, Earl of (ed). *The Encyclopaedia of Sport and Games.* Volume 4. London, England. William Heinemann, 1911.

Tait, Derek. *Devon at War 1939–1945.* Barnsley, England. Pen & Sword Books, 2017.

Tinling, Ted. *Sixty Years in Tennis.* London, England. Sidgwick & Jackson, 1983.

van Natta Jr., Don. *Wonder Girl: The Magnificent Sporting Life of Babe Didrikson Zaharias.* New York, Boston, United States and London, England. Little, Brown, 2011.

Walker, Randy. *On This Day in Tennis History: A Day-by-Day Anthology of Anecdotes and Historical Happenings.* New York, United States. New Chapter Press, 2008.

Ward, Fred W. *The 23rd (Service) Battalion Royal Fusiliers (First Sportsman's): A Record of Its Services in the Great War, 1914–1919.* London, England. Sidgwick & Jackson, 1920.

Williams, Jean. *A Contemporary History of Women's Sport, Part One: Sporting Women, 1850–1960.* New York, United States. Routledge, 2014.

Endnotes

Introduction

1 Details of where Dod died can be found on the website www.livesofthefirst-worldwar.org.

2 Information on the history of the nursing home was provided by staff when the author visited the facility on 26 July 2019.

3 Reported in the *Los Angeles Times*, 28 June 1960.

4 Quoted in the AP article that the *Morning News*, Wilmington, Delaware, ran on the match the next day, 28 June 1960.

5 As reported in the *Chicago Tribune*, 28 June 1960.

6 W. Methven Brownlee, *Lawn-Tennis: Its Rise and Progress. The Championship Meetings. Eminent Players. A Treatise on the Game.* J.W. Arrowsmith, London, England, 1889, p. 121.

7 Detail provided to Wimbledon librarian Alan Little by Ann Dod's son Geoffrey Worssam, in a letter dated 23 June 1983.

8 The fan was shown to the author by Lottie Dod's greatnephew, Bill Dod.

9 Wingfield's tennis patent is Royal Letters Patent No. 685. The text is displayed in the museum at the Newport, Rhode Island, International Tennis Hall of Fame.

10 The latter translation was the one used by Gwen Robyns in her history of Wimbledon, *Wimbledon: The Hidden Drama*. David & Charles, Newton Abbot, England, 1973.

11 Information provided in *We Have Come a Long Way: The Story of Women's Tennis*, by Billie Jean King, with Cynthia Starr; McGraw-Hill, New York, 1988, p. 6.

12 Lottie Dod kept a scrapbook of newspaper articles on herself. They were cut out of the papers and often didn't include the name of the source in which they were printed. Such is the case with these two quotes. The scrapbook is at the Kenneth Ritchie Wimbledon Library in the Wimbledon Lawn Tennis Museum.

13 Information on these tennis balls, which were used from 1879 to 1901, can be found in the Ayres catalogue, the relevant page reprinted in John Barrett's *Wimbledon: The Official History of the Championships*. HarperCollins, London, England, 2001. Two images of Dod's service motion are contained in

a rare set of tennis cartoons, from Wimbledon 1887, held in the Newport, Rhode Island, International Tennis Hall of Fame.

14 "Sports and Pastimes" the *Athenaeum*, no. 4263, 10 July 1909.

15 *The Encyclopaedia of Sport*, volume 1, edited by the Earl of Suffolk and Berkshire, Hedley Peek and F.G. Aflalo; published by Lawrence and Bullen, London, England, 1897. Dod's chapter is titled "Ladies' Lawn Tennis" and starts on p. 617.

16 Image of Bingley serving the ball contained in the set of 1887 Wimbledon cartoons. Op. cit.

17 Photographs of Dod are in black and white. However, the colour of her hair was detailed in a long article about her in the *Philadelphia Inquirer*, 3 October 1904.

18 *Pastime*, volume 9, 1887.

19 Ibid.

20 The ads can be seen on p. 435 of the book *The Birth of Lawn Tennis: From the Origins of the Game to the First Championship at Wimbledon*, by the tennis historians Robert T. Everitt and Richard A. Hillway. Vision Sports Publishing, Surrey, England, 2018 (limited edition). The ads were printed originally in *Pastime* on 17 August 1887.

21 A. Wallis Myers, *Twenty Years of Lawn Tennis: Some Personal Memories*. Methuen, London, England, 1921, pp. 167–168.

22 W. Methven Brownlee. Op. cit.

23 Information contained in Mrs. R Boys's essay "British Women on the Links", in *Golf* magazine, July 1904.

24 Gwen Robyns described the clubhouse in *Wimbledon: The Hidden Drama*. Op cit. When she visited it in 1973, the old grounds and courts had been taken over for use by the Wimbledon Girls' High School.

25 The price of the tickets is listed in Gwen Robyns's book, op. cit, p. 21.

26 Train timetables indicate that during the tournament up to four of these trains an hour would stop each afternoon at Wimbledon.

27 A. Wallis Myers, *Lawn Tennis: At Home and Abroad*. George Newnes, London, England, 1903, p. 47.

28 F.R. Burrow, *The Centre Court and Others*. Eyre & Spottiswoode, London, England, 1937, pg. 31.

29 The author spoke with some of the family's great-nieces and great-nephews while researching the book in 2019.

30 Information provided by Sally-Ann Dod, Anthony's granddaughter.

31 Detailed in Dod's death certificate, 30 June 1960.

32 *Westminster Gazette*, 20 July 1893.

33 Letter to tennis researcher Elizabeth af Jochnick from G.E. Worssam, in 1985; records kept at the Newport, Rhode Island, International Tennis Hall

of Fame archives.

34 As told to author Jeffrey Pearson in the 1980s, when he interviewed the surviving Dod descendants. Pearson recounted these conversations to the author, 18 January 2019.

35 Recollection of Jeffrey Pearson, from his conversations in the 1980s with Tony Dod's then elderly children.

36 *Evening Times-Republican*, Marshalltown, Iowa, 1 December 1904.

37 www.communist-party.org.uk/about-us/34-history/305-harry-pol-litt-1840-1960.html.

38 *Aberdeen Evening Express*, 27 June 1960. Accessed from the British Newspaper Archives.

39 *Birmingham Daily Post*, June 28, 1960, and *The Guardian*, 28 June 1960.

40 *Minneapolis Star*, 27 June 1960.

41 Information provided by Lives of the First World War archives, www.livesofthefirstworldwar.org. The probate amount was detailed on 10 August 1960, six weeks after Dod's death.

42 The author searched grave site records in Bebington and the surrounding area, and also in Sway and the surrounding area. In July 2019, he also looked at every legible gravestone in St Luke's Church, in the Sway cemetery and in the Lymington cemetery.

43 Kenneth Lash, "Imaginary Confrontations: W. Allen before *Broadway Danny Rose*". *North American Review,* volume 269, no. 2 (June 1984) pp. 12–13. Published by the University of Northern Iowa.

Chapter 1

1 Details of William Dod's finances, as well as the birth order of his and Mary's children, were provided to the author by Sally Dod, descendant of one of William's brothers, Thomas. Her father was in possession of a family tree going back eight generations. A copy of the family tree was shown to the author.

2 Reference to William Dod's Cheapside warehouse can be found in the *Liverpool Mercury*, 22 January 1847.

3 Details from the Find a Grave website. Their grave site is row 20, grave 49, memorial ID 134650060, in the St Hilary churchyard.

4 Jules Backman and M.R. Gainsbrugh, *Economics of the Cotton Textile Industry*. National Industrial Conference Board, New York, 1946, p. 22. Thomas Ellison's *The Cotton Trade of Great Britain;* table no. 1. Frank Cass (1968 edition). Originally published by E. Wilson, London, England, 1886.

5 Details on this can be found in Ellison's book, p. 206.

6 Nigel Hall, "The Governance of the Liverpool Raw Cotton Market, c. 1840–1914." *Northern History*, volume 53, 2016, no. 1, 2016.

7 Anthony Howe, *The Cotton Masters, 1830–1860*; preface. Clarendon Press, Oxford, England, 1984.

8 *Liverpool Mercury*, 24 March 1865.

9 In 1882, the *Liverpool Mercury* ran an article about the renovation of St. Mary's Church and Knox's tenure. The article can be found at www.stmarys-birkenhead.blogspot.com.

10 The Dod-Aspinall marriage notice appeared in the *Liverpool Mercury* on 12 September 1862.

11 Anthony Howe. Op cit., pp. 249–252.

12 As told to the author by Jeffrey Pearson, author of a 1988 monograph on Dod, who interviewed Dod's elderly surviving nephews and nieces for his research in the mid 1980s. Sir Anthony Dod's family history is listed in Sir Bernard Burke's volume *A Genealogical and Heraldic History of the Landed Gentry of Great Britain*, p. 356. Harrison, Pall Mall, London, England, 1879. Burke traces Anthony Dod's ancestry back as far as Henry II's England, in the second half of the twelfth century.

13 Details of the dining room and other living areas at Edgeworth can be seen, either by the naked eye or under a magnifying glass, in a series of photos that Lottie Dod saved.

14 See Smitha Mundasad's article for the BBC, September 27, 2014. www.bbc.com/news/health-28858090.

15 Conor Heffernan, "Indian Clubs in Victorian Britain." *Physical Culture Study*, 2 February 2015, www.physicalculturestudy.com/2015/02/02/indian-clubs/.

16 Images from the Victorian era, with dates attached, compiled in *The Lost Century of Sports*: www.youtube.com/watch?v=7luB6b3MgvA.

17 Details in Jeffrey Pearson's book *Lottie Dod: Champion of Champions – the Story of an Athlete*. Countyvise, Cheshire, England, 1988. Pearson reports that this anecdote was told as family lore down the generations.

18 The chess trophy was shown to the author by Sally-Ann Dod. She recollected stories of Anthony's ability to play multiple games while blindfolded.

19 Family photos show views of the courts from out of the windows of the east bedrooms.

20 Grand jury list published in the *Cheshire Observer*, Saturday, 20 October 1877.

21 Details provided in Gwen Robyns's *Wimbledon: The Hidden Drama*. David & Charles, Newton Abbot, England, 1973, p. 24.

22 This was written about by several journalists, including Denzil Batchelor in his 1949 article "All-Rounders: The First Lady of Wimbledon," published in *World Sports*, October 1949.

23 *Liverpool Mercury*, 2 December 1879.

24 Information provided by the Find a Grave website. The grave is in section J, plot 374, of the Bebington Cemetery.

25 In July 2019, Bill Dod showed the author a sketch of the family crest and motto.

26 A copy of Joseph Dod's will was provided to the author by the Office of Probate in the United Kingdom. It was proven in the probate division of the High Court at Chester, on 3 February 1880.

27 One such ad, in the *Liverpool Mercury* on Friday, 15 May 1885, offered for sale a "handsome" cow, about to calve for the second time.

28 Details of relatives gleaned from the family tree provided to the author by Sally Dod. Details on Joshua Pim's visits to Edgeworth House were mentioned in Denzil Batchelor's 1949 article, op. cit. Details on how and when visitors arrived discussed by Gwen Robyns, op cit.

29 Gwen Robyns, ibid.

30 For details on what schooling was available to nineteenth-century girls, see www.oxford-royale.co.uk/articles/history-womens-education-uk.html.

31 Information on the various careers the cousins chose can be seen on the Dod family tree, provided to the author by Sally Dod.

32 Photographs of Ann's studio are contained in Lottie Dod's photo album.

33 Details of Dod's early tennis wins are chronicled in then-Wimbledon archivist Alan Little's 1983 pamphlet, *Lottie Dod: Wimbledon Champion and All-Rounder Extraordinary*, published by the Wimbledon Lawn Tennis Museum.

34 From Lottie Dod's scrapbook. Date and publication unknown.

35 For a report on this tournament, and the Dod siblings' results, see the *Liverpool Mercury*, 28 June 1886.

36 *Pastime*, 29 June 1887.

37 On one of the pages of this album is a photo labeled, "R.O. Rawlins. Donor of this album."

38 As described by a reporter in the *Star* newspaper, London, England, 11 August 1888.

39 www.thoughtco.com/queen-victorias-golden-jubilee-celebrations-1774008.

40 Willam Peters Dole, "Carmen Acadium: Ode for the Jubilee Year of the Reign of Queen Victoria." Canada, 1887. The text has been archived by the Electronic Text Centre at the University of New Brunswick Libraries.

41 Described in the catalogue to the 1977 Royal Academy of Arts exhibition, "This Brilliant Year: Queen Victoria's Jubilee, 1887", pp. 9–13. Introduction written by Jeremy Maas. Visual imagery contained in John Charlton's oil painting *Queen Victoria's Golden Jubilee, 21 June 1887; The Royal Procession Passing Trafalgar Square*. Royal Collection Trust, RCIN 405285.

42 Visual description based on the oil painting, commissioned by Queen Victoria, of the event, by the Scottish painter William Ewart Lockhart, titled *Queen Victoria's Golden Jubilee Service, Westminster Abbey, 21 June 1887*. Original is in the Royal Collection, RCIN 404702. A black-and-white

monochrome reproduction is in the Hawaii State Archives in Honolulu.

43 www.foodhistorjottings.blogspot.com/2012/04/food-for-jubilees-and-other-royal.html.

44 Ibid.

45 David Lambert, *Jubilee-ation! A History of Royal Jubilees in Public Parks*. English Heritage, London, England, 2012.

46 Dod's attire was described in Gwen Robyns's book *Wimbledon: The Hidden Drama*. David & Charles, Newton Abbot, England, 1973.The description of her eyes is from the *Morning News*, Wilmington, Delaware, 6 October 1904. And the quote is from the *San Francisco Examiner*, 25 September 1892. Other commentators, from earlier in her career, also remarked on her poise under pressure.

47 The weather that day was described in *Pastime* on July 6, 1887; the magazines from 1887 were bound into volumes, which are stored in the Wimbledon archives. 1887, Volume 9, pg. 6.

48 The bowler-hat-wearing ball boys can be seen in photos of Dod's matches from the period.

49 Images of the audience, and where they were placed around the court, are in a series of photographs of Dod held in the archives at the Newport, Rhode Island, International Tennis Hall of Fame.

50 A photographic image of the crowd and the F.H. Ayres awning, from 1880, is contained in James Medlycott's *100 Years of the Wimbledon Tennis Championships*. Hamlyn Publishing Group, London, England, 1977, pg. 12.

51 Photographs of Centre Court from 1883, the photographer unknown, can be found in the Wimbledon archives and in a collection in Munich. The photos clearly show only singles lines were present on the courts. A more general history of the development of the stands around Centre Court in the 1880s can be found in Wimbledon librarian Alan Little's book *Wimbledon Compendium 2011* (21st edition). All England Lawn Tennis and Croquet Club, London, England, 2011, pp. 9–11 and 99.

52 Similar rackets held in the collection at the Newport, Rhode Island, International Tennis Hall of Fame weigh in the region of fourteen to fifteen ounces.

53 Gwen Robyns. Op. cit, p. 25.

54 *Pastime*, volume 11, 1888, pp. 68–69.

55 As reported in the *New York World*, 17 August 17 1888. The article was part of a series titled "England's Crack Tennis Players."

56 The poem is titled "The Tennis Worshippers" and was kept by Lottie Dod in her scrapbook.

Chapter 2

1 For details on this match, see James Medlycott's *100 Years of the Wimbledon*

Tennis Championships. Hamlyn Publishing Group, London, England, 1977, p. 15.

2 *Morning Post*, London, England, July 17, 1883, and *Derby Mercury*, 21 July 1886.

3 The series of Renshaw/Dod photos are in Dod's tennis photo album, in the Kenneth Ritchie Wimbledon Library of the Wimbledon Lawn Tennis Museum.

4 In a 1951 interview with Arnold Herschell, in *Lawn Tennis and Badminton*, Dod related this anecdote. She told Herschell that Bingley, her longtime rival, had personally told her about Ernest Renshaw's cross-dressing tennis exploits.

5 Details of William Renshaw's boast were captured in an article, date and publication missing, that Lottie Dod glued into her scrapbook.

6 A. Wallis Myer, *Lawn Tennis: At Home and Abroad*. George Newnes, London, England, 1903, p. 45.

7 Ibid.

8 Details on the three battle-of-the-sexes matches can be found in *Lottie Dod: Wimbledon Champion and All-Rounder Extraordinary*, a sixteen-page pamphlet written by the onetime Wimbledon librarian Alan Little, published by the Wimbledon Lawn Tennis Museum in 1983. There is also a reference to the Ernest Renshaw match in Floyd Conner's 2002 book *Tennis's Most Wanted: The Top 10 Book of Baseline Blunders, Clay Court Wonders, and Lucky Lobs*. Potomac Books, Lincoln, Nebraska, 2002.

9 Reproduced in the *Guardian*, 1 March 2019, www.theguardian.com/books/2019/mar/01/hallie-rubenhold-jack-the-ripper-victims#img-2.

10 See the time line of murders and letters created by the historian Richard Jones: www.jack-the-ripper.org/timeline.htm.

11 *Courier and Argus*, Dundee, Scotland, 9 October 1888.

12 *Yorkshire Herald and York Herald*, 13 October 1888.

13 *Bristol Mercury and Daily Post, Western Countries and South Wales Advertiser*, Bristol, England, 13 October 1888. And *Cincinnati Enquirer*, 7 October 1888.

14 Ibid. *Bristol Mercury and Daily Post*. The article is titled "A Whitechapel Affair in Paris," and detailed a murder attempt in which the woman was stabbed in the neck but survived.

15 As reported in the *Huddersfield Chronicle and West Yorkshire Advertiser*, 27 October 1888.

16 Match records contained in the Wimbledon Lawn Tennis Museum archives, and in newspaper reports from that summer's tournaments.

17 W. Methven Brownlee. Op. cit.

18 The date of the marriage was provided to Alan Little, during his research into Lottie Dod, by Ann's son Geoffrey Worssam. The letter is now contained in the Kenneth Ritchie Wimbledon Library.

19 Author interview with Pearson, 18 January 2019.

20 *Wright and Ditson Guide*, 1891. The guide is held in the archives of the Newport, Rhode Island, International Tennis Hall of Fame.

21 *Montgomery Advertiser*, 11 December 1904. The article was published beneath a large photograph of Dod, her face in profile, posed much like a Roman statue.

22 *Dispatch*, Moline, Illinois, 12 November 1904.

23 Interview with Dod in *Lady's Pictorial*, 1899.

24 *Pastime*, 30 July 1884.

25 From Dod's scrapbook, publication and date unknown.

26 Lottie Dod, "Ladies' Lawn Tennis," *The Badminton Library*. Longmans, Green, London, England, 1890, p. 307.

27 The photograph is now in the National Portrait Gallery in London, in the Cabinet Portrait Gallery section's collection of W. & D. Downey photographs from 1890–1894. www.npg.org.uk/collections/search/portrait/mw130811/Lottie-Dod?

28 A. Wallis Myers, *Lawn Tennis: At Home and Abroad*. George Newnes, London, England, 1903, p. 47.

29 As quoted in Denis Foster's book *Improve Your Tennis*. Findon Publications, London, England, 1950.

Chapter 3

1 Jaeger ran his ads in books such as W. Methven Brownlee's *Lawn-Tennis*. His company was Dr. Jaeger's Sanitary Woollen System Co. Ltd.

2 Lottie Dod, "Ladies' Lawn Tennis." Published in *The Badminton Library*, edited by the Duke of Beaufort. Longmans, Green, London, England. First edition published 1890. Dod's contribution starts on pg. 307.

3 Lottie Dod, "Ladies' Lawn Tennis," in *The Encyclopaedia of Sport*, volume 1, edited by the Earl of Suffolk and Berkshire, Hedley Peek and F.G. Aflalo. Lawrence and Bullen, London, England, 1897. Dod's contribution starts on p. 617.

4 Ibid.

5 Reported by Liz Pook in her article "Legends of the Ladies Links," published in the September 2007 issue of the British Golf Collectors Society magazine.

6 That Dod reached seventy-two on the Moreton golf course is extrapolated from a 1902 article in *Golf Illustrated*, in which the author says that after not playing for more than a year, Dod returned to Moreton and went a round of seventy-three, "only one above her record for the links."

7 Reported in the *Liverpool Mercury*, 24 May 1895.

8 Reported by Mrs R. Boys, "British Women on the Links." *Golf*, New York,

July 1904, pg. 26.

9 Song contained in archival holdings at the Newport, Rhode Island, International Tennis Hall of Fame.

10 Louie Mackern and M. Boys, *Our Lady of the Green*. Lawrence and Bullen, London, England, 1899.

11 The newspaper article is in Dod's golf album, shown to the author by Sally-Ann Dod. It is dated 19 May 1899, but it is unclear in which paper it was published.

12 A copy of this article was pasted by Dod into her golf album.

13 Queen Victoria's diaries, as quoted in Peter Arengo-Jones's *Queen Victoria in Switzerland*. Robert Hale, London, England, 1995, pp. 92–93.

14 James Tissot, *Captain Frederick Burnaby*, 1870. The painting was shown at the International Exhibition in London, in 1872; it now hangs in the National Portrait Gallery, London. Details provided in Nancy Marshall and Malcolm Warner's *James Tissot: Victorian Life/Modern Love*. Yale University Press, New Haven and London, 1999, pp. 54–55.

15 She described her stays in Chamonix in her first book, *The High Alps in Winter; or, Mountaineering in Search of Health*. Sampson Low, Marston, Searle and Rivington, London, England, 1883.

16 Details of Segantini's death were provided to the author by Katja Schneider of the Kulm Hotel.

17 Photographs of Segantini, of the Duchess of Manchester and of Lady Montagu can be found in Tony Dod's albums from this period.

18 These included Donald Smith, a Scotland-born Canadian millionaire, and his wife; the vicomte de Mouzilly; and the Honorable V. Gibson. Comprehensive guest logs from the period are held in the archives of the Badrutt's Palace Hotel.

19 Information in Main's photo albums, contained in the Martin and Osa Johnson Safari Museum, Chanute, Kansas.

20 Information on the annual Davos St Moritz ice hockey game was published in the *Sphere* magazine, 12 January 1902, p. 55.

21 From the Martin and Osa Johnson Safari Museum, Chanute, Kansas, the Elizabeth Main/Lizzie Le Blond collection, photo album six.

22 Elizabeth Alice F. Le Blond, *Mountaineering in the Land of the Midnight Sun*. J.B. Lippincott, Philadelphia and T. Fisher Unwin, London, 1908. Introduction, p. 3.

23 Le Blond, *High Life and Towers of Silence*. Sampson Low, Marston, Searle and Rivington, London, England, 1886, pp. 2–3.

24 Main photographed this column. The image is in an album kept at the Badrutt's Palace Hotel.

25 Details provided by Katja Schneider, at the Kulm Hotel.

26 Details on the various skating methods Dod had to perfect to pass this test

are contained in her St. Moritz photo album. The album was passed down to Tony's descendants, who then entrusted it to Stephen Bartley, honorary archivist of the St Moritz Tobogganing Club. Bartley showed the album to the author in London, 23 February 2019.

27 Ibid.

28 Anthony and Lottie Dod kept photographs of Main's living quarters. Photographs held by Stephen Bartley. Ibid.

29 Le Blond described Imboden's early career in her book *True Tales of Mountain Adventure: For Non-climbers Young and Old*. E.P. Dutton, New York, 1903, p. 31.

30 The English sports historian Madie Armstrong related this detail to the author in a phone interview, 26 January 2019. In Le Blond's memoir *Day In, Day Out*, she also recounts some of the details of the ice-skating season in St Moritz.

31 The names of the judges, and photographs of them judging, are contained in the Dod album. Op. cit.

32 Details on the day Lottie Dod passed the men's skating test are in Elizabeth Main's albums, now held at the Martin and Osa Johnson Safari Museum, in Chanute, Kansas.

33 Description of how one has to modify one's tennis game on the Kulm courts is based on the author's own observations from playing on them during the summer of 2019.

34 Elizabeth Main's albums. Op. cit.

35 The name of the dog is contained in Anthony Dod's photo albums from this period.

36 Elizabeth Main's photographs and handwritten captions document many of these details; the author also hiked these trails in the summer of 2019.

37 Le Blond, *True Tales of Mountain Adventure: For Non-climbers Young and Old*. E.P Dutton, New York, 1903.

38 Anthony Dod documented these expeditions, including the picnics and Pluto's presence, in his photographs and in the words accompanying them in the albums.

39 Le Blond, *The High Alps in Winter*. Op. cit, p. 179.

40 Details in Jean Williams's *A Contemporary History of Women's Sport, Part One: Sporting Women, 1850–1960*. Routledge, New York, 2014, p. 19.

41 These images are contained in Main's albums, held in the Martin and Osa Johnson Safari Museum, Chanute, Kansas. The page is titled "A Day's Climbing Near St Moritz", and is dated March 1896.

42 The author walked these paths in July 2019.

43 Details on Tony Dod's participation, as well as the names of the two guides and information about the peculiar weather conditions in the winter of 1896, can be found in a 1996 essay commemorating the centennial of the 1896 hiking winter, "One Hundred Years Ago," by C.A. Russell, published

in the *Alpine Journal*, www.alpinejournal.org.uk/Contents/Contents_1996_
files/AJ%201996%20227-233%20Russell%20100YrsAgo.pdf.

44 Main's photographs from this expedition are contained in an album held in
the archives of the Badrutt's Palace Hotel in St. Moritz.

45 Details of these climbs are contained in Jeffrey Pearson's book on Lottie
Dod. Op. cit.

46 Detailed in Anthony Dod's photos from the period. Op. cit.

Chapter 4

1 Sally-Ann Dod remembers being told about these parties by her father, Philip, who in turn had been told about them by his father, Anthony, as well as
his uncle William and aunt Lottie.

2 Photo album five, notes next to photo 5.125, in the Martin and Osa Johnson
Safari Museum archives.

3 Details provided in the Dods' album on this trip. The album was shown to
the author by Stephen Bartley, honorary archivist of the St. Moritz Tobogganing Club.

4 Description based on postcards from the period: www.amazon.com/
Bretagne-Florence-Original-Vintage-Postcard/dp/B00OYOG7KU.

5 Anthony Dod's album notes indicate they used Lake Geneva as a base from
4 May through to 25 May.

Chapter 5

1 Details on Topham's races on the Cresta in 1894 can be found in Sir Theodore Andrea Cook's *Notes on Tobogganing at St. Moritz*. Charles Scribner's
Sons, New York, 1894. The book is a modified version of an earlier article
that Cook published in the *New York World* newspaper.

2 The photograph, reproduced in *Notes on Tobogganing at St Moritz*, is unat-
tributed; but in the acknowledgments section, Cook wrote that most of the
photos in the book were taken by Elizabeth Main.

3 Ibid., pp. 25–26.

4 This is referenced in Jerrold M. Packard's *Farewell in Splendor: The Passing of
Queen Victoria and Her Age*. Dutton, New York, 1995, p. 157.

5 Sir Theodore Andrea Cook. Op. cit, p. 86.

6 This match, without a date listed, is mentioned in a 1942 article on Lottie
Dod in *Bulletin* magazine. It seems, however, to have been in the years after
she played the other four male players – Grove, the Renshaw brothers and
Pease. The *Bulletin* article noted that "she won as she pleased".

7 www.eyewitnesstohistory.com/duryea.htm.

8 Details provided by the Cresta Run's club: www.cresta-run.com/ride-the-cresta/facts-about-the-cresta/.

9 Harold Topham, "Toboggans and Tobogganing", *The Encyclopaedia of Sport and Games,* volume 4, edited by the Earl of Suffolk and Berkshire. William Heinemann, London, England, 1911, pp. 284–288.

10 Anthony Dod, who was experimenting with shutter speeds of up to 1/1000 of a second, managed to capture her in motion near the Cresta Leap portion of the course. She can be seen sitting upright as she hurtles down the slope.

11 Information provided by Stephen Bartley, honorary archivist at the St. Moritz Tobogganing Club.

12 Elizabeth Main's essay "Mountaineering in the Land of the Vikings", published in the *Queen: The Lady's Newspaper,* 22 October 1898.

13 Details on the chapel and the prayers against avalanches are contained in Le Blond's book *Adventures on the Roof of the World.* T. Fisher Unwin, London, England, 1904, p. 59.

14 Le Blond provided details of Roman's guiding career, including how he died, in her book *True Tales of Mountain Adventure: For Non-climbers Young and Old.* Op cit. The bulk of the description is on pp. 32–33, although other references are dotted throughout the book.

15 Ibid., preface, p. x.

16 The information on their packing Baedeker guidebooks, as well as the details of the itinerary they followed and some of the dangers they encountered, also comes from Main's "Mountaineering in the Land of the Vikings", combined with more general geographic research carried out by the author.

17 For information on Bertheau's career as a mountaineer, see www.hvitserk.com/therese-bertheau.

18 "Mountaineering in the Land of the Vikings". Op. cit.

19 In the Dod album of this trip is a photo of Anthony with his binoculars. He is accompanied by Lottie Dod and Imboden. It was, presumably, taken by Elizabeth Main.

20 Writing under the name Elizabeth Alice F. Le Blond, Main named this ship in her later book on the expeditions. *Mountaineering in the Land of the Midnight Sun.* J.B. Lippincott, Philadelphia and T. Fisher Unwin, London, 1908, p. 14. Details on the boats going between these cities can be found at www.norwayheritage.com/p_year.asp?ye=1897.

21 Photos of the fish market in 1890s Bergen are on the historian Sean Munger's website: www.seanmunger.com/2014/12/16/historic-photo-bergen-norway-waterfront-fish-market-1890s-compare-what-it-looks-like-today/.

22 Description based on Christian Krohg's 1905 painting *The Fish Market in Bergen,* displayed in the Bergen Art Museum.

23 Information on Grieg's itinerary in 1897, on his visitors, on his use of the hut as an escape and on his visits to the mountainous regions of Norway to

gain inspiration, were provided by the Edvard Grieg Museum at Troldhaugen, and in conversations with staff that the author had on 1 July 2019.

24 Descriptions of the boat ride are based on Elizabeth Main's writings. Additional landscape descriptions are based on the author's travels, by car and foot, through the region in July 2019.

25 Main's photographs of Imboden show him with his pipe sometimes at camp, surrounded by clotheslines from which were hanging their sweat-soaked socks to dry.

26 Details on Slingsby, including the use of this nickname, can be found in the biographical notice, written by Geoffrey Winthrop Young, which accompanied the 1941 edition of Slingsby's 1903 book *Norway: The Northern Playground*. Basil Blackwell, Oxford, England, 1941.

27 William Cecil Slingsby. Ibid. The section these passages reference is titled "The Conquest of Skagastölstind", pp. 94–112. Slingsby summited this peak on 21 July 1876.

28 From the Dods' album of this trip.

29 The hotel is now called the Turtagrø Hotel. The buildings are new, the original ones having burned down some years ago. Inside, old photos line the walls of the public areas; some of these include crowd scenes out front of the White House in the 1880s and 1890s. The author visited the hotel, and talked to staff there about the original White House, in July 2019.

30 The building standing where the second hotel used to be is now painted red; it is a part of the Turtagrø Hotel.

31 The author followed the route of the first day of their ascent up the mountain. Some of the descriptions contained in these passages are based on Elizabeth Main's writings; some are based on observations from the author's hike.

32 William Cecil Slingsby. Op. cit, p. 97.

33 Description based on photos in the Dods' album from this trip.

34 William Cecil Slingsby. Op. cit, p. 105.

35 "Mountaineering in the Land of the Vikings," op. cit.

36 Slingsby wrote, on p. 106 of his book, "A feeling of silent worship and reverence was more suitable than the jotting down of memoranda in a notebook. The scene was too overwhelming for notes."

37 From the photographs in the Dods' album, the hotel seems to have been the Macow Hotel, in the town of Oje.

38 From the Dods' album.

39 Op. cit. Main described the method of tying the climbers together on snow-fields in *Mountaineering in the Land of the Midnight Sun*, p. 295.

40 William Cecil Slingsby. Op. cit, p. 25.

41 Main described the smell of these rockslides on p. 300 of *Mountaineering in the Land of the Midnight Sun*. Op. cit.

42 Ibid.

43 Ibid.

Chapter 6

1 Le Blond, *Adventures on the Roof of the World*. Op cit. The chapter referencing the exploits of the unnamed lady is titled "A Stirring Day on the Rosetta."

2 *Bristol Mercury and Daily Post, Western Countries and South Wales Advertiser*, Bristol, England, 31 March 1900.

3 Dod's hockey trajectory was referenced in an article in the *Buffalo Times*, October 6, 1904. More general details can be found in Liz Pook's article "Legends of the Ladies Links," published in the September 2007 edition of the magazine for the British Golf Collectors Society.

4 Ibid, for details on women's hockey uniforms during these years.

5 Result reported in the *Freeman's Journal*, Dublin, Ireland, 21 February 1900.

6 See www.landforms.eu/shetland/storm%201900.htm.

7 *Freeman's Journal*, Dublin, Ireland, 2 March 1900.

8 A photograph of the Irish team wearing their uniform from an earlier game, in 1896, was provided to the author by the All England Women's Hockey Association.

9 *Freeman's Journal*, Dublin, Ireland, 2 March 1900.

10 Arnold Herschell wrote in the 1 January 1954, issue of *Lawn Tennis and Badminton* that he had known Dod for sixty years, and that she was "an expert horsewoman, rower, sculler and mountaineer."

11 Referenced in the ledger of the St Moritz Skating Association, kept in the Kulm Hotel.

12 The article, in an unidentified magazine, is dated 13 March 1908. It correctly identifies Ann Worssam, but then misidentifies her as having been known as "Miss L. Dod" before her marriage. The Worssams' doubts about Lottie Dod having played billiards were expressed by Geoffrey Worssam in a letter to Alan Little, Wimbledon librarian, dated 23 June 1983.

13 Jerrold M. Packard, *Farewell in Splendor: The Passing of Queen Victoria and Her Age*. Dutton, New York, 1995, p. 163.

14 Ibid, p. 187.

15 Ibid, p. 153.

16 Description of the Andover Road is based on the author's visit in July 2019.

17 Details from the 1911 census.

18 The author viewed William Dod's arrows, now in the possession of his great-nephew Bill Dod, who lives in London.

19 The scrapbook is contained in the Kenneth Ritchie Wimbledon Library.

20 Details of her early forays into golf are provided in Liz Pook's article "Legends of the Ladies Links," published in the September 2007 edition of the magazine for the British Golf Collectors Society.

21 For details on the Morris family, and photographs of Jack Morris, see www.charlesmicklegolfacademy.com/index.php?option=com_content&view=article&id=70&Itemid=80.

22 For details on Morris, see the Royal Liverpool's web page: www.liverpoolgolfcaptains.co.uk/brief_histories/royal_liverpool_golf_club/.

23 Scott subsequently wrote to Dod asking for a public endorsement of his equipment. Dod kept the letter in her golf album.

24 Mrs. R. Boys, "British Women on the Links." *Golf*, New York, July 1904. The article runs from pp. 25–31.

25 *Manchester Courier and Lancashire General Advertiser*. Manchester, England, May 17, 1904.

26 Mrs. R. Boys. Op cit, pg. 25.

27 The photograph is reproduced in Liz Pook's article. Op cit. The name of the original photographer is not known.

28 All of the correspondence was viewed by the author when looking over the golf album now kept by Lottie Dod's great-niece Sally-Ann Dod.

29 Ibid.

30 en.wikipedia.org/wiki/SS_Merion.

31 Information in *Publications Indexed for Engineering*, volume 4, 1906.

32 Information in N.R.P. Bonsor's book *North Atlantic Seaway*. Brookside Publications, St. Brélade, Jersey, 1955.

33 Numbers on private car ownership each year are available in Department of Transportation archives, www.fhwa.dot.gov/ohim/summary95/mv200.pdf.

34 A number of references to Dod's desire to acquire a family motorcar are contained in her personal correspondence, among the letters she received after her victory at Troon.

35 Article in the *Philadelphia Inquirer*, 3 October 1904.

36 Details of whom Dod was with were written up in the *Philadelphia Inquirer*, 3 October 1904.

37 *Buffalo Times*, 6 October 1904.

38 The loss was briefly reported on in the *Boston Globe*, October 15, 1904.

39 Details on the rain showers were written up in the *Morning Post*, Camden, New Jersey, 11 October 1904.

40 Rhonda Glenn, "Historical Highlights: Georgianna Bishop Wins Merion's First USGA Championship," 4 February 2013, www.usga.org/articles/2013/02/looking-back1904-us-womens-amateur-21474854305.html.

41 Numerous newspapers, including the *Buffalo Courier*, 12 October 1904, reported on the sclaffed shot.

42 *Trenton Times*, 12 October 1904, www.newspaperarchive.com/trenton-times-oct-12-1904-p-9/.

43 *Topeka State Journal*, Kansas, 23 November 1904.

44 *Morning News*, Wilmington, Delaware, 6 October 1904. The article described Dod as "a most charming and democratic young woman."

45 *Boston Daily Globe*, 26 October 1904, www.newspaperarchive.com/boston-daily-globe-oct-26-1904-p-5/.

46 The itinerary for this trip was published on 14 October 1904, in the *Baltimore Sun*.

47 *New York Times*, 4 December 1904.

48 Reported by the *Boston Globe*, 30 October 1904. The locales she played included Myopia Hunt Club in Hamilton; the Country Club, Clyde Park, in Brookline; and the Essex County Club in Manchester.

49 *Brooklyn Daily Eagle*, 4 November 1904.

50 *Brooklyn Daily Eagle*, 1 November 1904.

51 *Brooklyn Daily Eagle*, 5 November 1904.

52 Liz Pook. Op. cit.

Chapter 7

1 Jean Williams, *A Contemporary History of Women's Sport, Part One: Sporting Women, 1850–1960*. Routledge, New York, 2014, p. 71.

2 Details of Astor's fascination with archery can be found in the *Pittsburgh Press*, 5 August 1908.

3 Coubertin published a journal titled *Revue Olympique*. This quote is from its 1912 edition, p. 713, as referenced by the sports historian Martin Polley in his chapter "Sport, Gender and Sexuality at the 1908 London Olympic Games," published in the *Routledge Handbook of Sport, Gender and Sexuality*, edited by Jennifer Hargreaves and Eric Anderson. Routledge, London and New York, 2014.

4 Referenced in Billie Jean King's *Spectators No More: Women in the Olympics*, and also in Susan E. Cayleff's *Babe: The Life and Legend of Babe Didrikson Zaharias*, University of Illinois Press, Urbana and Chicago, 1995, p. 12.

5 Stephen Halliday, "London's Olympics, 1908." *History Today*, April 2008.

6 Information on these additional athletes comes from Martin Polley. Op cit.

7 British Olympic Association archives; British Olympic Council, "Olympic Games of 1908: Programme, Rules, and Condition of Competition."

8 Susan E. Cayleff. Op cit, p. 12.

9 Details on White City and the building of the Franco-British Exhibition can be found in Rebecca Jenkins's book *The First London Olympics: 1908. The Definitive Story of London's Most Sensational Olympics to Date*. Piatkus Books,

London, England, 2008.

10 *Times*, July 7, 1908. This article was the first in a series of long essays the newspaper published about the history of the games, ancient and modern.

11 *Observer*, "The Coming Olympiad," 15 March 1908.

12 The weather, and the "liquid mud" of the roads surrounding White City, are described in Keith Baker's *The 1908 Olympics: The First London Games*. SportsBooks, Cheltenham, UK, 2008, p. 24.

13 Ticket prices listed in a London *Times* article, from 20 July 1908. In the article, the writer mentioned that due to poor weekday sales, the ticket prices were being reduced. Those that had been one shilling were now selling for sixpence. The prices for all levels of tickets were likewise reduced.

14 *Winston-Salem Journal*, 14 July 1908.

15 These numbers are detailed by the University of Southampton sports historian Martin Polley, in his chapter "Sport, Gender and Sexuality at the 1908 London Olympic Games," published in the *Routledge Handbook of Sport, Gender and Sexuality*, edited by Jennifer Hargreaves and Eric Anderson. Routledge, London and New York, 2014.

16 A photo of the athletes' parade, by Bowden, can be found on the following sports blog, comparing the London Olympics of 1908 with those of 2012: www.blogs.loc.gov/inside_adams/2012/07/london-olympic-games-then-and-now-1908-2012/.

17 The order of events at the ceremony is listed in www.stillmed.olympic.org/media/Document%20Library/OlympicOrg/Factsheets-Reference-Documents/Games/Ceremonies/Factsheet-Opening-Ceremony-of-the-Games-of-the-Olympiad-October-2014.pdf.

18 Description of entrance "M," the royal box and the decoration opposite it can be found in an article in *The Observer*, 12 July 1908.

19 The time of the king's address to the White City crowd can be found in the *Times* coverage of the Olympics. The week before the Games opened, on July 7, the newspaper published a minute-by-minute schedule.

20 *Winston-Salem Journal*, 14 July 1908.

21 As reported in the *Evening Star*, Washington, DC, 19 July 1908.

22 *Butte Daily Post*, 24 July 1908.

23 *Buffalo Times*, 18 August 1908.

24 Details on the format of the archery contest can be found at www.sports-reference.com/olympics/summer/1908/ARC/womens-double-national-round.html.

25 A description of the arrows, and their being weighted by silver coins, as well as a description of the materials making up the target, can be found in "Archery: A Game of Antiquity," published in the *Buffalo Courier*, 2 August 1908. The film of Dod at the Olympics can be viewed on YouTube at www.youtube.com/watch?v=3IqE2KEqZJI.

26 *Guardian*, Olympic results, 20 July 1908.

27 The *Los Angeles Herald*, for example, wrote, "Oddly enough, the highest scores in both the ladies' and gentlemen's archery contests were made by members of the same family. W Dodd *[sic]* scored 403 points and his daughter Miss Dodd, 348 points." 18 July 1908.

28 On 2 July 1908, the *Guardian* reported that the Suffragettes were planning weekly Sunday gatherings at Heaton Park, and that on July 19 the meet would be modeled on a huge Suffragette protest that had recently been staged in London.

29 "Women Suffrage: The Demonstration in Heaton Park. A Great Gathering," was the headline on the *Guardian* story about it the next day, 20 July 1908.

30 Ibid.

31 Ibid.

32 Details of the events that night in London can be found in a long report filed for the *Hartford Courant*, in Hartford, Connecticut, the next day. It is titled "Suffragettes Try to Rush Commons," and was published on 14 October 1908.

33 As described by the University of Southampton sports historian Martin Polley, in his chapter "Sport, Gender and Sexuality at the 1908 London Olympic Games," published in the *Routledge Handbook of Sport, Gender and Sexuality*, edited by Jennifer Hargreaves and Eric Anderson. Routledge, London and New York, 2014, p. 36.

34 The full lyrics of the three-stanza song can be found at www.lyricstranslate.com/en/Haendel-See-Conquring-Hero-Comes-lyrics.html.

35 For details of the repeated singing of the Handel oratorio, see Rebecca Jenkins's *The First London Olympics: 1908*. Op cit, p. 232.

36 The order of the medalists was described in the *St. Louis Post-Dispatch*, 26 July 1908.

37 The author was shown the diploma by Sally-Ann Dod.

38 Details contained in *New York Times* coverage of the closing ceremony, 26 July 1908.

Chapter 8

1 The friend was Arnold Herschell. He reported this anecdote decades later in his 1951 *Lawn Tennis and Badminton* article "Early Wimbledons: Some Reminiscences from Miss Lottie Dod (Lady Champion 1887, 1888, 1891, 1892 and 1893)."

2 Details of Dod's nomination are contained in committee minutes held in the Royal North Devon Golf Club's archives.

3 Information on Dod's first aid training and a copy of Dod's VAD card were provided to the author by the Red Cross archives.

4 While Dod does not seem to have left detailed written records about her

training, others who went through comparable training did. One particularly evocative portrait, which contains information on the skills these women learned, is Enid Bagnold's *A Diary Without Dates*, written during the First World War. William Morrow, New York, 1935. Another is *Agatha Christie: An Autobiography*, published posthumously by Dodd, Meade, New York, 1977.

5 Katharine Furse, "The VADS: A Recruiting Letter from Katharine Furse," Winter 1917.

6 Agatha Christie. Op cit, p. 209.

7 Information on the origins of the VADs can be found at www.scarletfinders. co.uk/181.html.

8 Agatha Christie. Op cit, p. 211.

9 E. Sylvia Pankhurst, *The Home Front: A Mirror to Life in England during the World War*. Hutchinson, London, England, 1932, p. 15.

10 Details contained in minutes to meetings, held in the archives of the Royal North Devon Golf Club.

11 *Observer*, 20 September 1914.

12 Cunliffe-Owen's arthritis is described in www.sportsmansgazette.blogspot. com/2014/09/emma-pauline-cunliffe-owen.html.

13 As quoted in the British Legion essay on the Sportsman's Battalion, "The Amazing Mrs. Cunliffe-Owen and Her Sportsman's Battalions," 13 June 2016.

14 Ibid.

15 *Observer*, 17 January 1915, p. 12.

16 "The Sword on the Hearth" by Keble Howard; illustrated by George Van Werveke.

17 Details of the battalion's activities on Savoy Street and the Strand can be found in an article in the *Butte Miner*, 8 December 1914. And in Clive Harris and Julian Whippy's book *The Greater Game: Sporting Icons Who Fell in the Great War*. Pen & Sword Books, Barnsley, England, 2008, pp. 180–181.

18 The history of the Sportsman's Battalion, including the origin of this nickname, is told in Michael Foley's book *Hard as Nails: The Sportsmen's Battalion of World War One*. Spellmount, Stroud, England, 2007.

19 Ibid, p. 46.

20 *Guardian*, 17 December 1914.

21 An *Observer* article from 13 December 1914, reported that the War Office had called for five hundred additional recruits to the first Sportsman's Battalion, and 1,600 more to the second, and that the age limit had been raised to fifty-five.

22 As recorded in the British Legion history of the 23rd Battalion, www.britishlegion.org.uk/community/stories/remembrance/sport-remembers-the-amazing-mrs-cunliffe-owen-and-her-sportsman-s-battalions/.

23 The words to this poem, as well as a more general history of the battalion, are contained in a battalion history written by Captain Fred W. Ward and published after the end of the war. *The 23rd (Service) Battalion Royal Fusiliers (First Sportsman's)*, published in London by Sidgwick & Jackson, 1920. This book contains a series of oral history remembrances by members of the battalion who joined it at various points in the four-year conflict.

24 Ibid.

25 Michael Foley. Op cit, p. 72.

26 Ibid, p. 128.

27 William's poem was not published. He kept it stuffed between the pages of a family photo album, now in the possession of his great-niece Sally-Ann Dod. She showed the album to the author during a research visit in July 2019.

28 Michael Foley. Op cit, p. 142.

29 Dod's discharge documents, detailing his service with this branch, are available for viewing in the Royal Naval Reserve archives.

30 See *London Gazette* article, www.thegazette.co.uk/London/issue/29152/page/4264/data.pdf.

31 Royal Naval Reserves archives. Op cit.

32 "A Message from Katharine Furse, Commandant-in-Chief, British Red Cross Society Women's Voluntary Aid Detachments, to VADs Proceeding on Active Service." Probably written in 1915, when more VADs began being sent overseas.

33 Red Cross records, contained on p. 46 of a book of records listing London war hospitals, show that the Chelsea was in existence from March 17, 1915, through to 30 April 1919. During that time it treated 2,120 men, only three of whom are known to have died at the hospital. Listings of the VAD hospitals from the First World War can be found at: www.ezitis.myzen.co.uk/briefhistoryauxhosps.html. More detailed archival materials on some of the VAD hospitals can be found at the London Metropolitan Archives.

34 *The Times*, 18 June 1914.

35 A statue to Sir Robert, erected with funding by one of his descendants in 1997, stands at the corner of Grosvenor Crescent and Wilton Crescent. It shows Sir Robert standing with his left leg resting on a milestone that reads: "Chester: one hundred and ninety-seven miles."

36 Mr. Gillespie is listed in the Red Cross records for the Chelsea. His title is given not as doctor, but as "Hon. Surgeon Mr. Gillespie."

37 Details on VAD uniforms are contained in the British Red Cross archives. There are a number of photographs of VADs with their convalescing patients.

38 Information on VAD funding of the hospitals provided by the Red Cross.

39 Agatha Christie. Op cit, p. 216.

40 Vera Brittain, *Testament of Youth: An Autobiographical Study of the Years*

1900–1925. First published in 1933. The edition quoted from was republished by Victor Gollancz, London, England, 1980, p. 279–280.

41 Agatha Christie. Op cit, p. 227.

42 Enid Bagnold, *A Diary Without Dates.* William Morrow, New York, 1935, p. 6.

43 Ibid, p. 7.

44 Red Cross records on the London war hospitals, p. 47.

45 Royal North Devon Golf Club archives.

46 Details on the VAD uniforms, and the seniority of service allowing the white bar to be worn, can be found in the Scarletfinders' history of the VADs: www.scarletfinders.co.uk/185.html.

47 Article on the Red Cross blog, by Rosalind Knight, "The Record-Breaking Teenager who was the 'Little Wimbledon Wonder,'" 3 July 2017.

48 Enid Bagnold. Op cit, p. 64.

49 Ibid, p. 73.

50 The National Archives has records for roughly 15,000 nurses from the First World War years. Thousands of other records, however, were destroyed in the 1930s, during a housecleaning of the archives designed to provide more free space. Presumably Dod's records were among these.

51 For details on the munitionettes, and the health consequences of the work they did, see the Imperial War Museums' records on the topic: www.iwm. org.uk/history/9-women-reveal-the-dangers-of-working-in-a-first-world-war-munitions-factory.

52 *Suffragette,* 7 March 1913.

53 *Suffragette,* 18 July 1913.

54 *Suffragette,* 17 October 1913.

55 For a time line of the suffrage movement in the UK, see the following, compiled by researchers at the British Library: www.bl.uk/votes-for-women/articles/womens-suffrage-timeline.

Chapter 9

1 *Queen: The Lady's Newspaper,* 23 July 1892.

2 Dod is listed in the October 1924 electoral register, although her name is misspelled as "Dodd."

3 Early post–First World War programmes of the Oriana Madrigal Society are held in the rare books and music collection at the British Library.

4 The letter is contained in Lottie Dod's scrapbook, held at the Kenneth Ritchie Wimbledon Library. It is dated 15 March, but the year is not written down.

5 Details on the early Oriana Madrigal Society concerts are contained in Ron-

ald Peck's article "The Oriana Madrigal Society (1904–1954)," the *Musical Times*, October 1954.

6 For details of some of the Bach Cantata Club concert venues, see www. bach-cantatas.com/Bio/Scott-Charles-Kennedy.htm.

7 Ronald Peck. Op cit.

8 Charles Kennedy Scott's *Madrigal Singing: A Few Remarks on the Study of Madrigal Music with an Explanation of the Modes and a Note on their Relation to Polyphony*. Oxford University Press and Humphrey Milford, London, England, 1931, p. 3, foreword, and pp. 39 and 49.

9 Charles Kennedy Scott's notebooks are in the Trinity Laban Conservatoire of Music and Dance's library. The author visited the archives on 10 July 2019.

10 Part of a poem written in 1907 and titled "The Oriana Entreateth its Conductor to have Mercy." As quoted by Ronald Peck.

11 Ronald Peck. Op cit.

12 Philip Heseltine, *Frederick Delius*. John Lane, Bodley Head, London, England, 1923.

13 Details on first performances of Delius's works are found in an appendix to Heseltine's book. Ibid.

14 *Observer*, 24 May 1931.

15 *Times*, 18 April 1921.

16 *Observer*, 12 March 1922.

17 *Guardian*, 20 December 1928.

18 *Guardian*, 31 March 1927.

19 Details on Lottie teaching Philip tennis were told to the author by Sally-Ann Dod. Dod had heard this from her father and her aunts and uncles, who remembered Lottie and Philip on the court together.

20 For details on the Duke of York's Wimbledon appearance, see Lord Aberdare's *The Story of Tennis*. Stanley Paul, London, England, 1959, p. 145.

21 F.R. Burrow, *The Centre Court and Others*. Eyre & Spottiswoode, London, England, 1937, p. 131.

22 Pathé archival film footage from the ceremony, www.youtube.com/watch?v=VQXFcGCr2Do.

23 Both the *Women's World* and *Times* articles were published on 22 June 1926.

24 Photos of the Baddeley twins can be seen in John Barrett's *Wimbledon: The Official History of the Championships*. HarperCollins, London, England, 2001, pp. 33 and 36.

25 The photo of the ex-champions is attributed to Edwin Trim & Co., from 26 June 1926. Reprinted in Bob Everitt's article "1926 – Fifty Years of Champions."

26 The 1929 exhibition event at Roehampton is mentioned in an article, publication unknown, clipped by Lottie Dod and kept in her tennis scrapbook.

27 The *Telegraph* published a photograph of Dod and the other three players – Miss Ramsay, Mrs. Sterry, and Miss Ransome – on 28 September 1929.

28 The letter was kept by Dod in her scrapbook.

29 Foreword to Denis Foster's *Improve Your Tennis*. Findon Publications, London, England, 1950.

30 For details about Kingsway Hall, see www.kingswayhall.co.uk/d/kingsway-hallresponsive/media/Kingsway_Hall_history.pdf.

31 William Dod is listed in Oriana Madrigal Society programs from the early 1930s as an honorary member. The programs can be found in the Charles Kennedy Scott archives at the Trinity Laban Conservatoire of Music and Dance library.

32 Lottie Dod is listed as a subscriber in the Philharmonic Choir program from 26 March 1929, an event conducted by Charles Kennedy Scott at Queen's Hall.

33 The Stradivarius was bought for Lambert by her husband, Ernest E. Winterbotham, in 1922, for the price of £1,600. Details in *Solomon Ex-Lambert Stradivarius*, edited by Lambert Surhone, Miriam Timpledon, and Susan Karseken. Betascript Publishing, International Book Market Service, Mauritius, 2010. More details can be found in "Stradivarius: Still Priceless after All These Years," *The Independent*, 21 June 2011.

34 Gibbon's letter is contained in Lottie Dod's scrapbook, held at the Kenneth Ritchie Wimbledon Library.

35 An article in the *Bideford Gazette* that detailed Kipling's Westward Ho! connections was posted on the Westward Ho! History Group Facebook page. The date cannot be determined on the scan of this article.

36 Details of Westward Ho!'s role in the First World War can be found in Graham Smith's *Devon and Cornwall Airfields in the Second World War*. Countryside Books, Newbury, England, 2000. The opening chapter deals with the First World War.

37 Details of where Kingsley wrote his book can be found in S.P.B. Mais's *We Wander in the West*. Ward, Lock, London, England; and Melbourne, Australia, 1950, p. 65.

38 Charles Kingsley, *Westward Ho! or, The Voyages and Adventures of Sir Amyas Leigh, Knight*. It was first published in 1855. The edition quoted from was published by A.L. Burt, New York. No date appears on the publication page. Quote is from p. 8.

39 Ibid, p. 256.

40 As detailed at www.visitwestwardho.co.uk/history.

41 The pier was, according to an article in the local paper uploaded on to the Facebook page of the Westward Ho! History Group, completed in 1873.

42 The boarding school was called Buckleigh College, and was run by "The Misses Tatam, assisted by resident English & Foreign Governesses," as an 1895 ad for the institution phrased it. The grocery stores included "Barrett's."

43 In 1907, this particular issue caught the attention of locals, who wrote a series of letters to the local paper expressing outrage at such desecration of the Sabbath.

44 As related by Sally Dod, of Oxford, England, who recalled that her father had remembered his grandparents telling him about the sporting Dods and their sacrilegious behaviour. Discussed with author in a series of Facebook communications in 2019.

45 Details on the champion golfers who played on the Royal North greens can be found in the *Links* magazine article "Royal North Devon, England," published in 2019.

46 The golf manual was titled *Our Lady of the Green*, and was written in 1899 by Mrs Louie Mackern and M. Boys. It was published in 1899 by Lawrence and Bullen, in England. Dod's playing in this tournament at the Royal North Golf Club was described by the golfer and writer Liz Pook, in her September 2007 article for the British Golf Collectors Society magazine. The article was titled "Legends of the Ladies Links".

47 Details on the potwallopers and their relationship to the golf club were provided by Robert Fowler, historian of the golf club, in conversation with the author during a visit on 23 July 2019.

48 Song is titled "Westward Ho."

49 Helen Wills Moody, "How is Your Tennis?" *Nash's Pall Mall Magazine*, volume 91, no. 481, June 1933.

50 The Bideford Heritage Society collected memories of the Second World War, in which was reference to the removal of the ironworks from the front of buildings along Kingsley Street – labelled as Kingsley Road in the report, www.bidefordheritage.co.uk/life-in-bideford-during-ww2/recollections-bideford-ww2/.

51 The pylons were removed by Air Ministry contractors in 1957.

52 Information provided by Robert Fowler, historian of the Royal North Devon Golf Club.

53 There are photographs, owned by Anthony Dod's granddaughter Sally-Ann, of William Dod reading the newspaper in his house during this period.

54 Derek Tait, *Devon at War, 1939–45*. Pen & Sword Books, Barnsley, England, 2017, p. 42.

55 These photos, and the Archery Register volumes that once belonged to William, were shown to the author by Sally-Ann Dod.

56 Graham Smith, *Devon and Cornwall Airfields in the Second World War*. Countryside Books, Newbury, England, 2000, p. 115.

57 Derek Tait. Op cit, pp. 66–75.

58 Ibid, pp. 76 and 99.

59 The woodworking magazines and William Dod's books were shown to the author by Sally-Ann Dod, who also provided information on how the Dod siblings would likely have entertained themselves with poetry and music.

60 Henry Buckton, *Devon at War Through Time*. Amberley Publishing, Stroud, England, 2012, p. 53.

61 Details on the speeds the experimental Giant Panjandrum could pick up can be found in Derek Tait's book *Devon at War 1939–45*. Pen & Sword Books, Barnsley, England, 2017, p. 151.

62 Graham Smith, *Devon and Cornwall Airfields in the Second World War*. Countryside Books, Newbury, England, 2000, p. 113.

63 Details of the Baedeker raids can be found in Henry Buckton's *Devon at War Through Time*. Amberley Publishing, Stroud, England, 2012. Details on Westward Ho! residents and Bideford residents being able to see the fires from those raids can be found in the Bideford Heritage oral history collection on residents' memories of the war. Op cit.

64 Bideford Heritage oral history collection. Op cit.

65 Henry Buckton. Op cit, p. 58.

66 Bideford Heritage oral history, John Davies recollections. Op cit.

67 Charles Kingsley. Op cit, pg. 634.

68 Details on troop numbers for the D-Day invasion can be found in Henry Buckton's *Devon at War Through Time*. Amberley Publishing, Stroud, England, 2012.

69 Details provided in the Bideford oral history project, www.bidefordheritage.co.uk/life-in-bideford-during-ww2/recollections-bideford-ww2/.

70 Royal North Devon Golf Club committee meeting minutes.

71 The grand opening "Gala Night" dance was held on 27 November 1946.

72 S.P.B. Mais. Op cit, p. 67.

Chapter 10

1 Herschell published this letter as part of an article he wrote for the Festival of Britain edition of *Lawn Tennis and Badminton* in July 1951. The article was titled "Early Wimbledons: Some Reminiscences from Miss Lottie Dod (Lady Champion 1887, 1888, 1891, 1892 and 1893)."

2 This information was told to the author by two of the women currently living in the building. It was also written about in an article in *The Independent* newspaper on 5 November 2013.

3 Information on local restaurants during these years was provided to the author during street interviews with long-time residents of the area.

4 Details provided by Anthony's granddaughter Sally-Ann Dod.

5 The travel trunk is now in the possession of Bill Dod; it still has the red address labels inside (they would, presumably, originally have been attached externally) on which is written "5 Trebovir Road."

6 Lottie Dod's last will and testament was signed on 19 April 1951. A codicil,

written after William Dod's death, was added on 17 January 1955. It removed the £1,000 she had intended to leave to William, and also reallocated
her "personal chattel" away from Doris Winifred Worssam.

7 The list is now in the possession of Dod's great-niece, Sally-Ann Dod, who
provided the author with a copy.

8 Dod clutching raspberries was reported in a first-hand account by the author
Gwen Robyns, who actually saw Dod on the train station with the basket
of fruit. Gwen Robyns, *Wimbledon: The Hidden Drama*. David & Charles,
Newton Abbot, England, 1973.

9 George Kirksy, United Press; as quoted by Susan E. Cayleff in *Babe: The Life
and Legend of Babe Didrikson Zaharias*. University of Illinois Press, Urbana
and Chicago, 1995, p. 65.

10 Date and publication unknown. The article was kept by Lottie Dod in her
tennis scrapbook.